# LEGAL WRITING

# LEGAL WRITING

## Academic and Professional Communication

PAULA BARON AND LILLIAN CORBIN

OXFORD
UNIVERSITY PRESS
AUSTRALIA & NEW ZEALAND

OXFORD
UNIVERSITY PRESS

Oxford University Press is a department of the University of Oxford.

It furthers the University's objective of excellence in research, scholarship, and education by publishing worldwide. Oxford is a registered trademark of Oxford University Press in the UK and in certain other countries.

Published in Australia by Oxford University Press
253 Normanby Road, South Melbourne, Victoria 3205, Australia



First published 2016



National Library of Australia Cataloguing-in-Publication entry

Creator: Baron, Paula, author.

Title: Legal writing: academic and professional communication/Paula Baron, Lillian Corbin.

ISBN: 9780195593938 (paperback)

Notes: Includes index.

Subjects: Legal composition.
Legal correspondence.
Communication in law.
Law—Interpretation and construction.
Business communication.

Other Creators/Contributors: Corbin, Lillian, author.

Dewey Number: 808.06634



Edited by Trischa Baker
Text design by Sardine Design
Cover image: Stocksy/Simone Becchetti
Typeset by diacriTech, Chennai, India
Proofread by Carolyn Leslie, AE
Indexed by Karen Gillen
Printed by Sheck Wah Tong Printing Press Ltd.

# CONTENTS

# PREFACE

## HOW TO USE THIS BOOK

This is a book about legal writing. In it, we provide a process for legal writing that begins with reflection: reflection upon **audience**, **purpose**, **genre** and ethical obligations. So, in the spirit of practising what we preach, we begin with this reflective stage.

Our audience? This book is written to provide an ongoing reference – for writers across the curriculum and beyond. In the first instance it is written for novice legal writers who want to know the fundamentals of legal writing, with a view to developing a professional identity as legal writers in the longer term. But we also seek to assist more experienced legal writers, such as students completing honours, postgraduate students, and legal professionals.We envisage that these writers may wish to improve their legal writing and understand more clearly the ethical obligations inherent in their writing practice. Lastly, the book is also written for legal writing teachers, particularly those who want to teach legal writing as a professional skill which is linked to the ethical and professional obligations of lawyers.

Our purpose is twofold: first, we want to emphasise the fundamental importance of good legal writing to **professionalism** and to lawyering. 'Good legal writing' in this context we define as writing appropriate for the intended audience, written with a clear sense of purpose and cognisant of the writer's ethical obligations. Second, building on this last point, we want to emphasise the inextricable links between legal writing and ethics.

The genre? This book is, in a sense, a 'how to' book. But we wanted this work to be firmly based in the literature about writing, so its approach is academic in the sense that it seeks to provide a **scholarly** approach to legal writing, and to evidence and reference material that supports our approach.It is *not* primarily a book about grammatical structure, nor is it a text on **plain language** drafting, though these topics are addressed. Rather, we seek to provide a more holistic view of legal writing, both professional and academic.

Our ethical obligations? Like all legal writing, we have sought to produce work that is competent, honest and upholds professional obligations of civility. In our view, good legal writing is always an ethical practice. It is ethical, as we explain in the next chapter, in at least three ways: it calls for and depends upon ethical awareness of, and respect for self and other; awareness of the norms and conventions of the **community of practice**; and fundamental professional ethical obligations such as honesty, civility, competence, duty to law and duty to the client.

The book is divided into three main sections. These are: 'Part 1: General and Academic Writing'; 'Part 2: Professional Writing'; and 'Part 3: Learning Materials'. This preface and Chapter 1: 'Writing as an Ethical Practice' act as an introduction to this book. In them, we explain why good writing is always inherently ethical.

Part 1: General and Academic Writing, deals with the writing process, which is applicable to all forms of legal writing as well as the main forms of academic writing. It contains five chapters: 'Pre-writing', 'Researching for Writing' and 'Drafting, Revising, Editing and Proofreading'; and then chapters on the specific forms of academic writing commonly encountered by undergraduate and postgraduate students: 'Case Briefs and Problem Questions' and 'Essays, Theses and Dissertations'.

Part 2: Professional Writing, deals with specific forms of legal professional writing. It is divided into seven chapters: 'Balanced Writing', which deals specifically with the client letter and internal memoranda; 'Persuasive Writing', which deals specifically with appellate briefs; 'Form Writing', which deals with standardised documents and the use of precedents; and 'Technical Writing', which deals with reports and legislation. We turn then to consider specific ethical issues. There is a chapter on writing with civility, which deals with the professional expectations of courtesy in legal writing and, in particular, examines the line between discourtesy and robust advocacy; and a chapter on reflective practice.

At the end of each chapter you will find a summary of the chapter, key points, questions for reflection, exercises and additional materials.

In Part 3, we provide learning material. This includes an account of different theories of writing, tables outlining professional rules, a grammar primer and a glossary.

Although we have made the distinction between academic and professional writing, either or both sections may have relevance to you as a reader. As a student, for instance, you may be faced with the need to prepare an essay, especially if you are completing Honours. The obvious path to take is to read about the writing process, that is, Part 1 of the book, which deals with general writing skills and with the specifics of essay writing. But having completed the essay, you might like to engage in some reflection on your learning process. Reading Chapter 12 is thus likely to be helpful. Similarly, more experienced writers are likely to find this chapter useful in their day to day practices.

It is also quite easy to 'dip in and out' of the chapters in the book if, for instance, you need some ideas on planning; you want to think about improving your research process; or you want to understand what is expected of a 'literature review'.

For legal writing teachers, we recommend beginning with legal writing as an ethical practice before exploring the writing process in Part 1. Particular genres can then be explored as needed. Chapter 11, 'Writing with Civility' can reinforce the professional expectations of courtesy in legal writing and Chapter 12 can encourage reflective practice.

Throughout the book we refer to 'lawyers'. When we do so we are referring to practising lawyers. To illustrate our points in relation to professional responsibility, we directly reference the **Australian Solicitors Conduct Rules (ASCR)**. At the time of writing, these have only been adopted by New South Wales, Victoria, Queensland, and South Australia. We provide tables in the Learning Materials which outline both the equivalent solicitors rules for the other states of Australia, and the equivalent Australian Bar Association Barristers' Conduct Rules (Bar Rules, which are now adopted in New South Wales, Victoria, Queensland, South Australia and Western Australia) and again the equivalent rules governing barristers in the other states.

Where appropriate we have provided diagrams to simplify and clarify structures and processes. Image, as well as text, can be a powerful aspect of legal communications. We have provided a glossary of terms, and where we first refer to a term that is in the glossary, you will find it in bold text.

# ACKNOWLEDGMENTS

The authors and the publisher wish to thank the following copyright holders for reproduction of their material.

Armed with Reason for extract from article *Shooting Down the Gun Lobby's Favorite 'Academic': A Lott of Lies* by Evan DeFilippis and Devin Hughes. www.armedwithreason.com; Carolina Academic Press for excerpt from David C Thomson, *Skills and Values Lawyering Process: Legal Writing and Advocacy* (2013); Carrie Menkel-Meadow for extract from '*Aha? Is Creativity Possible in Legal Problem Solving and Teachable in Legal Education?*' (2001) 6 Harv Negot L Rev 97, 141; Dartmouth Institute for Writing and Rhetoric for extract from *Considering Structure and Organisation*; Elsevier Science Ltd from extract from *Interdisciplinary Integration in Europe: The case of the fifth framework review* by A Bruce, C Lyall, J Tait and R Williams (2004) Futures 36, 457–470; Fordham Law Review for extract from John O McGinnis and Russell G Pearce, '*The Great Disruption: How Machine Intelligence Will Transform the Role of Lawyers in the Delivery of Legal Services*'; Griffith Law School for extract from website, 5000LAW – Interdisciplinary Research Project unit; Halogen Software for article *10 Rules of Effective Peer-to-Peer Communications* by Sharlyn Lauby at http://www.halogensoftware.com/blog/10-rules-of-effective-peer-to-peer-communications, dated 4 February 2014; International Risk Management Institute, Inc., Dallas, Texas, for extract from the Expert Commentary section of IRMI.com, copyright International Risk Management Institute, Inc. Reproduced with permission of the publisher. Further reproduction prohibited. Visit www.IRMI.com for more information; McGraw Hill Education for extract from *How to Write a Thesis* by Rowena Murray, Open University Press, 2011; Mercer Law Review for extract from '*One Small Step for Legal Writing, One Giant Leap for Legal Education: making the case for more writing opportunities in the 'practice ready' law school curriculum*' (2014) by Sherri Lee Keen; Sage Publishing for extract from *Teaching Sociology Journal*; State of Queensland for case extract from Queensland Civil and Administrative Tribunal (QCAT); *Sydney Morning Herald* for extract from *When Research Findings Explode* by Alok Jha, 2012; Taylor & Francis for extract from Educational Psychologist Journal; The National Writing Project for extract from www.nwp.org; The University of Sydney, Learning Centre for extract from *Writing a Thesis Proposal* adapted from Mauch, J.E. and Birch, J.W. (1989) (2nd ed.) Guide to the successful thesis and dissertation New York: Marcel Dekker. http://sydney.edu.au/stuserv/documents/learning_centre/Thesis_Proposal_2012.pdf; Thomson Reuters for extract from Stephen V Armstrong and Timothy P Terrell '*The Rhetoric of Persuasive Writing*' (2007) 15(3) in Perspectives: Teaching Legal Research and Writing; University of Chicago Press for excerpt from *How to Write a BA Thesis*

(2005) by Charles Lipson; University of Manchester for extract from Academic Phrasebank, http://www.phrasebank.manchester.ac.uk; Washington Law Review for excerpt from J Christopher Rideout and Jill J Ramsfield, '*Legal Writing: A Revised View*' (1994).

Every effort has been made to trace the original source of copyright material contained in this book. The publisher will be pleased to hear from copyright holders to rectify any errors or omissions.

# CHAPTER 1

# LEGAL WRITING AS AN ETHICAL PRACTICE

## I INTRODUCTION

In this book, we hope to encourage the development of legal writing skills, a love for the craft of writing, and an appreciation that legal writing is always an inherently ethical practice. In our view, good legal writing is based upon an ethical awareness of, and respect for, self and other; upon an awareness of the norms and conventions of the legal profession's community of practice; and upon fundamental professional ethical obligations such as honesty, civility, competence, duty to law and duty to the client. We believe that an appreciation of these ethical dimensions of legal writing can produce not only better legal writers but also better legal practitioners.

We often take writing for granted – possibly because it is so fundamental to contemporary life:

> Writing has become central in the workplace, in education, and to our personal lives. In the realm of the personal, much social communication has moved online, to such settings as e-mail, texting programs for mobile phones, blogs, vlogs, and social networks … In the professional sphere, written reporting of all kinds has become central to management, and as such, on-the-job writing has become a 'marker of high-skill, high-wage, professional work' … Finally, in terms of education, many states have mandated critical, persuasive, and **analytical writing** assessments, pushing teachers to include a greater emphasis on writing throughout the curriculum … All of these trends suggest that writing skills are becoming more vital than ever in the technology rich environments that have begun to infuse all spheres of our lives.[1]

1 Alecia Marie Magnifico, 'Writing for Whom? Cognition, Motivation and a Writer's Audience' (2010) 45(3) *Educational Psychologist* 167, 167 (refs omitted).

As a professional practice, writing is at the very heart of lawyering: it has been said that '[l]awyering is a craft at the center of which is communication'.[2] If you are a law student, learning legal writing is not only a matter of skill development. Learning legal writing is fundamental to your own development as a lawyer: writing has been described as 'thinking on paper',[3] so learning to 'write like a lawyer' is inextricably linked to learning to 'think like a lawyer' and so to the development of your own professional identity.

In this chapter, we begin by outlining the relationship between legal writing and legal professional ethics in legal education. We turn then to the conventional mode of legal writing instruction – formalism – and the criticisms that have been made of that approach. We then consider an alternative view of legal writing that emphasises process, **mastery**, awareness of the **discourse community** and appreciation of professional obligations. Finally, we consider the implications of this alternative mode of writing instruction and the benefits of breaking down the boundaries between legal writing and ethics.

At the most basic level, this chapter outlines the fundamental professional obligations in legal writing, such as competence and honesty. If you are a law student, understanding the approach your law school takes to legal writing will help you understand what is expected of you. More importantly, though, we hope this chapter will encourage you to reflect upon the ethics of legal writing and thus begin to develop your own professional identity as a legal writer within a wider community of practice.

We begin by outlining the conventional view of legal writing taken in many law schools, in both the US and Australia. From here, we outline the ethical aspects of legal writing. These include an ethical awareness of self and other; an ethical awareness of the community of practice; and an ethical awareness of professional responsibility.

Throughout this book, we model the ethical obligation of referencing the ideas and words of others. You will thus see that the book is footnoted throughout, using the style of the *Australian Guide to Legal Citation* (AGLC). Although correct referencing in legal writing is emphasised in all law schools, many students view this emphasis as a compliance issue rather than an ethical issue. But all writing builds on the work of others, and this work should be acknowledged. At the same time, good referencing is important to the reader, providing them with the information needed to follow up on a point or read further. Referencing in legal writing is thus an essential aspect of the ethical awareness of self and other, discussed below.

---

2 Terrill Pollman, 'Building a Tower of Babel or Building a Discipline? Talking About Legal Writing' (2002) 85 *Marquette Law Review* 887, 892.

3 Grant Wiggins, 'EJ in Focus: Real-world Writing: Making Purpose and Audience Matter' (2009) 98(5) *The English Journal* 29, 32, quoting the US National Commission on Writing.

## II THE RELATIONSHIP BETWEEN LEGAL WRITING AND LEGAL PROFESSIONAL ETHICS

In orthodox legal education in Australia, legal writing is taught either as a stand-alone subject or as part of an introductory course. It may be linked to the content of a substantive subject but it is rarely linked to professional ethics. Taught as a stand-alone course or embedded in one or more subjects, the tendency is to teach legal writing in a **formalistic** and **technocratic** way, focusing primarily upon grammar, structure and genre. We argue that legal education would benefit by breaking down the boundaries between legal writing instruction and ethics. As we have already noted, in our view, good legal writing is an inherently ethical practice: it is based upon an awareness of, and respect for, the other; upon **reflection** and **reflexivity**; upon an awareness of the norms and conventions of the legal profession; and upon the fundamental professional ethical obligations of honesty, civility, competence, and duty to law. We maintain that changing the way we teach legal writing by acknowledging its inherently ethical foundations could potentially enrich the instruction of legal writing, create better legal writers and develop legal practitioners who are more ethically aware.

When we look at the literature, although a good deal has been written about legal ethics, and about legal writing, the two are generally kept separate. There are some notable exceptions. As far as legal writing is concerned, over 15 years ago now, Bell and Pether argued that ethical considerations are ineluctably a part of legal writing;[4] some years earlier, Johns had argued that 'a legal writing course should cover the professional responsibility issues that arise in the writing assignments'.[5] More recently, Weresh suggests that 'by incorporating a study of ethics and professionalism into our courses, we can effectively teach a more ethical **discourse** practice'.[6]

In relation to writing more generally, Burke discusses the links between ethics and writing, particularly highlighting the issue of **authorial** responsibility,[7] and Pemberton and the authors who contribute to his book emphasise ethical issues in writing instruction.[8] In relation to writing in other disciplines, Blancett highlights

---

4 Daniel Bell and Penny Pether, 'Re/Writing Skills Training in Law Schools – Legal Literacy Revisited' (1998) 9(2) *Legal Education Review* 113, 124.

5 Margaret Z Johns, 'Teaching Professional Responsibility and Professionalism in Legal Writing' (1990) 40 *Journal of Legal Education* 501, 507.

6 Melissa H Weresh, 'Fostering a Respect for Our Students, Our Speciality, and the Legal Profession: Introducing Ethics and Professionalism into the Legal Writing Curriculum' (2005-2006) 21 *Touro Law Review* 427, 428.

7 Sean Burke, *The Ethics of Writing* (Edinburgh University Press, 2008).

8 Michael A Pemberton, *The Ethics of Writing Instruction: Issues in Theory and Practice* (Ablex Publishing Corp, 2000).

ethical pitfalls in scholarly writing and publishing in the specific context of nursing,[9] and Rhodes has written on the linkages between ethics and writing with reference to organisational studies.[10]

In this book, we view ethics more widely as including, but not limited to, the professional conduct rules, and we apply ideas from some of the wider literature specifically to legal writing. Our approach thus most closely aligns with that of Bell and Pether,[11] in that we believe that good legal writing is inherently ethical.

## III CONVENTIONAL AND PROGRESSIVE LEGAL WRITING

Australian law schools adopt various positions on legal writing instruction in the LLB or JD. For some, legal writing is taught as a stand-alone course;[12] for others, it is co-taught with legal research;[13] and for many, it is embedded – most commonly within a first-year introductory unit.[14] Some law schools also offer advanced legal writing units, ordinarily in postgraduate courses.[15] A few offer legal writing courses specifically to international students.[16]

Despite this diversity of positioning, there is relatively high consistency of approach, with a standard tendency to be formalistic, **instrumental** and technocratic. Such an approach

> focuses on the formal features of legal texts-that is, on their formats, organization, and language and style. In it, the primary concern of the writer is with the subject, and with a text that communicates that subject well. It is based on an unproblematized view of language – that language does not contribute to the construction of meaning, but rather is a transparent medium for meaning. Thus, the primary formal concern in the writing of the text is with clarity-in organization, in style, in word choice-and with accuracy.[17]

---

9 Suzanne Smith Blancett, 'The Ethics of Writing and Publishing' (1991) *Journal of Nursing Administration* 32.

10 Carl Rhodes, 'After Reflexivity: Ethics, Freedom and the Writing of Organization Studies' (2009) 30(6) *Organization Studies* 653.

11 Bell and Pether, above n 4.

12 See, for instance, 'Legal Writing and Drafting' (VU); 'Legal Writing (Griffith).

13 See, for instance, 'Legal Research and Writing' (Flinders); 'Advanced Legal Research and Writing' (University of Canberra).

14 See, for instance, 'Legal Method' (UQ); 'Legal Process and Research' (USQ); 'Studies in Law' (Newcastle).

15 See, for instance, 'Advanced Legal Research and Writing' (University of Canberra).

16 For instance UNSW.

17 J Christopher Rideout and Jill J Ramsfield, 'Legal Writing: A Revised View' (1994) 69 *Washington Law Review* 35, 49.

Here, the implicit assumption is that writing is primarily representational, so the focus is upon the mechanics of writing: structure, grammar, spelling, and the tenets of plain language. As an example of this approach, one stand-alone legal writing unit description, similar to many others, provides:

> Students will be taught principles of plain English, effective written communication and drafting legal documents, including court documents and how to apply them in practice. The unit will cover the function and operation of a document, stages in preparing a document and structuring a document. Students will also learn about style, appearance, content and presentation of documents. The unit will further address legal rules of construction that apply to documents such as agreements, the use of precedents and rules of evidence and procedure that apply to court documents.[18]

Students are encouraged to write clearly and persuasively, cognisant of academic conventions and sometimes also of professional conventions, such as writing a letter of advice to the client. But in many law schools, the focus still tends to be upon academic, rather than professional, conventions.[19]

In the US, where the professionalism of legal writing instruction is well developed, the limitations of this approach have been acknowledged. Rideout and Ramsfield argue that traditional views of legal writing:

> have crippled legal writing programs because they have ensured that the complex task of introducing novices to legal discourse cannot be reasonably undertaken. Without fully understanding the epistemic, social, and process dimensions of legal writing, law schools do not assign the proper resources to developing good legal writers.[20]

Bell and Pether maintain that '[t]o learn the language of the law, and of the legal cultures in which the law exists, requires a teaching environment that is critical and reflective, as well as instrumental'.[21] Weresh, citing Krieger, argues that a technocratic approach may contribute to student distress,[22] a problem that has received considerable attention in Australian law schools in recent years.[23]

The main differences between the two approaches are summarised in Figure 1.1.

---

18 Victoria University, available at http://www.vu.edu.au/units/BLB2120.

19 Particularly where legal writing is embedded in a first-year course, the emphasis appears to be upon academic writing. Stand-alone courses tend to cover both academic and professional writing.

20 Rideout and Ramsfield, above n 17, 51.

21 Bell and Pether, above n 4, 118.

22 Weresh, above n 6, 450.

23 See further, Paula Baron, 'Sleight of Hand: Lawyer Distress and the Attribution of Responsibility' (2014) 22(2) *Griffith Law Review* 261; and Paula Baron, 'Althusser's Mirror: Lawyer Distress and the Process of Interpellation' (2015) *Griffith Law Review* 1 and the references therein.

FIGURE 1.1

**Conventional legal writing**

- is taught in isolation from legal ethics and professionalism;
- focuses on writing as a product;
- emphasises the mechanics of grammar and structure;
- inculcates a technical approach to writing.

→

**Progressive legal writing**

- is taught in an integrated fashion with legal ethics and professionalism;
- focuses on writing as a process;
- emphasises the norms and expectations of the legal profession as a discourse community;
- inculcates a reflective approach to writing.

In response to such criticisms, progressive legal writing instructors advocate a process approach, rather than a product approach, to legal writing (that is, in formalism, the emphasis is on the final written product rather than on the process of writing).[24] A process approach treats the act of writing as not merely representing but 'constructing' the law; it involves processes of description, **synthesis**, application, reasoning, **analogising** and developing legal **arguments**,[25] and appreciates that the student-novice needs to develop mastery over time. The process approach acknowledges that this development of expertise is often a struggle. It also acknowledges the inextricable link between writing and thinking:

> Writing is not just the act of putting words on the page through pen or keystrokes; writing is a cognitive act in which we must exercise our brains to express ourselves through words. Before we can craft sentences and phrases we must consider not only what words and phrases we intend to use but also why we intend to use some words and not others. In this sense, writing and thinking are inextricably linked. One cannot engage in the process of writing without simultaneously engaging in the process of thinking.[26]

A process approach to writing causes the mind to act like a 'radar scope that plays continually over one's own text'.[27] Such an approach is well suited to legal writing, because the writer enters 'into a sustained and serious dialogue about the subject under consideration … resulting in a much fuller and richer consideration of

---

24 Rideout and Ramsfield, above n 17, 50.

25 Ibid 55.

26 Peter Kaufman, 'On Reflexivity: Scribo Ergo Cogito, Reflexivity through Writing' (2013) 41(1) *Teaching Sociology* 70, 70.

27 Phillip C Kissam, 'Thinking (By Writing) About Legal Writing' (1987) 40 *Vanderbilt Law Review* 135, 140 citing Richard Marius, available at http://heinonlinebackup.com/hol-cgi-bin/get_pdf.cgi?handle=hein.journals/vanlr40&section=12.

contradictory evidence, counter-arguments, and the complex elements of a subject'.[28] While we certainly maintain that a process approach is preferable to a formalist approach, we argue that good legal writing instruction needs to go beyond the process approach to acknowledge the ethical foundations inherent in legal writing.

## IV ACKNOWLEDGING THE ETHICAL FOUNDATIONS OF LEGAL WRITING

Ethical legal writers will consciously consider how their writing may be influenced by their own views; how their writing might affect others; and how it must comply with the norms and conventions of the discourse community and the fundamental professional ethical obligations of the legal profession. Our approach is summarised in Figure 1.2.

FIGURE 1.2

| | |
|---|---|
| **What are your ethical responsibilities to the other?** | • What is your purpose?<br>• Who is your audience?<br>• Reflect on the reader's needs, understanding and the consequences of potential interpretations. |
| **What are your ethical responsibilities to the community of practice?** | • What are the conventions, standards, responsibilities and genres of the community?<br>• What is your professional identity and voice within this community?<br>• Reflect on the legal community's expectations of voice, tone, structure, genre and presentation. |
| **What are your professional responsibilities?** | • What are the standards as expressed in the relevant professional rules?<br>• Reflect on the professional expectations of competence, diligence, honesty and civility as expressed in the ASCR. |

### *Ethical awareness of self and other*

Learning legal writing is a process of developing your own professional voice, of understanding and accepting authorial responsibility, and of appreciating the 'other' through an understanding of the importance of audience, purpose and **tone**. As noted above, the process of learning to write is often a struggle: as a law student, you must move from novice to mastery and in this process must learn to write with

28 Ibid 140–1.

care, understanding that your choices (of words, of the information you can and cannot convey) reflect not only on your competence as a legal writer but on your personal integrity. Indeed, Bell and Pether cite studies that indicate that good writing is tentative and cautious (a finding that may come as a surprise to novice legal writers): 'expertise in both reading and writing seems to entail less certainty, and far more caution, about words and language'.[29] A similar view is taken by Williams: 'the writer must be confident that he [sic] understands the law well enough to give up its concreteness'.[30] This calls for you, as a legal writer, to write with clarity, persuasively, and in a way that signals 'authority without depending for its power on mere verbal opacity'.[31]

Legal writing demands an understanding of the self. Good legal writers understand and acknowledge their own biases, their conflicts, their agency and power. They 'communicate in a voice of their own – as a lawyer and as a mind'.[32] As Bell and Pether point out, 'the genres of legal **discourse** [are] explicitly concerned with issues of power and authority'.[33] Good writing is reflexive.

Legal writing also demands awareness of the other. As a legal writer, you must sustain awareness that what you write has consequences for others *beyond* the person for whom the writing is intended. This requires you to 'take account of the other side, not as someone to be "bested" or beaten, but as someone with needs, interests, and goals as well'.[34]

Ethical awareness of self and other extends also to research. Those undertaking legal research need to be aware of the fact that they can potentially harm the research participants psychologically, socially, emotionally or culturally.[35] Such harm may follow when participants 'have not fully considered the consequences of the disclosure of their attitudes, beliefs and behaviour' with respect to the research question.[36] Researchers' own values and assumptions can influence the analysis and dissemination of their work, and they must not fabricate or invent data; falsify or distort the results[37] or misrepresent data in such a way that it fails to report the

29 Bell and Pether, above n 4, 119.

30 Joseph M Williams, 'On the Maturing of Legal Writers: Two Models of Growth and Development' (1991) 1 *Legal Writing: The Journal of the Legal Writing Institute* 1, 28.

31 Ibid 29.

32 Weresh, above n 6, 427.

33 Bell and Pether, above n 4, 119.

34 Carrie J Menkel-Meadow, 'When Winning Isn't Everything: The Lawyer as Problem Solver' (2000) 28 *Hofstra Law Review* 905, 915.

35 R Iphofen, *Ethical Decision Making in Social Research. A Practical Guide* (Palgrave Macmillan, 2009) 444.

36 Ibid.

37 Sanjay Singh, 'Ethics in Research' (2012) 78(4) *Indian Journal of Dermatology, Venereology, and Leprology* 411, 412.

truth.[38] While the question of ethical writing may seem to attach in particular to **qualitative** research, Iphofen notes that 'it is dangerous to assume that **quantitative** approaches have less reason to be concerned about, say, vulnerability, sensitivity and the complex distinctions between anonymity and confidentiality'.[39] As Kritzer points out, '[t]he lines between quantitative and qualitative social science are less clear than often presumed. Both types of analysis involve extensive interpretation, and tools of interpretation that have many fundamental similarities'.[40] In effect, the underlying **premise** is that the findings of all research are the product of interpretation. We discuss research and your ethical obligations in more detail in Chapter 4.

### *Ethical awareness of the community of practice*

Fundamentally, instruction in legal writing should serve to initiate you, as a law student, into the legal profession's community of practice. As some commentators have pointed out, as a law student, you ordinarily go on to become a professional writer, whether in legal practice or one of the other employment destinations for law graduates in the government or private sector.[41] Instruction in good writing is thus a core aspect of legal education, albeit too often neglected.

Legal writing is constrained by conventions, standards, responsibilities and genres. Learning to engage in legal discourse is an act of socialisation, not only cognition;[42] of engaging in a dialogue; and of gaining access to a community of practice, matters we discuss in more detail in the chapter on purpose and audience. Bell and Pether argue that 'expertise is a process of mastering the codes of entry into, and acquiring acceptance within, a disciplinary culture'.[43] At the same time, they eschew a simplistic approach to aspects of legal discourse, such as genre:

> It is important to understand genre not as a recipe-like description of the characteristics or rules of writing, but as an analysis of what it is that facilitates communication in any act of writing and/or speaking. In other words, understanding writing means going beyond the words on the page to recognise the material and interactive qualities of genre – or what has been called 'genre as social action'.[44]

---

38 David B Resnik, 'What is Ethics in Research & Why is it Important?', *National Institute of Environmental Health Sciences*, 1 May 2011, available at http://www.niehs.nih.gov/research/resources/bioethics/whatis/.

39 Iphofen, above n 35, 445

40 HM Kritzer, 'The Data Puzzle: The Nature of Interpretation in Quantitative Research' (1996) 40(1) *American Journal of Political Science* 1, available at http://www.jstor.org/stable/10.2307/2111692.

41 See, for instance, Wayne Schiess, 'Lawyers are Professional Writers' (2012) *Austin Lawyer* 11, available at http://papers.ssrn.com/sol3/papers.cfm?abstract_id=2274981.

42 Bell and Pether, above n 4, 119.

43 Ibid 117.

44 Ibid 119.

At the core of your obligation to the discourse community as a legal writer is the concept of the duty to the law. Legal writing entails responsibility to society[45] 'to insure the legitimacy of the legal system in society':[46]

> What distinguishes the legal community from other interpretive communities is the presence of order and justice at the center of our webs of belief about law, the principles of legitimacy, stare decisis, and legislative supremacy near the center, and the commitment to legal reasoning in bringing these values and principles to bear in particular cases. The legal conversation is a conversation about the implications of these values and principles in particular cases.[47]

## *Ethical awareness of professional responsibility*

Good legal writing requires the integration of a range of skills (problem solving, analysis, reasoning) and an appreciation of organisational responsibilities and constraints (time management, the need for strategic research, hierarchies). It also requires an appreciation of professional responsibility: the need to be honest, competent, and courteous, and duties to the law and to the client. Along with the applicable legislation, lawyers are governed by professional conduct rules which mandate certain standards of behaviour. A breach of these rules can attract disciplinary measures. For the purposes of this book we will primarily be referring to the Australian Solicitors Conduct Rules (ASCR) adopted by New South Wales, Victoria, Queensland, and South Australia. We then provide, in the Learning Materials, the equivalent references for the other states, and the rules governing barristers – again, primarily the Australian Bar Association Barristers' Conduct Rules (Bar Rules), now adopted by New South Wales, Victoria, Queensland, South Australia and Western Australia.

Provisions relating to competence and diligence, honesty and courtesy have direct implications for legal writing. Within practice, 'legal writing is generally done in service of a specific client or set of clients'.[48] But the effects of writing are much wider: As Fischer notes, 'a lawyer's writing not only embodies his or her sense of professionalism and ethics, but also affects clients, opposing parties, the courts, and the legal system'.[49]

45 Frank Pommersheim, 'Voices, Values and Community: Some Reflections on Legal Writing' (1988) 12 *Legal Studies Forum* 477, 478.

46 Ibid 479.

47 Ibid quoting Steven Burton, *An Introduction to Law and Legal Reasoning* (Boston, 1985) 209.

48 SR Kedia, 'Redirecting the Scope of First-Year Writing Courses: Toward a New Paradigm of Teaching Legal Writing' (2009) *University of Detroit Mercy Law Review* 147, 156.

49 Judith D Fischer, 'The Role of Ethics in Legal Writing: The Forensic Embroiderer, the Minimalist Wizard, and Other Stories' (2004) 9 *The Scribes Journal of Legal Writing* 77.

## *Competence and diligence*

Members of the public expect that lawyers, as legal experts, will be competent. ASCR r 4.1.3 enforces that expectation, stating that a solicitor must 'deliver legal services competently, diligently and as promptly as reasonably possible'. The rule does not elaborate on what competence entails, but it is generally understood that it includes the elements explicitly set out in the American Bar Association rules, the *Model Rules of Professional Conduct:* 'A lawyer shall provide competent representation to a client. Competent representation requires the legal knowledge, skill, thoroughness and preparation reasonably necessary for the representation'.

In terms of legal writing, the phrase 'thoroughness and preparation ... for the representation' are particularly important. This implies that clients can expect that their lawyers will carry out whatever legal research is required to enable their competent representation. However, this reference to preparation should not lead to verbosity as it is now well established that 'concise prose communicates and persuades better than wordy, cluttered legalese'.[50]

Poor legal research can also result in a lack of diligence – for instance, failing to recognise that the statutory limitation has expired for commencing a claim.[51] Lawyers also need to bring their skill of analysis to bear on the legal research they conduct. A failure to do so may result in 'substandard documents'.[52] Given the fact that the court relies on lawyers to 'elucidate the issues',[53] ungrammatical sentences, a poorly written argument, and failing to include pinpoint citations hinder the court from understanding a party's case.[54] A document that makes an unsubstantiated or frivolous claim may also attract a claim of incompetence, and be held to be a breach of ASCR r 21, which provides that a solicitor must not allege any matter of fact in, *inter alia*, court documents, unless they believe on reasonable grounds that the factual material already available provides a proper basis to do so.

Good legal writing also requires an awareness of any formal expectations of the written work – for instance, court rules such as the number of pages allowed; or the font to be used.[55]

---

50 Ibid 99, n 144, referring to a number of other authors.

51 Carol M Bast and Susan W Harrell, 'Ethical Obligations: Performing Adequate Legal Research and Legal Writing' (2004) 29 *Nova Law Review* 49, 57.

52 Fischer, above n 49, 93.

53 Ibid 96.

54 Bast and Harrell, above n 51, 53–6.

55 Ibid 54.

### *Honesty and courtesy*

Lawyers are required by the professional rules to 'be honest and courteous in all dealings in the course of legal practice' (ASCR r 4.1.2). The theme of honesty underpins all aspects of lawyering. It is the criterion used to determine admission as an Australian lawyer and continuing membership of the legal profession. As officers of the court, lawyers have an overriding duty to the court (ASCR r 3) which is particularly manifested in honesty. In this regard, lawyers are duty bound to ensure that they 'do not deceive or knowingly or recklessly mislead the court' (ASCR r 19.1) and must 'take all necessary steps to correct any misleading statement' they have made (ASCR r 19.2). In fact, this duty extends to require the lawyer to advise the court of any binding authority (ASCR r 19.6.1), even if this authority is damaging to the client's case (ASCR r 19.6.3). This requirement means that a document that fails to inform the court of all of the relevant legal research undertaken is deficient. In fact, it is suggested that 'when a lawyer errs by failing to cite relevant adverse authority, a court must spend valuable time and effort to perform its own analysis',[56] and this may cause the court to make a decision without referring to a relevant precedent.[57] Dishonest behaviour, according to ASCR r 5, can potentially 'be prejudicial to, or diminish the public confidence in, the administration of justice … or bring the profession into disrepute'. Of course, for law students, the requirement of honesty means that written work that is **plagiarised** may compromise admission. We address plagiarism in later chapters.

The requirements of civility and courtesy must be adhered to in communications. Effective and appropriate communications with clients, other practitioners, the court and third parties are fundamental aspects of good legal service delivery and professionalism. Courtesy or civility in a general sense is gaining prominence. For instance, the professional conduct rules in New South Wales prior to 1 January 2014 only required lawyers to be courteous to other practitioners, whereas ASCR r 4.1.2 (now adopted in New South Wales) extends the requirement for lawyers to be courteous in *all* dealings and presumably this includes clients, other practitioners, and third parties with whom the lawyer interacts. ASCR r 34, which specifically sets out how members are to deal with other persons and includes a direction to not mislead, intimidate, embarrass or frustrate others,[58] emphasises the importance of civility. It also provides a basis for complaint by anyone who believes that a lawyer

56 Fischer, above n 49, 77.
57 Ibid 83.
58 ASCR r 34.

is guilty of discourteous and inappropriate communications.[59] ASCR r 42 now also includes an explicit prohibition against discrimination, bullying and harassment by lawyers. In fact, civility in legal writing is so important, we have devoted a separate discussion to the topic in Chapter 11.

## V CONCLUSION

Writing can often seem like a solitary task, but at its heart it is fundamentally both social and ethical in nature. For the lawyer, writing is fundamental to professional practice; and to the student, writing is the gateway to the practice of law, the legal community, and the development of a distinct professional identity. In this chapter we have suggested that good legal writing entails an awareness of, and reflection upon, the self and other, the community of practice and the professional expectations as expressed in the relevant rules of conduct. In the chapters that follow, we hope to encourage an appreciation of good legal writing and its relationship to ethical conduct.

---

59 Further, there are rules relating to lawyers communicating with clients, ASCR r 7; opponents, ASCR r 22; witnesses, ASCR r 26; and clients of another solicitor. While these do not speak specifically of courtesy, they do call for clarity, and show intolerance for misrepresentations and efforts to gain an advantage using 'smart' practices.

# REVIEW MATERIALS

## SUMMARY

This chapter set out the reasons for arguing that good legal writing is always an ethical act. It covered the relationship between legal writing and legal professional ethics, the conventional and progressive approaches to teaching legal writing, and the ethical foundations of legal writing in awareness of self and other, in the legal profession's community of practice, and in one's own professional responsibility.

## KEY POINTS

1. Legal writing is a core aspect of lawyering.
2. Legal writing is an important aspect of professional identity.
3. Good legal writing reflects self-awareness and ethical awareness of others.
4. Legal writing is constrained by the conventions, standards, expectations, responsibilities and genres of the community of practice.
5. The ASCR imposes professional obligations upon written communications.

## QUESTIONS FOR REFLECTION

1. What does it mean to be part of a community of practice? How might membership of the legal profession's community of practice affect your legal writing?
2. What does it mean to have an ethical awareness of the 'other' in your writing? How might such an awareness reveal itself in your writing?
3. How might a letter to a client written by a lawyer differ from a letter written to a student by a lecturer?
4. What, in your view, makes for 'professional' written communication? Is it wording? The organisation of the text? The presentation?
5. Why are rules imposed on the conduct of lawyers in the ASCR? What sanctions do those rules impose for breaching them?

## EXERCISES

These exercises are constructed with a view to encouraging reflection on what might be your own biases and goals, your relationship with your reader and with others, and any consequences for the reader and others involved in legal writing.

1. Is it unethical for a student to hide the seminal text on the topic of a required essay that is held in the university library? If you saw a student hiding such a text, what would you do?
2. Group work is an important skill for future lawyers. While it can bring challenges, it also provides an opportunity for group members to present something of a higher standard, superior to what any single student can accomplish. However, a high degree of cooperation is needed to achieve that goal. Competitiveness or a desire to promote yourself may cause tension within the group, impeding effective decision making; it may even result in unethical behaviour. Consider the following issues, and discuss ways of avoiding or alleviating the problems raised.
   a. Four out of five members of a particular group come from a clique of students who went to high school together. They write a dishonest report about the contribution of the fifth member whom they dislike and with whom they disagree.
   b. Members of a particular group disagree strongly with the views of one member of the group. That person had conducted all of the research and the other members had either not read any of the material or skimmed lightly over it.
   c. A member of a particular group signs off on participation in the work, but, in fact, had made no contribution at all.
3. Would it be unethical for a law teacher to provide a reference for a student whom they taught more than five years ago?
4. Write a professional identity letter.[60]

   The purposes of this exercise are to identify your core values, to consolidate the commitments you want to make to yourself as a professional, and to begin to establish your professional identity.

   Write a letter to yourself that outlines your core values and explain why they are important. Explain how those values can be incorporated into your professional identity as a lawyer. You may find the following prompts helpful:

   - What motivated you to be a lawyer, and why? How does that motivation relate to your core values?
   - How do you want to treat your clients?
   - How you want to interact with other members of your profession?
   - How will you incorporate your core values into your practice of law?

---

60 Adapted from Institute for the Advancement of the American Legal System, Educating Tomorrow's Lawyers, 'Sample Professional Identify Assignments', available at http://iaals.du.edu/sites/default/files/documents/resources/5_sample_professional_identity_assignments_burgess.pdf.

- What type of reputation do you want to create in the legal community? Is there a difference between how you want your clients to know you and how want your colleagues, and those in the legal profession generally, to know you?

If you do this exercise in first year, you might want to read this letter periodically as you continue through your degree and when you become a lawyer.

## FURTHER RESOURCES

1. Examples of communities of practice
   - First-year law: http://fyhe.com.au/current-activities/communities-of-practice/
   - Health and law: http://globalhealth.org/event/community-practice-health-law/
2. Communication skills
   - Communication skills for lawyers: http://www.cuttingedgelaw.com/content/communication-skills-lawyers
   - Written communication skills: http://www.kent.ac.uk/careers/sk/written-communication.htm
   - Communicating with your client: https://www.lsc.qld.gov.au/__data/assets/pdf_file/0004/97753/FACT-SHEET-7-Communicating-with-your-client-June-2012.pdf.

# PART 1

# GENERAL AND ACADEMIC WRITING

# CHAPTER 2

# PRE-WRITING

## I INTRODUCTION

Writing skills are essential for legal professionals. As Pollman points out, legal professionals – lawyers, judges and law academics – write every day.[1] It is thus essential to become 'confident and comfortable with legal discourse and composition in practical, social and intellectual contexts'.[2] Yet it has been observed that '[p]erhaps no aspect of legal life is more important, yet more widely misunderstood, than legal writing'.[3]

The bad news is that proficiency in legal writing is not quickly achieved or simple to learn. Legal writing has been described as 'difficult, painful, progressive work that takes long, conscious reworking'.[4] This process of developing proficiency in legal writing is at once personal and professional: '[w]riting is always an act of asserting oneself as a being in the world'.[5] Boyd White has noted that the greatest opportunity offered by the study of law is 'not that one can manipulate forms, but that one can acquire a **voice** of one's own, as a lawyer and as a mind; not a bureaucratic voice but a real voice'.[6]

In this chapter, we introduce you to the importance of pre-writing, which consists of the process of reflection (particularly on purpose and audience) and **planning**. Research is also part of the pre-writing process in law, but we discuss this in a separate chapter.

---

1 Terrill Pollman, 'Building a Tower of Babel or Building a Discipline? Talking about Legal Writing' (2002) 85(4) *Marquette Law Review* 887.

2 J Christopher Rideout and Jill J Ramsfield, 'Legal Writing: A Revised View' (1994) 69 (35) *Washington Law Review* 35, 39.

3 James Boyd White, quoted by Pollman, above n 1, 892.

4 Rideout and Ramsfield, above n 2, 43–44.

5 Thomas DeVere Wolsey, Diane Lap and Douglas Fisher, 'Students' and Teachers' Perceptions: An Inquiry into Academic Writing (2012) *Journal of Adolescent and Adult Literacy* 714, 716.

6 James Boyd White, quoted by Pollman, above n 1, 892.

In the reflective part of the cycle, we also encourage you to reflect on the topic or problem that forms the basis of your writing task, the particular genre appropriate to your task and the ethical obligations, general and specific, that may apply to the task. Because these issues depend greatly on the particular writing task (are you writing a legal essay? Answering a hypothetical problem? Starting a PhD?), we encourage you to also read the chapter relevant to your writing task. This will help you determine the issues you need to address and also any specific ethical obligations that might apply.

Here, we begin by discussing the fundamental importance of reflection on the purpose for which you are writing and on your audience. These notions are not as straightforward as you might assume.

## II PURPOSE AND AUDIENCE

To learn legal writing is to assert your identity as a knowledgeable participant 'in and outside of the classroom, while constructing an identity with a unique voice within the learning community'.[7] Wiggins refers to this as '**authentic writing**', and he advises: 'say it *concisely*, have great *empathy* for your client/audience, and pay close attention to *context*. In other words: get serious, really serious, about Audience and Purpose'.[8] He argues that 'purpose' and 'audience' are not mere buzzwords; 'they are task-defining: the consequences of your writing matter for a specific audience in a specific situation'.[9] Wong argues that purpose and audience are always intertwined and affect the approach writers take. This is borne out by the study by Wong, who found that student writers who considered the audience to be the lecturer who was evaluating them wrote for the purpose of knowledge display, and were less willing to take risks. Writers who considered the audience to be someone other than the lecturer–evaluator tended to write for the purpose of 'writing to learn'. These writers were more ready to try out ideas and strategies.[10]

Some have suggested that a failure to consider purpose and audience is at the heart of accusations that legal writing is 'wordy, abstruse and unintelligible'. Thus Phelps argues that:

> [w]ordiness, abstruseness and unintelligibility result when legal writers fail to recognise that the discourse they produce is essentially a conversation with

7 Wolsey et al, above n5, 716.

8 Grant Wiggins, 'EJ in Focus: Real-world Writing: Making Purpose and Audience Matter' (2009) 98(5) *The English Journal* 29, 29.

9 Ibid 32.

10 Albert TY Wong, 'Writers' Mental Representations of the Intended Audience and of the Rhetorical Purpose for Writing and the Strategies that they Employed when they Composed' (2005) *System 33*, 29, 43–44.

> another or several others intended to solve problems and to discover answers to questions together. The law, thus seen, is a communal activity in which people speak and write for and to each other.[11]

Phelps's notion of writing as a conversation, although primarily focused on the relationship between writer and reader, also touches on the point that, although we tend to imagine writing as a solitary act, in practice much legal writing is done collaboratively, with teams of writers working together in **drafting** and editing a document.[12]

As we will see, however, despite widespread acknowledgment of the importance of considering purpose and audience, both terms have been contested and their meaning and application may depend on one's view of writing. Further, in legal writing, one's unique voice is always subject to the conventions of the community of practice. As Rideout and Ramsfield observe:

> law school offers an invitation into one of the richest and most complex of the professional discourses: a community that is demanding in its argumentative and analytical paradigms, challenging in its research and writing processes, and complicated by its social pressures.[13]

## *What is your purpose?*

The choices made to achieve the writer's desired purpose are set out in Figure 2.1. Purpose is essential to legal writing, and it has been argued[14] that legal writing is English for a specific purpose. One of the reasons purpose is so important to legal

FIGURE 2.1

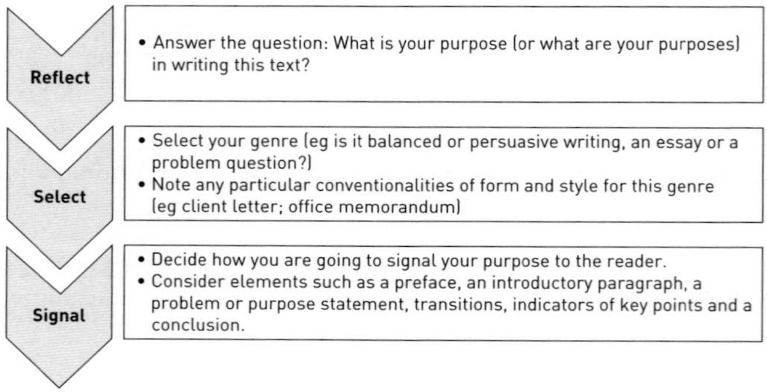


11 Teresa Godwin Phelps, 'The New Legal Rhetoric' (1986) 40 *Southwestern Law Journal* 1089, 1090.

12 Pollman, above n 1, 887.

13 Rideout and Ramsfield, above n 2, 99.

14 Ibid 43–4.

writing is that it is strongly linked to genre: Badger and White[15] observe that different kinds of writing, or genres, such as a letter to a client or law reports, are used to carry out different purposes. There is also a distinction to be made between purpose and impact. Arguing that 'the point of writing is to have something to say and to make a difference in saying it', Wiggins[16] observes that impact is rarely considered in writing instruction. Rather, the focus tends to be on process, and this, in turn, tends to be formulaic rather than purposeful.

Purpose is important for the reader, who draws on cues in the text and her own knowledge of genre and conventions to find an inner logic in the text based on a sense of the writer's purpose.[17] Indeed, Flower's study found a surprising number of participants resolved ambiguity in a text by rhetorical reading – that is, resorting to inferences about the author's purpose and structure.[18] For this reason, Flower emphasises the importance of signalling purpose to the reader.

Conventions for signalling purpose include the preface, the introductory paragraph, and the problem/purpose statement. Throughout the text, signalling devices such as **transitions**, and indicators of key points and conclusions indicate the linear plan that organises a document. The marking of purpose in the text explicitly gives 'the impression of orderly, linear, controlled intentionality and singularity of purpose'.[19]

Phelps[20] argues that, in legal writing, the writer is seeking to achieve one of two purposes: either to 'reveal and explain a particular reality' (for example, office memoranda or a client letter) or to persuade a reader' (for example, a brief to a barrister). We have used this distinction – between **balanced writing** and **persuasive writing** in this book, particularly in Part 3. The main features of each type are summarised in Figure 2.2.

Charrow et al[21] provide a more detailed statement of purpose. They claim that legal documents are written to:

- inform;
- elicit information;
- persuade;
- record;

---

15 Richard Badger and Goodith White, 'A Process Genre Approach to Teaching Writing' (2000) 54(2) *ELT Journal* 153, 155.
16 Wiggins, above n 8, 29.
17 Linda Flower, 'The Construction of Purpose in Writing and Reading' (1988) 50(5) *College English* 528, 542.
18 Ibid 548.
19 Ibid 531.
20 Phelps, above n 11, 1092.
21 Veda R Charrow, Myra Kerhardt and Robert P Charrow, *Clear and Effective Legal Writing* (Wolters Kluwer, 4th ed, 2007) 95.

- describe;
- satisfy court rules or federal/state laws;
- make someone act, or not act;
- give notice.

FIGURE 2.2

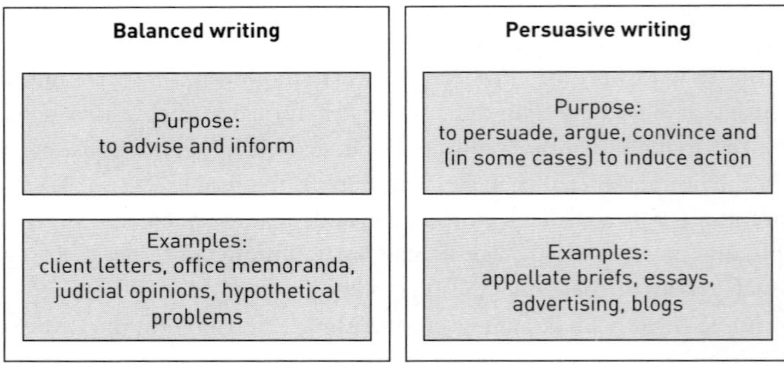


It is rarely the case, however, that a single, stable purpose is behind any piece of written work; rather, 'the purposes behind any rhetorical or any human act are multi-fold, entangled and even contradictory'.[22] Flower refers to a 'web' of purpose, that is, 'a multi-dimensional network of information – a web that radiates in all directions, anchored to points unknown'.[23] She notes that studies of writers show that purpose emerges as a dynamic structure that may remain under construction throughout the composition of a text: '[i]t is built and developed, and sometimes radically restructured at even the top levels, as the writer imagines possibilities and responds to new ideas or to his or her own developing text'.[24]

This is also true of legal texts, which can be written for multiple, sometimes even conflicting, purposes.[25] You may find it helpful to list your purposes and rank them. This is because purpose will often dictate your writing strategy. For instance, Charrow et al[26] observe that if, for example, your primary purpose in a particular piece of legal writing is to inform, then you will need to:

- 'Find out what your audience does or does not know;
- Gather relevant information, anticipating questions;

22 Flower, above n 17, 528.
23 Ibid 531.
24 Ibid 534.
25 Charrow et al, above n 21, 95.
26 Ibid 98–9.

- Know the relative importance of different bits of information;
- Put the information into a logical sequence …;
- Highlight the information you want the reader to be most aware of;
- Guide the reader through the document.'

On the other hand, if your primary purpose is to elicit information, you will need to:

- 'Decide what information you need;
- Find out what information your audience is likely to have;
- Ask relevant questions;
- Order your questions to fit your needs.'

### *Who is your audience?*

Like purpose, a consideration of audience is said to be crucial to good writing. One characteristic of the expert writer is that they 'use their conception of audience to narrow their focus and to solve specific writing problems'.[27] Magnifico suggests that 'expert writers tend to consider the elements of purpose, discourse type, and audience at roughly the same time, suggesting that the choice of an audience helps to constrain the form and presentation of the writing'.[28] In legal writing, a client letter will require a different approach from that taken in a memorandum to a senior partner, for instance.

Ethically, we show consideration for our readers by thinking about their needs and writing 'empathically, clearly and concisely'.[29] Wiggins asks: 'who is your audience? what are their expectations, needs, interests?' and he argues that empathy comes from redrafting with specific audiences in mind.[30] For lawyers, that specific audience might be judges and other lawyers, but may also be individual clients, business clients, government agencies or lay people who are not clients.[31] Neumann and Simon[32] suggest that the members of the typical audience for legal professional writing generally share three characteristics, and we should keep these in mind when we write:

- they must make a decision of some kind and need you to provide exactly the material necessary to make that decision, no more and no less;
- they will be busy – they must read quickly and do not have time to read twice;
- they are likely to be sceptical and will look for gaps and weaknesses in your analysis.

---

27 Alecia Marie Magnifico, 'Writing for Whom? Cognition, Motivation and a Writer's Audience (2010) 45(3) *Educational Psychologist* 167, 170.

28 Ibid 169.

29 Wiggins, above n 8, 32.

30 Ibid 32.

31 Charrow et al, above n 21, 108.

32 Richard K Neumann Jr and Sheila Simon, *Legal Writing* (Wolters Kluwer, 2008) 3.

This last point is also taken up by Schmedemann and Kunz, who note that readers come to a text with expectations about grammar, punctuation and word usage. The more formal the prose, the more likely it is that such reader will anticipate that their expectations will be met. Legal writing is very formal prose, so reader expectations are high. If the text is grammatically correct and easy to read, the reader will think more of the substantive analysis. The opposite is also true, so a reader faced with a poorly constructed or presented text will become increasingly sceptical about the content.[33]

In law school, the audience for your legal writing will most commonly be your lecturer or tutor. You need to keep in mind while writing that this reader will not, unlike other readers, be reading for information. Rather, that person will be reading to evaluate what you have learned and how well you can communicate it.[34] It is also helpful to realise that your lecturer or tutor is not an 'isolated, idiosyncratic, individualised reader'.[35] Rather, she represents the community of scholars and teachers in the field. It is thus helpful to assume that you are writing to a law-trained reader who does not have particular expertise in the area in which you are writing. This assumption will help you get the right balance in your writing.

But while reflecting on audience, we need to also keep in mind our professional identities as writers. Writing is also 'an exploration of ideas, a quest for purpose, and a projection of oneself'.[36] Thus, although our client letter and our intra-office memorandum require different approaches, they both say something about us as legal professional writers.

Although audience is extensively used as a subject for theory and for the teaching of writing, and the concept is thus considered 'obvious' and 'crucial', it has also been described as 'remarkably elusive'.[37] Park notes that there is a distinction between 'readers' and 'audience' but that the distinction is often tacit and ambiguous.[38] He also observes that there are two divergent meanings of 'audience'. One meaning is 'toward actual people external to a text, the audience whom the writer must accommodate'; the other is implied in the text itself as 'a set of suggested or evoked attitudes, interests, reactions, conditions of knowledge which may or may not fit with the qualities of actual readers'.[39] He argues that 'we are too often unaware of the rich ambiguity of the term 'audience' and depend too heavily upon the

---

33 Deborah A Schmedemann and Christina L Kunz, *Synthesis: Legal Reading, Reasoning and Writing* (Wolters Kluwer, 4th ed, 2014) 311.

34 Linda H Edwards, *Legal Writing: Process, Analysis and Organization* (Aspen, 2006) 154.

35 Mary Kay Mulvaney and David A Joliffe, *Academic Writing: Genres, Samples and Resources* (Pearson Longman, 2005) 2.

36 Barry M Kroll, 'Writing for Readers: Three Perspectives on Audience' (1984) 35(2) *College Composition and Communication* 172, 183.

37 Douglas B Park, 'The Meanings of "Audience"' (1982) 44(3) *College English* 247.

38 Ibid 247.

39 Ibid.

concrete image of audience as the readers external to the text'.[40] Magnifico defines audience as 'the person or people addressed by a speech or a piece of writing'.[41] She argues that the audience occupies a middle space between the writer and her topic. On this view, 'audience' in the abstract helps the writer to frame her intentions and plans about the writing; and 'audience' in the sense of a social group of readers provides external feedback about how successfully the writing communicates its ideas.[42]

Why is there such ambiguity in our understanding of 'audience'? The answer is that 'audience' has multiple meanings in contemporary work on written composition, and the pedagogy of writing is based on different theoretical perspectives, notably, the **'rhetorical'**, the **'formalist'**, the **'cognitive'** and the **'social'** perspectives. Figure 2.3 sets out the elements of each of these theories and suggests examples where they apply. An outline of these theories of writing is included in Appendix 2.

FIGURE 2.3

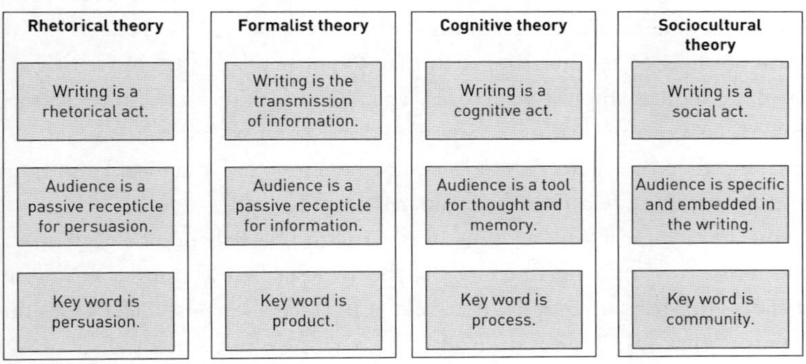


## III PLANNING

We have discussed the importance of identifying purpose and audience prior to planning. Markman[43] argues that as a writer, you must first articulate your purpose and audience and know the framework within which you write. Only then can you effectively begin to plan, draft and revise.

---

40 Ibid.

41 Magnifico, above n 27, 169.

42 Ibid 176.

43 Natalie A Markman, 'Bringing Journalism Pedagogy into the Legal Writing Class' (1993) 43 *Journal of Legal Education* 551, 559.

## *Planning as part of a (messy) recursive process*

In this section, we are concerned with this process of planning, or what some writers term the 'pre-writing', stage of the writing process. The writing process is often modelled on three stages: planning, drafting and **revising**. In planning, the writer generates ideas and organises them into a writing plan. In drafting, the writer gets her thoughts down on paper. In revising, the writer attempts to improve a draft.[44] All three stages are important. Developing your own strategies for planning, drafting and revising text is not only effective in improving your performance if you are a struggling writer, but also enhances your writing if you are already skilled.[45]

Although we will discuss these stages of the writing process in a linear fashion, it is important to keep in mind that in the actual writing process, the three stages of writing overlap and intertwine.[46] In other words, writing is often messy! This is because all writing, including legal writing, is not mechanical or straightforward. Rather, writing is always 'exploratory, **recursive**, reflective and responsive'.[47] Rather than engaging in a clear-cut linear progression from beginning to end, the legal writer moves back and forth among planning, drafting, and revising. Revising, for instance, often generates more planning.[48]

If you are new to legal writing, this may seem surprising. Legal writing is often portrayed as logical, highly structured and formal. Although more formal and elaborate, however, the writing components of a law text are the same as those of a poem, an article or a letter. The ideas must be generated, organised and translated into text. In turn, the text must be evaluated and revised.[49]

If you are a logical person who likes structure, it will not be welcome news that this process of making meaning has been described as 'messy, slow, tentative, full of starts and stops, a complex network of language, purposes, plans, options and constraints';[50] that '[p]rogress is unsteady'; that writing is not a methodical movement from small to large or from large to small: writers 'as frequently work from wholes

---

44 John R Hayes and Linda S Flower, 'Writing Research and the Writer' (1986) 41(1) *American Psychologist* 1106, 1107–8.

45 Steve Graham, Karen R Harris and Charles MacArther, 'Explicitly Teaching Struggling Writers: Strategies for Mastering the Writing Process' (2006) 41(5) *Intervention in School and Clinic* 290, 294 citing Graham and Harris 2003 and 2006.

46 Teresa Godwin Phelps, 'Writing Strategies for Practicing Attorneys' (1987/8) 23 *Gonzaga Law Review* 155, 160; Hayes and Flower, above n 44, 1106.

47 Linda L Berger, 'A Reflective Rhetorical Model: The Legal Writing Teacher as Reader and Writer' (2000) 6(57) *Journal of the Legal Writing Institute* 57, 63.

48 Teresa Godwin Phelps, 'The New Legal Rhetoric' (1986) 40 *Southwestern Law Journal* 1089, 1095.

49 Britt-Louise Gunnarrson, 'Text Comprehensibility and the Writing Process: The Case of Laws and Lawmaking' (1989) 6 *Written Communication* 86, 87.

50 Linda L Berger, 'Applying New Rhetoric to Legal Discourse: The Ebb and Flow of Reader and Writer, Text and Context' (1999) 49 *J Legal Ed* 155, 155.

to parts as from parts to wholes' and that they 'leap back and forth between local concerns. Perhaps the reason for this is that:[51]

> writing, in general, can be understood as an ill-defined construction task of the sort seen in musical composition, architecture, or design … That is, the problem-solver is not only building his or her own representation of the problem and its goals, but the problem or task itself changes as the constructed product grows. The writer's draft and the designer's sketch feed new constraints back into the planning[52] about words and global concerns about the shape of the total piece.[53]

Although **iterative** and messy, there are certain identifiable stages in the legal drafting cycle. Figure 2.4 is our diagram of these stages. Editing and proofreading are not on this diagram – these are the final stages, once your work is complete. Before you get to these stages, however, you may find that you have to go through this cycle a number of times.

FIGURE 2.4

## *What is planning and why is it important?*

Planning is important, despite the 'messiness' of writing. Research shows that it is an essential part of effective writing.[54] It marks a significant difference between

51 Linda Flower, Karen A Schriver, Linda Carey, Christina Haas and John R Hayes, *Planning in Writing* (Carnegie Mellon, 1989) 4.

52 Ibid.

53 Berger, above n 50,160.

54 Paul Maharg, 'Contracts: An Introduction to the Skills of Legal Writing and Analysis' (1996) *Journal of Information, Law and Technology* 1; Bruce Saddler, Susan Moran, Steve Graham and Karen R Harris, 'Preventing Writing Difficulties: The Effects of Planning Strategy Instruction on the Writing Performance of Struggling Writers' (2004) 12(1) *Exceptionality: A Special Education Journal* 3, 3–5; Sandra Stotsky, 'On Planning and Writing Plans. Or Beware of Borrowed Theories' (1990) 41(1) *College Composition and Communication* 37.

experienced and inexperienced writers. Inexperienced writers often do very little planning and tend to identify writing with text production.[55]

Planning has been described as 'a strategic response to the task, as the writer sees it, and to the representation of knowledge the writer currently holds'.[56] Markman[57] argues that the legal writer is at an advantage in this stage of the process because they 'can strategically structure an entire document around what the audience needs and wants to know'.[58]

In turn, the quality and integration of planning is important. Effective writers use their planning time to consider the entire rhetorical problem[59] and the organisation of the text as a whole,[60] make far more connections among their goals than novice writers[61] and are conscious of constraints imposed by the genre and the needs of the reader.[62]

Planning is particularly important to legal writing. Good legal writing is 'plain, simple and direct',[63] that is, concise and to the point. This is because much of the subject matter is complex. Legal writing thus requires *more planning and time in the pre-writing stages* than other forms of writing:

> Starting to write without any pre-planning is a recipe for wasting time and a poor final product. Writing with insufficient pre-planning is also inefficient, hampering your efforts and making the process more difficult than necessary. A simple outline – which might have worked for you in the past – will usually not be sufficient to help you produce a good piece of legal writing. Rather, a "thick" outline with detailed instructions to yourself about which section will discuss which case, and what parts of that case will be emphasized in that section, is what you need to prepare before you start writing. If you spend the time doing that sort of work in advance, the final product will always benefit because it is much easier to write plain, simple, and direct prose when you understand the problem thoroughly and know exactly what comes next in your explanation of it.[64]

---

55 Flower et al, above n 51, 48.
56 Ibid 2.
57 Markman, above n 43, 567.
58 Ibid.
59 Ibid 51.
60 Saddler et al, above n 54, 3–5.
61 Hayes and Flower, above n 44, 1109.
62 Saddler et al, above n 54, 3–5.
63 David C Thomson, *Skills and Values Lawyering Process: Legal Writing and Advocacy* (Carolina Academic Press (CAP), 2013) 5.
64 Ibid.

## *Planning strategies*

There is no single 'right way' to plan.[65] Despite the almost unanimous view that planning is an essential part of good writing, there is little consensus on what the process entails and it has been said that 'writers may take significantly different paths in developing [their] plans'.[66] At the higher levels, there is some consensus that planning involves 'preliminary decisions about purpose, audience, major ideas, and organizing strategies'[67] but beyond this, there is little agreement about what kinds of plans should result from planning and there is no consistency in examples used. Writers vary in the strategies they use: some writers begin with a detailed outline; some use a flow chart; others use bubble charts; and others free write.[68]

You should experiment to find the method that suits you best.[69] Part of the process of learning legal writing is developing your own style, not only in terms of your professional voice but in terms of your own strategies for planning, drafting and revising. We have collected here a few recommended strategies. We suggest that you experiment to find the strategy that best suits you and your particular writing task. Of course, you need not confine yourself to one strategy – you may find it helpful to mix and match some strategies.

### *The IRAC planning strategy*

Most legal documents follow a particular convention:[70] they are divided into four parts: a statement of the issue or concern; an explanation of the legal rules that are applicable to that issue; an application of the rule to a client's facts; and a conclusion that summarises the explanation and application provided. If more than one issue needs to be fully analysed to solve the client's problem, this form is repeated to address each issue in turn. This outline strategy brings us to what is known as IRAC.

IRAC stands for **I**ssue, **R**ule, **A**pplication, **C**onclusion. If you are writing for assessment, keep in mind that not all law teachers are wedded to IRAC; others may want you to follow IRAC carefully; still others will insist on a method of their own, so you need to clarify expectations with them. Much material on using IRAC suggests it should not be used too rigidly, but it is a useful way to structure legal

65 Pamela Samuelson, 'Good Legal Writing: Of Orwell and Window Panes' (1984/5) 46 *University Pittsburgh Law Review* 149, 150.

66 Ibid 50.

67 Stotsky, above n 54, 42.

68 Suzanne E Rowe, 'Legal Research, Legal Writing and Legal Analysis: Putting Law School into Practice' (2000) 29(4) *Stetson Law Review* 1193, 1205.

69 Ibid 1205.

70 Thomson, above n 63, 4.

analysis for problem questions, particularly at the planning stage, and particularly if you are new to legal writing. We cover IRAC in more detail in Chapter 5 'Case Notes and Problem Questions', but in essence, it uses the following structure:

- *State the issue:* This is the legal question or questions posed by the facts. What has gone wrong and for whom? Identify the plaintiff and defendant and their respective issues. Some IRAC guides suggest you begin by listing the known facts, and determining whether there is information that you need to make a determination, but is not given. Using Markman's journalistic analysis (below) can be helpful at this point in the process.
- *State the law:* This is the legal principle or principles applicable to the question, derived from judicial decisions and/or legislation. Often the principle will contain a number of elements that must be established in order to, for instance, determine liability of a party. You may need to consider definitions of particular words in your principle; exceptions and limitations to the general rule; and available defences.
- *Apply the law:* This is the heart of your analysis. You should match each element of the legal rule or rules you have identified as relevant with a fact. Your analysis should identify the facts that help prove the elements of the rule and which might further the public policy underlying the rule. At the same time, you need to identify the counter-arguments that can be raised by opposing counsel. The core of legal analysis is in the processes of analogising and **distinguishing**.
- *Conclude:* There is not necessarily a right or wrong answer. You should identify the argument you think is the strongest, but state your conclusion as a probable result.

## *Other law-specific planning strategies*

### *Put your strongest case first*

Samuelson[71] advises:

- Your plan should break the argument up into its basic components.
- It should reflect the order in which the strongest case for your position can be made. You should play with the ordering of the elements. Ask yourself why what you put first needs to be there.
- Allow yourself to revise your structure as you go along if, as you write, you find yourself dissatisfied with your initial organisation.

---

71 Samuelson, above n 65, 155.

- Reread the paper after you've written it to see if the organisation you tried has been successful. If not, try to rework it in outline form before rewriting the whole paper.

### *The journalistic approach*

Markman[72] advises that adopting journalism's 'five W's and an H' (Who, What, When, Where, Why and How) can assist planning and organisation of writing. This strategy helps to focus on the most significant facts as you gather and convey information. Law students can use this **heuristic** to frame their issues, begin their research, and synthesise their materials. It can help to quickly and concisely articulate legally relevant information in a given fact pattern or case.

### *The reflective approach*

Phelps[73] recommends a reflective approach[74] and advises that the writer begins by asking themselves:

- 'What question(s) should this document answer?
- What is my answer (no more than a few words)?
- Who is my reader? Implications for word and content choices.
- What is my reader's relationship to me? Implications for word and content choices.
- How much does my reader know about the subject and my answer? Implications.
- What is my reader's attitude about the subject and about my answer?
- What does my reader need to know to understand my answer? List in "need to know" order.
- Why am I writing this?' (ie why does this legal document need to come into existence? What problem needs to be solved? What are the issues?)

Phelps advises that '[i]n order to write an accurate and effective legal document the writer must be able to identify and state the issue or issues properly; otherwise, the writer answers the wrong question and the entire document misses the mark'.[75] In addition:

- Generate your outline. This may be a list or a cluster of ideas.
- Begin to draft but continue to plan as you go.[76]

---

72 Markman, above n 43.
73 Phelps, above n 46, 164.
74 For more on reflective approaches, see Chapter 12.
75 Phelps, above n 48, 1099.
76 Ibid.

## *General strategies for planning writing*

### *A structured approach*

Williams and Gregory, whose particular focus is on developing and communicating an argument, recommend the following planning approach, which would work well for law essays:

- On one page, sketch the problem or question and a potential solution or answer.
- At the top of separate pages, write the main reasons that would persuade readers to agree. Assume you will need between two and five reasons.
- After each reason, sketch the evidence or additional reasons that support the main reason.
- At the bottom third of each page, sketch relevant objections or alternatives your reader might raise, and respond to these.
- On another page, sketch a conclusion.[77]

### *The web*

Other writers propose strategies that are not directed explicitly to legal writing, but may be helpful. Graham[78] recommends:

- Brainstorm all you know and you would like to know about the topic.
- Organise your ideas by main points and details on a web, where main ideas and subordinate ideas are linked together through the use of lines and arrows.
- Read to find new information and verify the accuracy of already generated material (add delete and modify information on the web as necessary).
- Write using information from the web you created, but continue planning as you write.
- Check to be sure that you used everything that you wanted from the web.

### *A formal approach*

Hayes and Flower[79] advise more generally that planning can be distinguished by four features, which vary with the skill of the writer. First, writers develop an initial statement of the task and a body of goals that in turn guide and constrain the writing. Second, the body of goals is hierarchically organised: that is, writers set up top-level goals that they develop with plans and subgoals. Third, at the same time, these goals are also connected in a network in which one action can carry out multiple goals and individual plans or goals can be linked by a web of associations to other parts of this network. Fourth, this network of goals is dynamic. It is

---

77 Joseph M Williams and Gregory G Colomb, *The Craft of Argument* (Longman, 2nd ed, 2003) 48.
78 Graham et al, above n 45, 291.
79 Hayes and Flower, above n 44, 1109.

constructed, developed and sometimes radically *restructured* as the writer responds to new ideas or to their own text. The relative importance of the parts of this structure will also change as the writer works. 'Priorities change; attention wanders; writers forget. However, writers often return to goals that they established earlier but had seemingly abandoned. Thus, writing goals may persist even if they are currently inactive'.[80]

## IV CONCLUSION

In this chapter, we have considered the first two aspects of pre-writing: reflection on purpose and audience, and planning. It has been said that 'planning activities, analysis, and writing are inextricably linked'.[81] It is thus recommended that 'writers start projects by systematically recording purpose, audience, scope, and context'.[82]

Reflection and planning are essential to good writing, but are often neglected by novice writers in the interests of getting on with the writing task. Novice writers tend to 'plunge' in; or draw up a brief plan which they then adhere to rigidly. But reflection and planning are complex processes. Research suggests that planning is evolutionary and ongoing; that writers often generate multiple plans, make and sometimes forget plans;[83] that some plans fail;[84] and plans change over time and during the writing process.[85] Planning has been described as a 'demanding cognitive process' for novice and expert writers alike.[86] Most writers will develop their own, unique planning style, but in the beginning heuristic devices, such as IRAC, can help you to identify issues and relevant information, and assist in the ordering of the written text.[87] At the same time, experts recommend that a good plan is flexible and that modifying writing goals may be essential for good writing. Writers stymied by writer's block appear to have more difficulty changing goals and plans than do other writers, so flexibility is key. [88] We turn now to researching for writing.

---

80 Ibid.
81 Ibid 96.
82 Ibid 94.
83 Flower et al, above n 51, 49–50.
84 Ibid 50.
85 Ibid.
86 Hayes and Flower, above n 44, 1109.
87 Phelps, above n 48, 1099.
88 Hayes and Flower, above n 44, 1109.

# REVIEW MATERIALS

## SUMMARY

This chapter focused on general and academic writing: its purpose and audience, the planning process, the importance of reflection, and strategies to achieve an excellent result.

## KEY POINTS

- As a lawyer, you are, in effect, a professional writer.
- A key difference between novice and expert writers is that experts spend more time and take more care with the planning process than novices do.
- Always begin your writing with a consideration of audience and purpose.
- The process leading to good writing is rarely linear. It tends to be recursive and messy.
- Experiment to find which planning strategy suits you best – there is no 'right' way to plan your writing.

## QUESTIONS FOR REFLECTION

1. When you are given a writing task, how do you plan to manage your time? Do you build in sufficient time for planning at the beginning, and for editing and proofreading at the end? What proportion of your time should you build in to your writing task for planning/researching/drafting/revising/editing and proofreading?
2. If you were a lecturer, what would you look for in a legal writing task? What would distinguish good writing from poor writing from a student?
3. Choose five articles from a variety of online sites or magazines. Who is the intended audience? What is the purpose of the article? How do audience and purpose shape the written text?
4. What distinguishes formal writing from informal writing? Can you think of three examples of each? How would you plan, respectively, for a piece of formal writing and a piece of informal writing?
5. What is your reaction to being told that writing is a messy and iterative process? Are you relieved? Anxious? Challenged? Why do you have that reaction?

## EXERCISES

1. Writing for an audience[89]

   Imagine that you recently had an accident at university which probably occurred because you were under the influence of drugs.

   If you had to write and tell your parents about the accident, what might you say? Imagine how you might tell the story differently if you were telling your friends about what happened. How might this version be different from the one you tell the insurance company? What details would you emphasise? Are there some details you might tell your friends that you might not emphasise or even mention at all in your letter to your parents or the insurance company? Would the order in which you told the various details be different? What does this exercise tell you about the relationship between author and their audience?

2. Different voices[90]

   Choose a sentence or two from a draft essay that you are writing now and rewrite it as if you are:

   - a politician;
   - a judge;
   - a barrister;
   - an academic.

   Read your original sentence to the class, and then your new sentences.

   Ask your peers whether they can pick which voice relates to your new sentences.

   Discuss what has changed (for instance diction, tone, length, vocabulary).

3. Different audiences

   Use the sentences you constructed in the 'Different voices' exercise immediately above and this time assume you are writing to:

   - a member of your family;
   - a used car salesman;
   - someone you want to impress;
   - someone you dislike.

   Reflect on the ways in which your writing style changes depending on your audience.

---

89 The following scenario has been adapted from one published on the University of Maryland University College 'Writing for an Audience', available at https://www.umuc.edu/writingcenter/writingresources/writing_for_audiences.cfm.

90 This exercise has been adapted from Lauren Holm, 'Lesson Plan: Exercises for Voice and Audience, University Writing Program at Brandeis University, available at www.brandeis.edu/writingprogram/.

## FURTHER RESOURCES

1. Audience analysis checklist[91]
   Student presentations are a common form of assessment in universities, but students often fail to consider their audience. If you have a presentation coming up, you might like to use this checklist.
   a. What is the approximate size of your audience? Are you addressing just one or two people, or a sizeable group?
   b. What information do you have about the demographic makeup of your audience (age, gender, education level, ethnicity), and how might you use that information to develop and shape your speech or report?
   c. What personal and professional traits do you have in common with the members of your audience?
   d. Are there any cultural considerations that might influence the way your audience responds to the speech or report?
   e. Will your audience expect to be entertained as well as informed?
   f. Will you be targeting certain members of your audience, and if so, *which* members?
   g. Thinking about the subject of your speech or report, how much knowledge or expertise will audience members already possess?
   h. Will audience members recognise your authority and implicitly trust your credibility (or ethos) or will you have to earn their trust by *demonstrating* your knowledge or expertise?
   i. What preconceptions or biases about your subject might some members of your audience hold?
   j. In general, will your audience have a favourable, unfavourable, or neutral attitude toward your subject?
   k. What common misconceptions about your subject will you need to correct during the course of your speech or report?
   l. In general, will your audience have an interest in your subject, or will you have to generate that interest?
   m. What expectations will your audience have about the length of your speech or report?
   n. What expectations will your audience have about the format of your speech or report?
   o. To follow your line of reasoning, how much background information will the audience need?
   p. What key questions will your audience expect you to answer?

91 This checklist has been adapted from Richard Nordquist, available at http://grammar.about.com/od/ab/g/audienceanalysisterm.htm.

q. What key objections are audience members likely to raise?
r. To connect to the needs and interests of your audience, what particular appeals should you include in your speech or report?
s. What tone or general attitude do you want to convey to your audience – objective? authoritative? collaborative? supportive?
t. What do you want your audience to know or be able to do as a result of listening to your speech or reading your report?

2. Sentence starters[92]
Do you find it difficult to start a writing task? Do you procrastinate, or suffer from writer's block? Reflection can be a valuable way of engaging with pre-writing. The following suggested sentence starters may be useful as a way of overcoming writer's block and engaging with a writing task.

| Cognitive Strategies: Sentence Starters | |
|---|---|
| Planning and goal setting<br>• My purpose is ...<br>• My top priority is ...<br>• To accomplish my goal, I plan to ...<br>Tapping prior knowledge<br>• I already know that ...<br>• This reminds me of ...<br>• This relates to ...<br>Asking questions<br>• I wonder why ...<br>• What if ...<br>• How come ...<br>Predicting<br>• I'll bet that ...<br>• I think ...<br>• If, then ...<br>Visualising<br>• I can picture ...<br>• In my mind I see ...<br>• If this were a movie ...<br>Making connections<br>• This reminds me of ...<br>• I experienced this once when ...<br>• I can relate to this because ...<br>Summarising<br>• The basic gist ...<br>• The key information is ...<br>• In a nutshell, this says that ...<br>Adopting an alignment<br>• The character I most identify with is ...<br>• I really got into the story when ...<br>• I can relate to this author because... | Forming interpretations<br>• What this means to me is ...<br>• I think this represents ...<br>• The idea I'm getting is ...<br>Monitoring<br>• I got lost here because ...<br>• I need to reread the part where ...<br>• I know I'm on the right track because ...<br>Clarifying<br>• To understand better, I need to know more about ...<br>• Something that is still not clear is ...<br>• I'm guessing that this means, but I need to ...<br>Revising meaning<br>• At first I thought, but now I ...<br>• My latest thought about this is ...<br>• I'm getting a different picture here because ...<br>Analysing the author's craft<br>• A golden line for me is ...<br>• This word/phrase stands out for me because ...<br>• I like how the author uses to show ...<br>Reflecting and relating<br>• So, the big idea is ...<br>• A conclusion I'm drawing is ...<br>• This is relevant to my life because ...<br>Evaluating<br>• I like/don't like because ...<br>• This could be more effective if ...<br>• The most important message is... |

92 These sentence starters are reproduced from http://www.nwp.org/cs/public/download/nwp_file/8538/Booth_Olson,_Carol,_et_al.pdf?x-r=pcfile_d.

## CHAPTER 3

# RESEARCHING FOR WRITING

## I INTRODUCTION

'Legal research' refers to the steps that are taken to solve a problem. It requires finding the relevant primary materials – cases or legislation – that can help answer a legal question. Legal research also means accessing secondary sources such as journal articles or reports to aid this process. Legal research and legal writing are interdependent activities,[1] and both are fundamental to the practice of law: '[a] major portion of the work which lawyers do is legal research, and the application of the fruits of that research [result in] some kind of writing'.[2]

Legal research has ethical dimensions. For legal practitioners, research skills are related to the professional expectation of competency. Legal argument and advice must be based upon accurate and up-to-date information, and must acknowledge information that both supports and detracts from their position.

For other legal writers – such as academics, law reform advocates, and government employees – legal research is undertaken for the purpose of disseminating knowledge. In this sense:

> research is a way of thinking: examining critically the various aspects of your day-to-day professional work; understanding and formulating guiding principles that govern a particular procedure; and developing and testing new theories for the enhancement of your practice. It is a habit of questioning what you do, and a systematic examination of the observed information to find answers, with a view to instituting appropriate changes for a more effective professional service.[3]

---

1 Terry Hutchinson, *Researching and Writing in Law* (Lawbook Thomson Reuters, 3rd ed, 2010) 5.

2 Wesley Gilmer, 'Teaching Legal Research and Legal Writing in American Law Schools' (1972–1973) 25 *Journal of Legal Education* 571, 571.

3 Ranjit Kumar, *Research Methodology: A step-by-step guide for beginners* (Pearson Education Australia, 2nd ed, 2005) 2.

Legal research is thus work that seeks to add to the existing knowledge about a topic and ultimately tries to 'increase society's wellbeing'.[4] Legal writers should be confident that what is written is based on verifiable data and that interpretations are sound. Implicit in this approach is the writer's acknowledgment that if their writing is less than sound, then those relying on their writing may be 'harmed' – something that will be discussed below with respect to writing ethically. And, of course, legal writers must acknowledge the words and ideas of others.

The chapter begins with a note about the different sources in law before considering research for legal problems, from analysis to communication, including more on the IRAC method. We then turn to researching for other forms of legal writing, such as dissertations, articles and policy advice. Here, we outline a process of planning, doing and reflecting. The *planning* stage involves identifying the research issue and developing a research plan; and determining whether to take a **doctrinal** or **interdisciplinary** approach and considering whether an **empirical** study is needed. The section on the *doing* stage is not a detailed discussion of how to conduct legal research, but it makes some important points, particularly about evaluation of sources. The chapter will conclude with the *reflecting* stage, stressing the importance of reminding researchers of their ethical obligations to those who will read and who may be affected by the findings.

## II A NOTE ABOUT 'PRIMARY', 'SECONDARY' AND 'TERTIARY' SOURCES

Before you begin to research, you need to understand the difference between primary, secondary and tertiary resources.

*Tertiary resources* compile, list or digest information from other sources. They include dictionaries, encyclopedias, digests, citators and Wikipedia. Tertiary sources are not considered acceptable material on which to base academic legal research, but they can be very valuable as a starting point. They can provide you with an overview of the area and background to your issues, and help you focus your research.[5]

*Secondary resources* analyse, discuss, explain, interpret and assess the law. They include scholarly articles, reports and books.

*Primary resources* are the original material in the field. In law, this category includes legislation, bills, treaties, regulations, judicial decisions and original legal documents (such as wills or contracts). If you are undertaking an empirical study, data created through your original research is also a primary source.[6]

---

4 Hutchinson, above n 1, 6.

5 Hopkins, 'Primary, Secondary and Tertiary Resources', available at http://www15.uta.fi/FAST/FIN/RESEARCH/.

6 Ibid.

There has been a significant increase in recent years in the volume of case law and statutory material. Secondary sources have increased considerably as well. Legal researchers are faced with a voluminous amount of information and it is thus important to learn how to identify relevant material and to be discriminating in your use of material.

## III RESEARCHING A LEGAL PROBLEM

In many cases, particularly in earlier years of law studies, you will be given a hypothetical problem as an assignment that can be answered using cases that have already been studied or provided. However, at some point, you will be expected to conduct legal research of primary and secondary materials to solve the problem. Of course, as a lawyer, you will be expected to have legal analysis, research and problem-solving skills. Researching a legal issue can sometimes seem overwhelming, and it is helpful to have a structured approach. Different strategies can be used but their core approaches are very similar, and can be summarised as in Figure 3.1.[7]

FIGURE 3.1

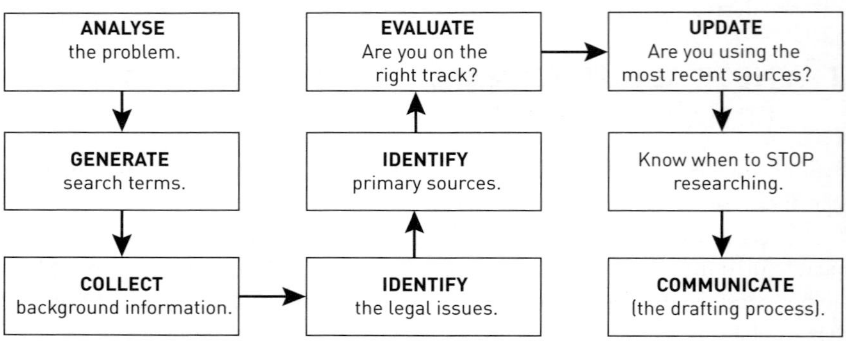


### Step 1: Analyse your problem

Legal issues are fact-dependent and for this reason, the first step is to go through the facts of your problem carefully and thoroughly. Issue identification is key to effective research. Some researchers use the journalistic 'who, what, when, where, why and how' approach to analyse their facts. Others recommend what is colloquially known as the 'TARP' method:

---

7 This structure is adapted from Paul L Boley Law Library, 'Legal Research Strategy', available at https://law.lclark.edu/library/help/strategy/.

- T stands for **THING** or subject matter, place, or property in dispute. We also suggest, at this point, identifying the jurisdiction in which your fact scenario takes place.
- A stands for cause of **ACTION** or grounds of defence. Is this a tort or a breach of contract, for instance? Does the party you are advising need to raise a defence to a legal action?
- R stands for **RELIEF** sought. What do the parties want? Monetary damages? An injunction? Not to be found guilty of a crime?
- P stands for **PERSONS** or **PARTIES** involved. What is the relationship of the parties to one another? Does your problem involve a group? A corporation? Employer–employee? Family members?

## Step 2: Generate a research vocabulary and develop a note-taking system

Having completed your initial analysis of the facts, consider terms and phrases that might be relevant to your research. Once you have generated some terms, broaden your search by developing **synonyms** and **antonyms** for your original terms. Consider too, related terms, both broader and narrower than your original terms. For this step, you might like to rely on a law dictionary, a thesaurus (legal and general), and *Words and Phrases*.

It is important that you develop a workable note-taking system from the beginning of your research and that you take notes on your sources – with full citation details – as you go along. A note system helps to avoid duplication of effort, particularly if you note which search terms are useful and which are not. And it is extremely frustrating to have to chase up a reference later on if you have not taken good details from the beginning.

## Step 3: Collect background information

First, identify what information you already have. Then, using your research vocabulary as an index, conduct a search using online and/or manual sources. Here are some tips that can be helpful:

- *Start from the general and move to the more specific* as you gain in understanding. For instance, you might like to start with your legal text books before moving to legal articles.
- *Start with tertiary or secondary sources*. These sources will summarise and interpret the law in a narrative format. They also provide you with background information and references to relevant further secondary and primary resources.[8]

---

8 'Basic Legal Research Techniques', available at http://www.aallnet.org/chapter/scall/locating/ch3.pdf.

- *Start from the most recent publications*. These will be more up-to-date on the applicable law, and they will also generally give you references to earlier works on the topic.

## Step 4: Identify and frame the legal issues raised by the facts

Different legal issues can drive your legal research in different directions. It is very important that you learn to identify the legal issues: if they are wrongly identified or some are missed completely, your answer will be incorrect or incomplete. There may be sub-issues to your issues. You may find it helpful to map your issues at this point to sharpen your focus and your research.

## Step 5: Identify primary authorities that relate to your legal issues

Are there appropriate legislative provisions and/or judicial authorities? How would they affect the outcome of the legal issues you have identified? In some instances, there may be conflicting decisions, or no binding authority. You may need to look to other jurisdictions for guidance. With judicial authorities, start with decisions from higher courts, and start with the most recent decisions (these will often refer to and/or discuss earlier decisions).

As you research your cases, it may be helpful to chart them. Charting can help you identify similarities and differences between your case (or legal problem) and decided cases. It also helps you to see patterns emerging in the law and so be better placed to predict likely outcomes.[9] And it can help you choose the best and most relevant cases for your analysis. Coughlin et al are keen proponents of charting as a research tool and they suggest two different types of charts, depending on your purpose.[10] So, the first chart is based on the elements of an action. The chart would list as many cases as you deem relevant:

| Case name | Facts | Element 1 | Element 2 | Element 3 | Element 4 | Holding | Like or unlike my case |
|---|---|---|---|---|---|---|---|
| Case 1 | | | | | | | |
| Case 2 | | | | | | | |
| Case 3 | | | | | | | |

---

9 Christine Coughlin, Joan Malmud Rocklin and Sandy Patrick, *A Lawyer Writes: A Practical Guide to Legal Analysis* (Carolina Academic Press, 2nd ed, 2013) 68.

10 Ibid.

The second chart is based on a single element in an action:

| Case name | Rules about element | Facts about element | Holding about element | Additional reasoning re: element |
|---|---|---|---|---|
| Case 1 | | | | |
| Case 2 | | | | |
| Case 3 | | | | |

## Step 6: Re-evaluate and re-analyse the issues and your research

The research process can be messy and it is certainly not linear. Sources consulted, and the order in which they are consulted, will vary with the knowledge of the individual researcher and the particular facts of the problem. Having undertaken your analysis, and read relevant authorities, you may now find new issues; or certain facts may take on new significance; or you may have found that issues you thought were raised were, in fact, not relevant. You need to re-evaluate your research **methodology**, particularly if you are struggling to find sources. Re-assess your work at this point and ensure your plan is relevant and your research has covered all the relevant issues. You should also cross-check your research from other sources, so you are not relying on a single source.

## Step 7: Update and verify to ensure the authorities you have chosen still apply

The law is constantly changing. Your primary sources may have been overruled or amended. Online databases such as Casebase or Timebase can help ensure your authorities are up to date.

## Step 8: Know when to STOP researching!

Often students become overwhelmed by the research process and they don't know when to stop researching. This can happen when you research a legal problem; or in some instances of qualitative empirical research; or where you are researching for an essay or policy-based document. The general rule is that you will reach what is called a 'saturation' point, that is, you will keep reading the same legal rule or hearing the same information repeatedly. You can usually accept this as an indication that your research has been sufficiently complete to provide you with a reliable answer.

### Step 9: Communicate your findings

You use the law you have found and apply it to the facts by comparing, contrasting, and **synthesising** relevant cases and/or by interpreting and applying statutes. We discuss this more closely in Chapter 6 on answering hypothetical problems.

## IV RESEARCHING AN ESSAY, DISSERTATION OR ARTICLE

We turn now to consider research for an essay, dissertation or article. We recommend a three-stage process here, of planning, doing and reflecting (Figure 3.2). If you are embarking on an essay, dissertation or article, we also refer you to Chapter 7.

FIGURE 3.2

### *The PLANNING stage*

The first few steps towards producing an essay, a dissertation or writing a publishable article involve a considerable amount of planning. As noted in the previous chapter, lack of planning is often the downfall of the novice legal writer.

### 1 *Identifying the research topic/question*

The initial step is to identify a topic. While the obvious place to start may be to suggest that you should have some knowledge of the topic you choose, the main determinant should be that the topic is one in which you are interested and that you believe is important or significant. For academics, this factor also tends to underpin even those situations where they are asked to research a specific topic chosen by a community organisation or a corporation on a consultancy basis, since they are being approached because of their prior research. There are cases where researchers associated with law reform commissions may find themselves researching topics that have been determined by others, perhaps by government bodies. Generally, however, if a researcher has the opportunity to choose a topic, in most cases that topic comes from the researcher's prior experience and interests.

Sometimes a researcher can identify a topic that hasn't been addressed previously, but more often than not, a research question builds on what has already been discussed. Thus, what is produced incrementally adds to what is known. The research issue is generally something that has arisen through investigating another matter, and usually begins to formulate in the mind of the researcher as a question.[11] This should not come as a surprise, given the definition mentioned above, which implied that research is carried out to find answers to questions to increase knowledge and/or something that will benefit the public generally.

There are, however, instances where it is more intuitive to express the research question as a **hypothesis**, for example, when conducting experimental or quantitative types of descriptive research.[12] A hypothesis is a strong statement that if participants are doing certain things, then a certain outcome will emerge. It follows then, that a hypothesis be used if the researcher is fairly confident of the answer that the research findings will produce.[13]

While authors in the legal writing field generally discuss ways to identify a research topic, Millman[14] wrote a short article in 1998 that sets out what he describes as the 'nine most productive ways of identifying a research topic' in the field of education. Five of these may provide some guidance for you as a legal writer:

- *Hitch your Wagon to a Star*: gain inspiration from the projects of a group with which you might be involved, or the work of a mentor – someone whose work you admire.
- *You can See a Lot by Looking*: noticing anomalies, puzzling observations, and contradictory studies.
- *Dig for Gold in Them Thar Hills*: examine the data gathered by national organisations.
- *Look a Gift Horse in the Mouth*: take notice of the questions raised by reputable academics as a result of some research they have performed.
- *Read Much About Little*: become an expert in some aspect of your field.

Kumar refers to two further factors that you should take into consideration when formulating a topic: availability of data and ethical issues.[15] While topics that examine how the law or its processes affect society are very interesting and worthwhile, the evidence required to come to an educated finding can be impossible to access. For example, if researchers wish to pursue a topic that questions how well consumers of

---

11 Lisa Webley, *Legal Writing* (2nd ed, Routledge-Cavendish, 2010) 44.

12 Daniel J Boudah, *Conducting Educational Research: Guide to Completing a Major Project* (Sage, 2011) 26.

13 Webley, above n 11, 45.

14 Jason Millman, 'Strategies for Identifying a Research Topic in Educational Measurement' (1998) 17(2) *Educational Measurement: Issues and Practice* 37–9.

15 Kumar, above n 3, 44.

the family law system are treated, then they would need access to those consumers. The question is then: how could this be achieved? The data that is required to answer this question may be difficult to obtain.

This example also serves to illustrate that some topics attract particularly difficult ethical issues. For instance, if a researcher is interested in determining the effectiveness of the family law system, and if participants in that system can be accessed, the researcher would need to be very careful to ensure that the participants were not 'adversely affected by some of the questions (directly or indirectly); deprived of an intervention; expected to share sensitive and private information; or expected to be simply experimental "guinea pigs"'.[16]

Many of the factors that relate to the choice of a topic are also relevant to planning a research strategy.

## 2 *Developing a plan*

The planning process now becomes much more focused. The generally worded topic, research question, or hypothesis is examined in detail in order to produce a series of sub-issues or questions. If you find that you have a very extensive list of issues or questions, this may indicate that your topic is too broad and therefore unmanageable.[17]

Armed with a research topic/question or hypothesis, and a set of sub-issues or questions, some researchers will then consider how they will go about their research. Kumar suggests that there is a further step beyond listing a set of sub-issues or questions, suggesting these questions be translated into a set of actions. For instance, he gives an example where the researcher has chosen the topic: 'what are the effects of alcoholism on the family'?[18] From this he raises three questions:

1. What impact has alcoholism on marital relations?
2. How does it affect the various aspects of children's lives?
3. What are the effects on the family's finances?

He then suggests that the researcher should formulate a set of objectives, transforming research questions 'into behavioural aims by using action-oriented words such as "to find out", "to determine", "to ascertain", and to "examine"'.[19] With respect to the topic of alcoholism, Kumar suggests that the objectives could be stated as follows:
*Main objective:* To find out the effects of alcoholism on the family.

---

16 Ibid 44.
17 Ibid 46.
18 Ibid 47.
19 Ibid 46.

*Specific objectives:*

1. to ascertain the impact of alcoholism on marital relations
2. to determine the ways in which alcoholism affects the different aspects of children's lives
3. to find out the effects of alcoholism on the financial situation of the family, etc.[20]

He then suggests that these objectives be assessed in light of some practical or resource questions. For instance:

- the work involved;
- the time available to you;
- the financial resources at your disposal;
- your (and your research supervisor's) technical expertise in the area.[21]

Hutchinson adds a further question for students: '[d]o you have access to a supervisor with the knowledge of the area you want to work in and knowledge of what work has been done?'[22] and one specifically relevant for academics: '[d]oes your topic coincide with the research strengths of the faculty?'[23]

## 3 *Choosing your approach: doctrinal, empirical or interdisciplinary research?*

Further thought needs to be given to what type of research is required to respond to the topic/answer the question. Before we consider that in more detail, it is useful to note the distinction between doctrinal and interdisciplinary research.

### *The doctrinal approach and its critics*

Traditionally, legal researchers have taken a doctrinal approach (which means researching within legal parameters of a specific jurisdiction) or a comparative doctrinal approach involving other jurisdictions. In effect, the doctrinal approach is predominantly a textual analysis of the law's rules, principles and concepts found in case law, legislation and other legal documents: 'legal **doctrine**, is basically studying law as a **normative** system, limiting its "empirical data" to legal texts and court decisions'.[24] While Van Hoeck has concluded that, since Roman times, legal doctrine has been practised as 'a mainly **hermeneutic** discipline', he also notes that

20 Ibid 47.

21 Ibid.

22 Hutchinson, above n 1, 161.

23 Ibid.

24 Mark Van Hoecke, 'Legal Doctrine: Which Method(s) for What Kind of Discipline?' in Mark Van Hoecke, *Methodologies of Legal Research: Which Kind of Method for What Kind of Discipline?* (Hart, 2011) 2.

it includes 'empirical, argumentative, logical and normative elements'.[25] In terms of hermeneutic, he acknowledges that 'texts and documents are the main research object ... interpretation ... is the main activity of the researcher'.[26] McCrudden, too, points to the empirical aspects, but he notes that if empirical work is conducted, then only those who are legal actors dealing with this knowledge are canvassed concerning the effectiveness of its knowledge and processes.[27]

This perceived narrow approach taken by legal researchers has been criticised. For instance Vick[28] refers to a number of authors who suggest that legal or doctrinal research is 'rigid, dogmatic, formalistic, and close-minded';[29] that it encourages '"intellectual tunnel-vision" through an unhealthy preoccupation with technicalities';[30] it places 'an intellectual strait-jacket on understandings of law and society';[31] and leads to 'impoverish[ing] the questioning spirit of both law student and teacher'.[32] These criticisms suggest that researchers taking a pure doctrinal approach fail to appreciate the context in which law is practised and therefore do not appreciate its effect. In addition, it has been suggested that doctrinal researchers or 'academic lawyers are only interested in what law-makers actually do'[33] that is, only interested in what those on the 'inside' do.

### *The interdisciplinary approach*

Criticisms of the doctrinal approach lead us to a discussion of interdisciplinary research. Much legal education is so focused upon a doctrinal approach that the possibilities of interdisciplinarity are not even raised. There are, however, at least two reasons to consider an interdisciplinary approach to an essay, dissertation or article. First, law regulates our lives and has potential impact upon people in a variety of ways: psychologically, economically, politically and so on. Second, law also regulates the interaction of other disciplines with society. For instance, it determines how psychologists deal with patients and how schools deal with students.

---

25 Ibid 17.

26 Ibid 4.

27 C McCrudden, 'Legal Research and the Social Sciences' (2006) 122 (Oct) *Law Quarterly Review* 632, 633.

28 Doulas W Vick, 'Interdisciplinarity and the Discipline of Law' (2004) 31(2) *Journal of Law and Society* 163, 181.

29 Grant Gilmore, *The Death of Contract* (Ohio State University Press, 1974) 12–13.

30 R Cotterrell, 'Subverting Orthodoxy, Making Law Central: A View of Sociolegal Studies' (2002) 29 *Journal of Law and Society* 632, 633.

31 R Collier, 'The Changing University and the (Legal) Academic Career – Rethinking the Relationship Between Women, Men and the "Private Life" of the Law School' (2002) 22 *Legal Studies* 1, 27.

32 Ibid 19.

33 Mathias M Siems, 'The Taxonomy of Interdisciplinary Legal Research: Finding the Way Out of the Desert' (2009) 7(1) *Journal of Commonwealth Law and Legal Education*, 5, 5.

An interdisciplinary approach examines law in its 'reality, law as it is'.[34] This is often referred to as socio-legal studies, an approach that considers law's effect, that is, law within a context of social and political theories. In this chapter, we use the following definition of interdisciplinary:

> We define *interdisciplinary understanding* as the capacity to integrate knowledge and modes of thinking in two or more disciplines or established areas of expertise to produce a cognitive advancement – such as explaining a phenomenon, solving a problem, or creating a product – in ways that would have been impossible or unlikely through single disciplinary means.[35]

At the same time, we should note that there are multiple terms used for research that is not purely doctrinal. However, in providing some explanations of the meaning of the terms we should point out that there is no general agreement on either the categories or their meanings, even though there is agreement that there are different types of interdisciplinarity.[36] For instance, Siems refers to the different categories of multidisciplinary, interdisciplinary, transdisciplinary and cross-disciplinary.[37] He also notes that there are authors who suggest that these can be viewed as a 'continuum in interdisciplinary research, ranging from lesser to greater degrees of synthesis'.[38] Davies and Devlin also take this approach. They define multidisciplinary research as disciplines coexisting – when a couple of disciplines are involved and the researchers proceed to discuss these separately.[39] There is no actual integration or attempt to blend.[40] Davies and Devlin also use the term 'cross-disciplinarity', which they define as one discipline 'peering' into another. It is a situation where a researcher from one area (say law) is investigating a topic using the knowledge from another discipline (about which they are not an expert) to explain their findings. In this instance, there is some shared discourse about the research problem. Finally, the term 'transdisciplinary research' has been used to denote an approach that 'highlights

---

34 Van Hoeck, above n 24, 2.

35 V Boix Mansilla and E Duraising 'Targeted Assessment of Students' Interdisciplinary Work: An empirically grounded Framework Proposal' (2007) *78(2) Journal of Higher Education* 215, 219.

36 Siems, above n 33, 5.

37 B Nicolescu, *Manifesto of Transdisciplinarity* (State University of New York Press, 2002) cited by Siems, above n 33, 5.

38 Siems, above n 33, 5. See also M Nissani, 'Fruits, Salads, and Smoothies: A Working Definition of Interdisciplinarity', (1995) 29 *Journal of Educational Thought* 121; and Bart Van Klink and Sanne Taekema, 'A Dynamic Model of Interdisciplinarity: Limits and Possibilities of Interdisciplinary Research into Law' (2008) Tilburg University Legal Studies Working Paper No. 010/2008; Tilburg Working Paper Series on Jurisprudence and Legal History No. 08-02, available at SSRN: http://ssrn.com/abstract=1142847 or http://dx.doi.org/10.2139/ssrn.1142847.

39 Martin Davies and Marcia Devlin, 'Interdisciplinary Higher Education: Implications for Teaching and Learning' Centre for the Study of Higher Education, University of Melbourne, 2007.

40 Annie Bolitho and Mark McDonnell 'Interdisciplinarity in Research at the University of Melbourne' Melbourne Sustainable Society Institution, University of Melbourne, 14 July 2010.

an external issues focus, which is likely to reflect a mix of disciplines associated with each issue'.[41] To visually represent these variations, Bolitho and McDonnell include the diagram in Figure 3.3, published by Lyall, Tait and Williams.[42]

FIGURE 3.3

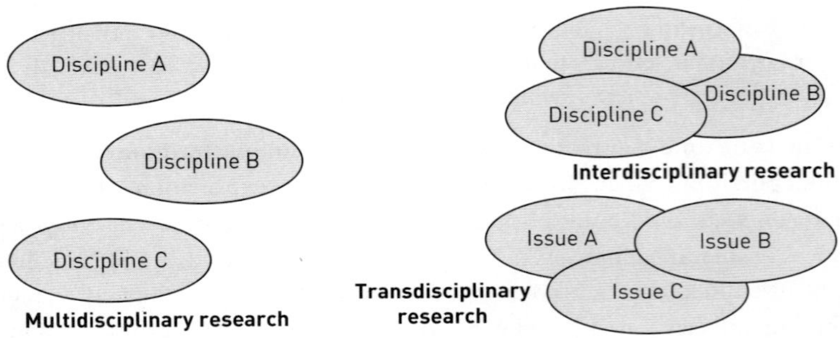


While much of the literature discussing doctrinal and interdisciplinary approaches to research tends to argue that one research method is better than another, Schrama provides a simple way to determine the appropriate research approach to apply. She maintains that it depends on whether the topic or question relates to the internal or external effectiveness of law.[43] For instance, if the topic raises an internal legal question, then doctrinal research is the approach that should be taken.[44] As an example, a doctrinal approach is appropriate if the question relates to the internal consistency of legislation. When a new piece of legislation is being introduced, it is important that it does not contradict the dictates of another piece of legislation.[45] This would require a researcher to consider questions such as: What is the appropriate law, and the special sections that deal with this topic/question? What cases have analysed these sections? Have these sections been amended and why – should they change? This is obviously a textual analysis of legislation and case law. More specifically, it would require the researcher to analyse the legislation, taking note of whether there have been any amendments, and using the statutory interpretation principles (including examining the explanatory notes and second reading speeches); to analyse

41 Ibid.
42 A Bruce, C Lyall, J Tait and R Williams, 'Interdisciplinary Integration in Europe: The Case of the Fifth Framework Review' (2004) *Futures* 36, 457–470, cited in Bolitho and McDonnell, above n 40.
43 Wendy Schrama, 'How to Carry Out Interdisciplinary Legal Research: Some Experiences with an Interdisciplinary Research Method' (2011) 7 (1) *Utrecht Law Review* 147, 148.
44 Ibid.
45 Ibid.

the relevant case law; and perhaps to investigate whether there are any proposed changes to the legislation such as government policy inquiries.

On the other hand, a question that asks whether law is externally consistent in that it effectively achieves its purpose in society points to the need to conduct interdisciplinary research.[46] Taking this approach moves the focus away from the discipline to the problem. As Karl Popper explained: '[w]e are not students of some subject matter, but students of problems. And problems may cut right across the borders of any subject matter or discipline'.[47]

The key elements of the doctrinal and interdisciplinary approaches are captured in Figure 3.4.

FIGURE 3.4

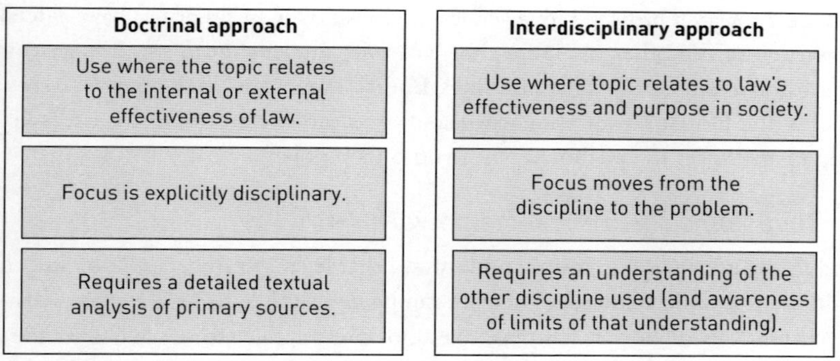


Should you take an interdisciplinary research approach in your essay or dissertation? You may find the following prompts helpful:

- Does the topic or issue need an interdisciplinary approach?
- Which discipline/s will be employed?
- Why is it important for each discipline to be involved? What substantial contribution will information from that discipline make? How does it present a clearly distinct perspective (a different way of knowing)?
- What would be missing if this discipline were not represented?
- How will the use of the other discipline (to law) enhance the findings?[48]

46 Ibid.

47 Karl Popper, *Conjectures and Refutations: The Growth of Scientific Knowledge* (Routledge and Kegan Paul, 1963) 68.

48 Clinton Golding 'Integrating the disciplines: Successful interdisciplinary subjects' University of Melbourne, Centre for the Study of Higher Education, November 2009, 12.

Using this structure, Golding suggests that it is necessary to consider a number of disciplinary perspectives to deal with a problem relating to environmental planning:

- Understand that there are several important disciplinary perspectives that are relevant to every environmental decision, such those of an engineer, zoologist, landscape sociologist and architect, and lawyer;
- Understand the perspective of each relevant discipline;
- Judge how important each perspective is for the issue at hand;
- Evaluate the evidence or reasons supporting each of the perspectives;
- Balance, weigh up or accommodate the pressures from the different perspectives in order to reach a reasonable and creative decision or outcome; and
- Make a case for why this decision or outcome is better than alternatives.[49]

You might find this approach surprising, especially if you are undertaking an individual research project. However, it is not absolutely necessary to have a detailed knowledge of the other discipline. For example, concepts from psychology can be understood and used to explain findings. But it is important in all research to set out honestly the limitations of your work; and to acknowledge when it is necessary to bring in an expert to collaborate with you on a problem.

## 4 *Choosing a theoretical framework*

In addition, it is now commonly understood that legal research should be informed by theoretical understandings. Theories can be descriptive (to help explain what the law currently is or how it has developed); or prescriptive (to set out what the law *should* do, and suggest potential reforms). Traditionally, the theories employed by legal researchers have related to legal philosophy – as occurs with natural law, liberalism, economic analysis of law, critical legal studies, feminism, critical race theory, and postmodernist arguments.[50] However, an interdisciplinary approach allows legal researchers to draw on the underlying theories that inform other disciplines such as psychology, or regulatory theory or public policy theories. The most common theories used in legal research are discussed briefly below.

### *Neo-liberalism*

Neo-liberalism is currently the predominant political theory in Australia. It is often described as a reinvention of classical liberalism with elements of rights and libertarianism, but it prioritises individual rights and freedoms through the lens of productive efficiency operating in a market environment. For example, it

49 Ibid 4.
50 Hutchinson, above n 1, 52–63.

has been argued that Australian governments operate according to the theory of neo-liberalism. They treat education as a 'trading commodity' and therefore regulate universities by funding those which operate in accordance with those values. In this environment, universities are expected to tailor their offerings so that only those degrees that meet student demand are offered.[51]

### *Critical studies*

Liberalism assumes that all individuals are equal and have equal rights, that they are autonomous, rational and are capable of making decisions independently, and have the rights to own property, be educated and have access to justice. This is correct in the formal sense, but substantively there are many inequalities, such as those stemming from gender, race or power imbalances.[52]

### *Economic theory*

Many have found that the concepts of economic theory have value to a study of legal issues. The theory is used to analyse the law in terms of efficiency. The theory assumes that individuals are rational, autonomous and pursue self-interest. It could be argued that economic theory is often applied in judgments even though there is no explicit reference to economic concepts. For instance, when studying law, we recognise that there are some assumptions underlying what are often referred to as 'black-letter' rules in say contracts, torts, and administrative law. Some would say that these are probably based on the principle of economic efficiency or rational choice theory.[53]

### *Regulatory theory*

While the aim of both classical liberalism and neo-liberalism is that individuals should be free to determine how they will live and be free from state intervention, we are actually very heavily regulated. It is therefore important for questions to be asked as to why this regulation is needed, as it heavily influences our society. Some questions could be:

- Why is the regulation needed?
- What is it trying to achieve, or what mischief is it trying to cure?
- Have all of those who will be affected been considered?

---

51 Paula Baron and Lillian Corbin, 'The Academic Role: Service, compliance, freedom' in A Kwan, E Wong, T Kwong, P Lau and A Goody (eds), *Research and Development in Higher Education: Higher Education in a Globalized World* (HERDSA, 2014) 10–19.

52 See, for example, Suzanne Jamieson, 'Feminist theory, Globalization and Comparative Labour Law: Women Workers in Australia and Ireland' (2004) 15 (3) *The International Journal of Human Resource Management* 459.

53 See, for example, Giovanni B Ramello, 'What's in a Sign? Trademark Law and Economic Theory' (2006) 20 (4) *Journal of Economic Surveys* 547-65.

- Is the regulation achieving its goals?
- Are there unintended consequences?
- Is the regulation being interpreted as was intended?[54]

### *Psychological theory*

Psychology and law have much in common. Both disciplines focus on the individual and in predicting and controlling behaviour. Psychology is particularly used in law as a way of explaining human behaviour. For instance, studies are now starting to refer to the theories of self-awareness, self-identity, and cognitive dissonance. Recent theory also suggests that people operate in stressful environments and often use judgment heuristics – shortcuts, 'rough judgments' or 'rules of thumb' to save time and reduce their decision-making load.[55]

### *History*

Legal history research takes a critical approach and seeks to ascertain whether what has been traditionally understood about certain events, is, in fact the truth. The research typically concentrates on gathering the perspectives of as many as possible and examining all of the available documents and accounts, even those only tangentially relevant.[56]

## 5 *Empirical studies*

The above discussion has focused on whether the research topic or question requires a purely textual analysis or an interdisciplinary approach. Researchers might also need to consider undertaking empirical work such as observations or other kinds of qualitative or quantitative studies. It is not our intention to discuss these methods in detail, but some comments will be made. For instance, as we noted earlier, even in doctrinal research empirical work can be useful, but commonly empirical studies are conducted to determine law's external effects.

Quantitative methodologies rely upon measurements - the quantity of something rather than its quality. Generally, quantitative work is premised on a stated hypothesis, and the results are often used to predict future outcomes. Quantitative methodologies are linked to **positivism**. Qualitative methodologies seek to understand the characteristics of a thing or phenomenon, as opposed to measurements based on quantity. Often, they focus upon the experience or understandings of participants.

---

54 See, for example, Benedict Sheehy and Donald Feaver, 'Designing Effective Regulation: A Normative Theory' (2015) 38 (1) *University of New South Wales Law Journal* 392.

55 See, for example, Christine S Scott-Hayward 'Explaining Juvenile False Confessions: Adolescent Development and Police Interrogation' (2007) 31 *Law & Psychology Review* 53.

56 See, for example, Tim Rowse, 'Indigenous Heterogeneity' (2014) 45 (3) *Australian Historical Studies* 297–310.

In many cases, qualitative work allows a hypothesis to develop from the research. Qualitative methodologies are linked to **postmodernism**.[57]

There are a number of empirical strategies, but broadly speaking the three commonly used in relation to law are: observations, quantitative surveys, and qualitative interviews (or a mix of these). In fact, it is often suggested that researchers triangulate their findings by conducting different research strategies, such as a survey and qualitative interviews. It is also the case there are a number of interviewing styles. Structured interviews are where the participants are asked a set series of questions. The interviewer keeps to the script. The advantage of this is that it allows the researcher to compare the answers easily (while not within a research environment, a good illustration of this approach is a job interview). Unstructured interviews are those where the interviewer asks an open question and structures the next question in accordance with the participant's response. These can be one-on-one interviews or focus groups.

## 6 *Crafting a research proposal*

Once all of these decisions have been made, then in some instances, the researcher may find it necessary to produce a research proposal. Although producing a proposal is common for postgraduate students and academics, in some instances, a proposal will be required from undergraduates, either for an honours **thesis** or as part of the **scaffolding** of a major piece of assessment.

A research proposal is a concise explanation of a research idea that seeks to persuade others of the value of pursuing a particular research goal. While the presentation of the topic needs to be primarily descriptive, the proposal must also show why the topic is significant in that it will solve a problem or serve the purpose of filling a gap in the literature that has been identified. In effect, all research assignments need to include a statement that aims at showing the significance of the topic in the introduction, and at the research level, the proposer must show that the topic is interesting, has a purpose, and that there is a reasonable likelihood that the research goals will be met.

There is no one fixed way to achieve this, although some institutions or assessment tasks may prescribe this. Our suggestions are as follows:

a *State the research question:* At the very least, a research proposal should state the research topic or question, or both. It is also helpful to note the limits of the work: that is, outline the parameters of your topic, acknowledging that certain aspects of the topic will not be considered. Since it is sometimes difficult to keep your focus on the specific topic, it is advisable to state your hypothesis or your

57 Hutchinson, above n 1, 107.

thesis. This is your opinion of what you expect to conclude at the end of the study. It encapsulates your argument or your view on the research question or topic.

b *State the significance of the work:* This should be outlined by reference to some preliminary reading into the existing literature. This review of the literature serves to demonstrate knowledge about the topic and also that the work is necessary to provide a solution or fill a gap in the literature.

c *Describe the research methodology and methods to be employed to answer the research question* (as discussed above).

d *Outline any potential problems and obstacles* that you might encounter and which might affect your ability to complete the project on time, and any access issues (such as gaining access to the required data).

e *If empirical work is to be conducted, note the subjects you need to observe, survey or interview*, and note that you will probably need to request ethics approval from your institution, which will require you to identify any ethical issues that may arise.[58]

Once these steps have been completed, you are ready to put the research plan into action: that is, you enter the DOING stage.

### The DOING stage

While the technical aspects of legal researching will not be discussed,[59] we would like to emphasise two points. First, '[r]esearch means just that – re-search and re-search'.[60] As we have discussed, writing is a recursive process. You will do an initial plan, research, write, then return to the cycle as the gaps in your knowledge become apparent or you find new issues arising that you have not seen before. Second, as a researcher, you must gather the necessary knowledge and to do this, you need to know how to locate both primary materials (cases and legislation) and relevant secondary materials (that is, journal articles, commentaries, reports, news items and so on). Your task is to read, analyse and link 'the new information to that already established'.[61]

---

58 For a more detailed approach to completing a research proposal see Kumar, above n 3, Chapter 13. Also note the discussion under *The REFLECTING stage – ethical obligations* included below, with respect to an institution's ethics approval requirements.

59 We suggest that you consult Peter Cane and Herbert M Kritzer, *The Oxford Handbook of Empirical Legal Research* (OUP, 2010).

60 Queen's University, 'Steps in Legal Research', available at http://library.queensu.ca/law/lederman/steps.

61 Hutchinson, above 1, 38.

## Using primary and secondary materials

### *Primary*

In accessing legislation and regulations, be sure to check their currency and jurisdictional relevance. Some prompts you might find helpful are:

- Are you searching the legislation relevant to the jurisdiction to which the research issue relates?
- Is the legislation as it is now in force, the applicable law for the issue you are researching?
- If the current legislation is required, is the version you are examining the current law that takes account of any recent amendments?
- Are the regulations relating to the legislation also relevant?
- Are there any plans to reform the legislation?

The statutory interpretation rules, as set out in the *Statutory Interpretation Acts* of both the Commonwealth and the states, depending on the jurisdiction of the research issue, might also require you to access Hansard or the Second Reading Speech and the Explanatory Notes relating to the legislation.

For case law, again you need to check currency and jurisdictional relevance. Some prompts that you may find helpful are:

- Have you found the most recent decisions?
- Do the cases you have found still have precedential value?
- Have these cases been decided in the superior courts of states and territories, or in the High Court?
- Have these cases been cited in recent cases? Do these recent cases affirm the court's previous interpretations, or have the earlier principles been modified? Does this modification suggest that the issue you are dealing with would be treated differently by the courts if heard now?

### *Secondary*

You should also research secondary sources: journal articles, government submissions, reports and commentaries, newspapers and public media reports.

With respect to journal articles you should keep in mind that some journals are more authoritative than others. For instance, scholarly academic journal articles that are peer reviewed are considered to be more credible than articles published in practitioner journals. You will find that Ulrich's *Periodical Directory* provides detailed information on journals. Although academic/scholarly journals take time to publish, practitioner journals articles can be very useful in relation to commenting on recent case law.

You may find these prompts useful when determining the credibility of a journal article and the author:

- Is this a peer-reviewed journal?
- Is this a specialist journal that deals with this topic?
- What is the journal's jurisdiction? Is that authoritative for Australia?
- Who is the author? A practitioner, an academic, a judge, someone from another field, a layperson? What do you know of their other work?
- Is s/he an authority on the topic?
- When was the article published?
- What was the social and political context in which it was written?
- Was the article published in reaction to other articles? Did it form part of a wider trend in legal thinking?
- What seems to have motivated the author to write in the first place? What inspired their research questions?
- Does the author persuade you regarding the importance of the topic? If not, why not?
- What is the author's thesis?
- What are the main arguments?
- Is there a logical structure to the arguments? Does the author come to logical conclusions?
- Are the arguments presented clearly? Does the author provide sufficient evidence for the arguments asserted? What sources did the author explicitly rely on in the text of the article? Are there other influences which seem implicitly to affect their thinking?
- Does the author refer to counter-arguments and logically persuade you to agree with their thesis? Would you have taken a different approach?
- How does the article fit within a broader context? How does it relate to other readings you've looked at?
- Does it add to your understanding of the topic; the subject; other subjects you've studied or are studying; or law in general?
- Does it raise further questions?

How you write the introduction, the methodology chapter and the paper itself will be discussed in Chapters 5–8. The following section, on the REFLECTING stage, discusses the need for you to reflect on the impact of what you write.

## *The REFLECTING stage – ethical obligations*

In Chapter 1 we suggested that all writers should reflect on the effect of their writing on others. This section discusses the ethical obligations of researchers or legal writers in more detail.

All legal writers are expected to write objectively, and in so doing, they are expected to present arguments that may, in themselves, conflict. This is required so that clients or readers generally are presented with the whole picture. Webley argues: '[e]xcellent written work … does not end at description, but also provides analysis. Your analysis (your authoritative opinion, [which aligns with your **thesis statement**]) needs to be well evidenced with authoritative research that adds credence to what you are saying'.[62] While legal writers in practice generally do not receive feedback on their writing, law students are often provided with very detailed comments on their submissions. Therefore, if you want to aim for the best mark, then it is important that you learn how to critique your own work.[63] This reflection of your work should incorporate a consideration of your sentence structure, grammar, writing style, tone, and in keeping with the theme of this book, questions of whether your writing is ethical – that it presents the true picture of what you have studied:

> Ethics is about supporting values such as respecting people and their communities and benefiting individuals and society. In this context, this includes doing valid research, respecting research participants and their communities in all the ways that pertain to the particular context, creating socially beneficial policies, and effectively disseminating and applying findings.[64]

As we have noted, research may involve questioning law's effects. How we conduct a survey or interview actual participants could dramatically affect those involved. We suggest that ethical constraints ought to be part of our thinking *regardless* of what we are writing and whatever methods we adopt. There are always consequences, particularly when written work is taken seriously and systems or procedures are changed on that basis for the participants and the public generally. Research is about building knowledge and so it is important that each piece of the building is reliable.

There is an overarching Code that governs how research is conducted. This is the Australian Code for the Responsible Conduct of Research which is administered by the Australian Government's National Health and Medical Research Council.[65] This Code[66] provides guidelines to academic and research institutions on how to develop procedures within research investigation to ensure that students and academics practice responsibly and with integrity. As a student or an academic, you are therefore

62 Webley, above n11, xi.

63 Ibid ix.

64 JE Sieber, 'Empirical Research on Research Ethics' (2004) 14 *Ethics and Behavior* 397, 402.

65 Australian Code for the Responsible Conduct of Research, available at https://www.nhmrc.gov.au/guidelines-publications/r39.

66 Ibid.

required to seek the approval of your institution's ethics committee to conduct empirical quantitative and qualitative research. The process asks the researcher to provide the committee with advice on who will be surveyed/interviewed and the questions being asked. You will also be required to obtain the approval of the committee for an Information Sheet, which should be written from an objective perspective, to be provided to the potential participants; and a Consent Form. Ethical research requires informed consent, participants having full information so that they give their permission to be involved completely and in an understanding of the implications of their involvement in the study. In particular, ethics committees will be concerned with surveys or interviews conducted on vulnerable participants, such as children or those who would be considered to have dealt with or are still dealing with 'sensitive issues'.

Although clear guidelines are provided to researchers by ethics committees, researchers may still encounter dilemmas. For instance, the following are some questions that feature in a report funded by the European Commission's Information Society Technologies (IST) Programme and published by the Institute for Employment Studies Brighton UK: [67]

- How can the interests of the range of different stakeholders be balanced?
- How can the interests of other stakeholder groups, who may not be directly involved in the research project, be protected?
- Who decides what constitutes harm and benefits?
- How can the different understanding of what these are for different groups be reconciled?
- Is conducting research purely for the pursuit of knowledge ethically justifiable?
- Is it, in principle, ethically sound to randomly assign human subjects to comparative groups for the purpose of 'controlled' experiments?
- Is contravening the law ever acceptable?
- Which laws apply to Internet research?
- What should happen in situations of conflict between the law and ethical standards/philosophy?
- Do particular research methodologies discriminate against women or men?
- Are there practical mechanisms for ensuring that gendered language and concepts are not included in any aspect of the research design, conduct or reporting?
- How can it be ensured that members of research teams are treated in relation to their contribution and expertise, rather than due to their gender or seniority?

67 Sally Dench, Ron Iphofen, and Ursula Huws, 'An EU Code of Ethics for Socio-Economic Research', European Commission's Information Society Technologies (IST) Programme and published by the Institute for Employment Studies Brighton UK IES Report 412 2004, available at http://www.respectproject.org/ethics/412ethics.pdf.

- Do particular research methodologies discriminate against people from different racial, ethnic, religious and cultural backgrounds?
- By what means can it be ensured that different groups are properly represented in research studies, and if not, that this is due to considered rationale rather than omission or accident?
- How can it be ensured that racist or xenophobic language and concepts are not included in any aspect of the research design, conduct or reporting?
- How can it be ensured that members of research teams are treated in relation to their contribution and expertise, rather than because of their nationality, skin colour, religion, culture or ethnicity?

We will now briefly refer to some more general issues arising in quantitative and qualitative research.

### *Surveys and statistical analysis*

Surveys are often subject to statistical analysis and while statistics are often used just to describe a phenomenon, in many instances they are relied upon to make predictions and decisions. Obviously then, it is important that the statistics are correct. Some of the elements that can produce incorrect statistics include sample size (for instance, using a very small sample to draw inferences about a large number of people); and randomness (for instance, drawing a sample from a group of first-time car buyers would not substantiate a car manufacturer's claim that a particular low priced car is model of choice for the community in general).[68] These examples suggest that if you have not studied statistics, then using this method may require you to get expert help. Publishing findings based on misinterpretations would be, of course, unethical.

### *Interviews*

**Sample size** and **randomness** are also matters that may affect the validity of the results of interviews. However, bias may be the main concern for researchers conducting interviews. This may not be a big problem for structured interviews where, regardless of a participant's response to a question, the researcher moves to the next question as planned. However, for unstructured interviews, researchers must be very careful that what amounts to their conversation with the participant does not imply a preference for a particular view on a topic. While it is not unethical for a researcher to hold a specific subjective opinion, making statements that attempt

---

68 The Center for Informed Decision-making, 'Statistics', 1998, available at http://cygnus-group.com/CIDM/stats.html.

to influence or bias responses from participants would be unethical.[69] When asking for a participant's consent researchers assert that they will keep their responses confidential. It would obviously be unethical to abuse this privilege.

As has been noted, interpretation plays a role in what is reported. So in order to achieve reliability, some researchers use computer software. However, this method relies on the identification of keywords, which may result in some data being missed. Another method employed by researchers in seeking to achieve authenticity in reporting on data is '**bracketing**'. However, its effectiveness depends on the rigour with which the researcher acknowledges what beliefs, assumptions and preconceptions, ought to be suspended (excluded from consideration) when interpreting the data that is collected.[70]

## V CONCLUSION

In this chapter we have outlined researching for legal problem solving and researching for essays, dissertations and articles. We have noted the distinction between primary and secondary sources, and between doctrinal, interdisciplinary and empirical research. We have provided prompts and methods to help you in the research process. We have also sought to show that there is a tension between extending knowledge and causing social harm. This responsibility falls on researchers and so it is important that they are aware of their ethical obligations and just what that may entail.

69 Kumar, above n 3, 214.

70 Wendy Walker, 'Ethical Considerations in Phenomenological Research' (2007) 14 (3) *Nurse Researcher* 36, 42.

# REVIEW MATERIALS

## SUMMARY

This chapter explained the appropriate use of sources and sets out the steps involved in researching for legal writing. It described the stages of research for legal problems and for different kinds of specialised academic writing, along with their ethical requirements.

## KEY POINTS

1. In legal writing, you need to be cognisant of the differences between primary, secondary and tertiary resources.
2. When researching, start with the most recent information and work backwards; and start with more general information sources and work towards the particular.
3. Know when to stop researching: many students spend too much time in the research phase of writing. You know you have researched an issue sufficiently when you reach saturation point.
4. Ensure that your research approach and methodology are appropriate to your research question.
5. Research is not value-neutral, and the process carries with it ethical obligations.

## QUESTIONS FOR REFLECTION

1. In answering each of the following fictitious questions, would you use a doctrinal or an interdisciplinary approach? Why?
   The *Family Law Act* contains a number of new provisions.
   a. What elements must be present for the court to grant a divorce?
   b. Are these elements similar to Family Law Acts of other jurisdictions?
   c. Are the provisions regarding custody applied fairly?
2. Why are ethical obligations imposed on investigators to protect the rights and interests of research participants? What, in your view, might make a research participant particularly vulnerable in a law-related research study, and thus 'high risk'?
3. What ethical obligations might someone who is reviewing a manuscript for potential publication in a law review owe to the author of the research?
4. What are some of the limitations of quantitative research? Of qualitative research?
5. Why might it not be sufficient to only rely on journal articles that interpret legislation or case law as support for an argument you are making?

## EXERCISES

1. Brad and Amy are colleagues at a Sydney university. Brad has fixed Amy's roof after a recent downpour. As a mark of gratitude, Amy has written a paper on judicial interpretation in migration cases and includes Brad as a co-author. Although Brad works in the area of migration law, he has had nothing to do with the research or the writing of the paper. Brad is delighted as his university has high research publication expectations which he struggles to meet. Is the attribution of authorship appropriate in these circumstances? Discuss.
2. The reduction in government funding and the heavy reliance by promotion committees on published research may provide reasons for the recent instances of fabrication of data by researchers. What are the potential harms, if any, the following case studies may cause researchers, their discipline, research participants and the community generally, financially, psychologically, socially, emotionally or culturally?
   a. Case 1:[71]
   'Dirk Smeesters had spent several years of his career as a social psychologist at Erasmus University in Rotterdam studying how consumers behaved in different situations. Did colour have an effect on what they bought? How did death-related stories in the media affect how people picked products? And was it better to use supermodels in cosmetics ads than average-looking women?
   The questions are certainly intriguing, but unfortunately for anyone wanting truthful answers, some of Smeesters' work turned out to be fraudulent. The psychologist, who admitted "massaging" the data in some of his papers, resigned from his position in June after being investigated by his university, which had been tipped off by Uri Simonsohn from the University of Pennsylvania in Philadelphia. Simonsohn carried out an independent analysis of the data and was suspicious of how perfect many of Smeesters' results seemed when, statistically speaking, there should have been more variation in his measurements.'
   b. Case 2:
   Dutch psychologist Diederik Stapel 'was found to have fabricated data for years and published it in at least 30 peer-reviewed papers, including a report in the journal *Science* about how untidy environments may encourage discrimination.'

71 Alok Jha, 'When Research Findings Explode', *Sydney Morning Herald*, September 20, 2012, available at http://www.smh.com.au/world/science/when-research-findings-explode-20120919-2674r.html/.

c. Case 3:[72]
   - 'More guns, less crime.
   - Guns are used more in self-defence than in criminal acts.
   - The vast majority of mass shootings occur in gun-free zones.
   - Good guys with guns stop mass shootings.
   - Guns make women safer.

   All of these claims are staples of the gun lobby, and all of them rely on the research and advocacy of Dr John R Lott.

   John Lott is, without exception, the most prolific and influential writer on the topic of gun violence and gun control. He has credentials that would make most academics envious – with various stints at Stanford, Rice, UCLA, Wharton, Cornell, the University of Chicago and Yale.

   …

   The lobbying arm of the National Rifle Association, the Institute for Legislative Action (NRA-ILA), has spotlighted Lott's scholarship at least 140 times on their website. After every mass shooting or national gun violence tragedy, Lott is the de facto talking head for the pro-gun community on news programs such as *Fox News*. He has also testified numerous times in front of Congress and state legislatures, having been a critical voice in the expansion of Right-to-Carry (RTC) laws.

   …

   Lott's research relied heavily on advanced econometrics, a highly specialized sub-field of economics. Using an econometric model with a blistering array of controls, including 36 independent demographic variables, John Lott analyzed a total of 54,000 observations for 3,056 counties over an 18-year period. Such a massive dataset would ostensibly permit Lott, for the first time, to identify the specific effect of concealed carry laws on crime with great precision.

   The book was extremely well-received by the pro-gun community, being described as the bible of the gun lobby, and has since sold 100,000 copies. His book inaugurated a new era in the pro-gun movement: for the first time ever, organizations like the National Rifle Association could articulate their advocacy in the language of public health, rather than in constitutional terms. To this day, legislators continue to cite John Lott's work as the basis for votes against gun control.

   The only problem? Nearly nothing in the book is correct.'

---

72 Evan DeFilippis and Devin Hughes, 'Shooting Down the Gun Lobby's Favorite "Academic": A Lott of Lies', Armed with Reason, available at http://www.armedwithreason.com/shooting-down-the-gun-lobbys-favorite-academic-a-lott-of-lies/.

## FURTHER RESOURCES

1. Helpful links:
   - Law dissertation topics and ideas: http://www.lawteacher.net/law-dissertation-topics/
   - Current legal topics: http://www.loc.gov/law/help/current-topics.php
   - Need a research topic? http://faculty.law.lsu.edu/ccorcos/biblio/RESEARCHTOPICPAGE.htm
2. Research proposal template:

   This template has been adapted, with permission, from that used by Griffith Law School in 5000LAW – Interdisciplinary Research Project unit.

### RESEARCH PROPOSAL

| |
|---|
| **Instructions** – Complete this form and keep a copy for your records. |

| Name: *(last name, first name/initials)* | |
|---|---|
| **Student number** | |
| **Email address** | |
| **1. Topic area and/or draft title** | *(If possible, state your proposed topic as a preliminary draft title for your paper)* |
| **2. Theory/other discipline** | *(e.g. liberalism, regulatory theory, economic, sociology, psychology, environmental science, public policy)* |
| **3. Area(s) of legal Knowledge** | *(e.g. commercial law, torts, criminal law, constitutional law, etc)* |
| **4. Research question/ hypothesis** | *(State the research question which your project is seeking to answer.)* |
| **5. Significance** | *(Why is your research question important, original and/ or interesting – to you, others, or both? Why does it help answer a significant problem?)* |
| **6. Methodology** | *(Explain the research and analytical steps that you will follow in order to answer your research question.)* |
| **7. Ethics** | Will you be conducting interviews?<br>If so, please complete the attached ethics information form. [Attach form required by your university] |

CHAPTER 4

# DRAFTING, REVISING, EDITING AND PROOFREADING

## I INTRODUCTION

In this chapter, we consider the writing process itself. We want to stress here the importance of redrafting and of writing as a recursive process. Too often, inexperienced writers present a first draft as the final work. Experts agree, however, that good writing comes from the revision process: '[r]evision, editing and rewriting are what make mediocre writing good and good writing great'.[1]

Two points arise from this. First, the importance of revision means you need to do some good strategic thinking about time management, as the revision process can be time-consuming. It is common for novice legal writers to spend a long time in the research phase of their writing, leaving insufficient time for the all-important revision process. Second, writing is, as we have noted, a recursive process: we have talked about identifying your audience and purpose and outlining your work before you begin, but because good writing is not a linear, but a circular process, you will need to return to issues of purpose, audience, and organisation as you write.

## II DRAFTING AND REVISING FOR ACCURACY, BREVITY AND CLARITY

You will recall our diagram of the drafting cycle (see Figure 2.4). Having completed your reflection, initial planning and your research, you are ready to start drafting.

---

1 Wayne Schiess, 'Legal Writing is Not What It Should Be' (2009–2010) 37 *Southern University Law Review* 1, 15.

### *The initial draft*

> I'm writing a first draft and reminding myself that I'm simply shovelling sand into a box so that later I can build castles.[2]

There are two rules for the initial draft. They are: write early; and do not be distracted by detail. These are linked, but let's start with the direction to 'write early'. In our experience, students at both levels, undergraduate and postgraduate, put off writing the first draft. Skilled writers spend more time revising, editing and proofreading than they do writing.[3] The trick is thus not to stress too much about the initial draft. Start writing as soon as you think you understand the problem and the likely solution(s).[4] Indeed, write *to* understand the problem and the likely solution(s).

For some inexperienced writers, this direction will be very hard to follow. Often procrastination over the first draft is due to anxiety about confronting a blank page or getting things 'perfect'. Both anxieties can create a number of problems. First, they give rise to time pressures and can lead to poor work if there is insufficient time for the all-important revision process. Anxiety about starting the first draft can create a vicious circle, so that the longer you delay writing the more stressed you become. Second, students often continue researching for far too long before writing, which can lead to negative results. You may have fallen into this trap. You may be overwhelmed by the material you accumulate; tend to gather material that is marginal or irrelevant to the task at hand; or you may discover too late that there were other areas of research that you did not originally think of, and now have no time to pursue.[5]

The first draft does not have to be – indeed, cannot be – perfect. The important thing is to *start* the writing process. At this point, you should not be distracted by details or by matters of form (spelling, grammar etc).[6] The important thing is to get your ideas down in writing:

> As you write, some of your ideas will crystalize. Others will crumble. Concepts you thought you understood will be difficult to explain. If ideas are jumbled in your head, they are likely to come out jumbled on paper. As you write and then revise, you will learn what you know, and realize where you need to spend more time on your analysis.[7]

---

2 Shannon Hale, author.

3 Adina Radelescu, 'The Pitfalls of Simplifying Legal Writing' (2012) 4(2) *Contemporary Readings in Social Justice* 367, 369.

4 Reed Dickerson, 'Legal Drafting: Writing as Thinking, or, Talk-Back from your Draft and How to Exploit It' 29(4) *Journal of Legal Education* 373, 376.

5 Ibid 376.

6 Ibid 377.

7 Suzanne E Rowe, 'Legal Research, Legal Writing, and Legal Analysis: Putting Law School into Practice' (1999–2000) 29 *Stetson Law Review* 1193, 1205.

If you are having difficulty starting to write, or you are procrastinating, it may help to try **'freewriting'**, a technique we discuss in more detail in Chapter 6. In essence, all you do is set a timer, then write *something* – even if you write about how difficult it is to write. This will often break the writer's block and enable your work to get moving.

## *Revising*

> I enjoy rewriting much more than I do first drafts. Rewriting, at least you have something to work with. I find writing first drafts extremely difficult.[8]

Once the first draft is done, it often takes away much of the initial anxiety, and the process of revision can begin. A number of points about revising are important to keep in mind.

First, it may be necessary to revise a work several times. Many people are resistant to this idea, but there is an important point about the revision process which goes back to an idea we discussed earlier: the link between knowledge and writing:

> [G]ood writers know that successive drafts are better not simply because their word choices are better but because with each draft they seem to know more about their subject and are better able to organize their ideas coherently.[9]

In other words, successive drafts tend to improve your understanding of the subject matter.

Revision can be time consuming.[10] Students are often subject to a number of competing deadlines for written work. In legal practice, too, 'deadlines, billable hours and heavy workloads'[11] can make it difficult to set aside time for revision. Good writing requires some careful and strategic thinking about time management and, particularly, about dedicating a good amount of the available time to the revision process. And to complicate this, it is often helpful to have enough time to set the written piece aside for a while. It is easy to get too close to a text and thus have difficulty seeing its flaws. If your schedule does not allow for this, it may be helpful to ask someone else to read the piece, thus supplying that fresh perspective.

Third, because the writing process is recursive, and because '[n]o rhetoric is effective except to the extent that it is devised for a particular audience and occasion', you need to return to issues of organisation, research, audience and purpose as you revise. As we will see, this is often the key to clear and effective legal writing.

---

8 George RR Martin, author.

9 Fredric G Gale, 'Logic, Rhetoric, and Legal Writing' (1996) 10(2) *Journal of Business and Technical Communication* 203.

10 Schiess, above n 1, 15.

11 Ibid 15.

Lastly, it is important to recognise that producing clear and effective legal writing is hard work and, like any other skill, such as playing the piano or becoming good at tennis, it requires practice.[12] Legal writing improves with practice.

Osbeck observes that: 'good legal writing is writing that facilitates the reader's ability to extract information from the document that will aid the reader's professional decision-making'.[13] He argues that there are three core qualities in legal writing: clarity, conciseness and engagement. These can provide helpful prompts for the revision process.

### *Is your work clear and concise?*

Clarity has been described as the 'most basic' and the 'paramount goal of legal writing'. This is because the reader must be able to understand and utilise the communication in their decision-making: '[t]he aim of any writing is to be easily understood'.[14] The writer needs to revise the work to ensure that it can be understood by the reader.[15] Osbeck considers that conciseness is at the core of good legal writing because it helps readers make effective use of their limited time. He argues that legal readers are ordinarily time-poor. The writer should thus ensure that their writing makes its point efficiently and with an appropriate level of detail so as not to waste the reader's time.[16]

Revising your work for clarity and conciseness thus requires, as a first step, a reconsideration of audience and purpose. What information does the reader need? What is the appropriate level of formality?[17] Is the work organised clearly so that the reader can find the information they need easily, and understand the points made? Is the language used clear and appropriate for the audience?

The first advice from expert legal writers is: get to the point.[18] They recommend that, unless a rule requires otherwise, all analytic writing should have a summary of the issue(s) and conclusion *at the beginning*. For instance, in a letter, the first paragraph should summarise the point of the letter; in a piece of legal analysis, the central issue(s) and conclusion should be stated at the beginning.[19]

Thereafter, the text needs to be organised at the micro and macro levels: is the organisation of the document logical? Have you used clear and descriptive titles,

---

12 Ibid 24.

13 Mark Osbeck, 'What is "Good Legal Writing" and Why Does it Matter?' (2012) 4(2) *Drexel Law Review* 417, 439.

14 David Ross, 'Legal Writing' (2005) 1(4) *Original Law Review* 85.

15 Osbeck, above n 13, 436.

16 Ibid 439.

17 Schiess, above n 1, 20.

18 Joseph Kimble, 'First Things First: The Lost Art of Summarizing' (2001) 38 *Court Reviw* 30, 30.

19 Wayne Schiess, 'The Five Principles of Legal Writing' (2003) *Practical Lawyer* 11.

headings and subheadings?[20] Are paragraphs and sentences connected smoothly, so the **transitions** are clear? Do paragraphs build on each other or introduce new topics?[21] Clarity also demands the use of the **active**, rather than the **passive** voice,[22] 'ordinary words and simple sentence structures'.[23] Many writers advocate keeping sentences short, with one issue in each sentence.[24] One rule of thumb is to keep sentences to no more than 22 words, although this should not be adhered to rigidly – see our suggestions below about the importance of varying sentence length.

Clarity requires conventional grammar, spelling and punctuation. As Osbeck points out, the reason for this is 'that language has to have certain agreed-upon rules to govern its basic functioning. Otherwise, there would be no possibility of shared meaning, and therefore no possibility of language itself'.[25] Disregarding these rules makes it difficult for the reader, accustomed to following these rules, to understand the writer's message.[26] This brings us to issues of the plain language movement.

To some extent, as Radelescu observes, 'the language of the law is bound to deviate from common speech in favour of technical or professional language'.[27] However, lawyers are often criticised for use of '**legalese**': use of Latin words or archaic words unnecessarily; use of complex words unnecessarily; overuse of the passive voice and **nominalisations**; sentences that are too long; and use of insider jargon, even when the communication in question is not directed to 'insiders'.[28] Schiess argues that lawyers tend to resort to legalese either to impress, or because they are very busy and simply revert to more formal prose because they read so much of it in law school.[29] He argues that too much legal writing is 'stuffy and formal' and that 'experts should shed legalese'.[30] Wherever you can, you should cut 'fluff', Latin, old-fashioned words, and useless jargon.

Some critics of the plain language movement, however, argue that focusing on ordinary, rather than technical terms, affects the precision of legal writing. That is, ordinary terms are often vague and ambiguous, while technical legal terms can provide

---

20 Ibid.
21 Ibid.
22 Ross, above n 14, 86. Consult our 'Grammar Primer' if you don't know the difference between the active and the passive voice.
23 Osbeck, above n 13, 429.
24 Ross, above n 14, 86.
25 Osbeck, above n 13, 428.
26 Ibid 429.
27 Radelescu, above n 3, 371.
28 Schiess, above n 1, 17–18.
29 Ibid 19.
30 Ibid 18.

greater precision.[31] Osbeck argues that we should understand the prescription to use plain language as a more nuanced rule, that is:

> When you use distinctive technical or legal terms, consider whether the terms add any value beyond their ordinary language equivalents. If not, use the ordinary term. If so, then consider the nature of the audience to determine whether the increased precision resulting from the technical term outweighs any loss of clarity that may result from using a term that may not be familiar to all members of the intended audience.[32]

In other words, the use of plain language should be contextual and involve a consideration of audience and purpose. You will find some prompts for plain language writing in our Grammar Primer.

### *Is your work engaging?*

Osbeck's third quality of good legal writing is engagement. Engagement is not necessarily something most people would immediately associate with legal writing. Osbeck argues, however, that it is essential: '[w]riting that does not engage the reader's attention makes it more difficult for the reader to glean necessary information from a document because it makes the reading process more laborious. And that in turn hinders the reader's ability to make professional decisions based upon the document'.[33] He breaks down the elements of engagement as: variety; voice; and tone. To these elements, we would add presentation, as in Figure 4.1. You can thus make your work more engaging by utilising some simple ideas.

FIGURE 4.1

| | |
|---|---|
| **Variety** | • Vary your sentence structures, vocabulary and sentence length. |
| **Voice** | • Your writing conveys an image of you as a legal professional. Your own voice can only develop with practice. |
| **Tone** | • Legal writing should be clear, concise, confident and courteous.<br>• It should have an appropriate level of formality without being pretentious. |
| **Presentation** | • Good document design can make your documents easier to read and more engaging for the reader. Pay attention to the details: font, font size, white space, headings, spacing, text alignment. |

31 Osbeck, above n 13, 431.
32 Ibid 433–4.
33 Ibid 442.

### *Vary sentence structures, vocabulary and sentence length*

Using varied sentence structures, vocabulary and sentence length can make writing more engaging. This variation creates a more natural flow that helps maintain the reader's interest.[34] We noted above that short sentences, of about 22 words, can help clarify your writing. Certainly long sentences can be confusing (and boring) for the reader. But varying sentence length can create a rhythm and interest to your writing.

### *Develop your own voice*

We referred to voice earlier: the aim of good legal writing is to develop an authentic professional voice, one that has character and individuality.[35] Developing your own professional writing voice helps to engage the reader. This is, of course, something that can only develop over time and with practice, but if you write with the desire to connect with your audience, this will help to develop your authentic voice:

> Law, as you can see, is … a kind of writing, at its heart less of an interpretive process than a compositional one. The central task for the lawyer from this point of view is to give herself a voice of her own, a voice that at once expresses her own mind at work in its best way and speaks as a lawyer, a voice at once individual and professional.[36]

There are many examples of authentic voice in legal writing. Perhaps one of the most famous is that of Lord Denning, whose judgments often had a quality of storytelling. His account of the facts in *Beswick v Beswick* [1966] 1 Ch 538 provides a good example:

> Old Peter Beswick was a coal merchant in Eccles, Lancashire. He had no business premises. All he had was a lorry, scales and weights. He used to take the lorry to the yard of the National Coal Board, where he bagged coal and took it round to his customers in the neighbourhood. His nephew, John Joseph Beswick, helped him in the business. In March, 1962, old Peter Beswick and his wife were both over 70. He had had his leg amputated and was not in good health. The nephew was anxious to get hold of the business before the old man died. So they went to a solicitor, Mr. Ashcroft, who drew up an agreement for them. The business was to be transferred to the nephew: old Peter Beswick was to be employed in it as a consultant for the rest of his life at £6 10s. a week. After his death the nephew was to pay to his widow an annuity of £5 per week, which was to come out of the business.[37]

---

34 Ibid 443.

35 Ibid 443–4.

36 Ibid 444, quoting James Boyd White, *The Legal Imagination*, xv (abr ed 1985).

37 *Beswick v Beswick* [1966] 1 Ch 538, 549.

In contrast, in the same case, Lord Salmon wrote:

> Throughout this judgment I will, for the sake of clarity, refer to A, B, and C. A is the late Mr. Peter Beswick and also the plaintiff standing in his shoes in her capacity as administratrix. B is the defendant and C is the plaintiff in her personal capacity.[38]

### *Pay attention to tone*

*Tone* is the expression of the writer's attitude towards the subject, audience and self. Attention to tone means ensuring that you have adopted the right degree of formality and that the subject matter of the document and the writing style are in harmony.[39] Tone is primarily conveyed in writing through **diction**, **syntax**, and the appropriate level of formality. In legal writing, the tone should be clear, concise, confident and courteous. While legal writing must be sophisticated, it should not be pretentious, and while courteous, should not be overly familiar or informal.

### *Pay attention to presentation*

An often-neglected aspect of good legal writing is presentation. Good presentation of your written work can make reading easier and more engaging for your reader. The presentation should be sharp and professional without drawing undue attention to the design itself.[40] It is helpful to read about good document design and take note of documents you like as a reader. Consider issues such as:

- *Text alignment*: readers generally prefer left justification with a ragged right margin for letters, court documents and contracts.[41]
- *Headings*: ensure these are sufficiently distinct. Ordinarily, headings are on the left margin, rather than centred in bold and/or italics, but some style guides, such as the AGLC, dictate both the placement of margins and their typeface (eg bold, italicised, small caps).
- *Spacing*: often double-spacing is a requirement. If so, use it, though some commentators, such as Schiess,[42] recommend using increased font size and single space with increased space between paragraphs to improve the readability of the text.
- *Fonts*: generally a serifed font is used for the main body of text in legal documents to give the appropriate sense of formality. Non-serif fonts are considered informal. Courier should never be used.[43]

---

38 Ibid 563.
39 Ibid 454.
40 Schiess, above n 19.
41 Ibid.
42 Ibid.
43 Ibid.

- *White space*: Ensure there is sufficient white space on the page to facilitate ease of reading.

## *Giving and receiving feedback*

In our diagram of the drafting process, you will see that we advise that, once you have a substantially revised draft, you should seek feedback. Students are sometimes invited (or required) by their lecturers to submit a pre-finalised draft for feedback. If this is not the practice at your university, you can seek feedback from a peer mentor, if your university has such a system. If not, a family member or friend can provide feedback. They do not have to understand the legal technicalities. In fact, sometimes it is helpful if they don't. You want them to provide feedback on the text: can they follow the argument? Is it easy to understand? Does it flow? If you are in practice, a colleague can provide feedback. We recommend this particularly for client letters. If you have no one who can provide feedback, try to ensure that you have enough time to put the writing away for a couple of days. When you come back to it with fresh eyes, you will often be able to see problems that were difficult to spot while you were drafting and revising.

Increasingly, students are asked to work collaboratively to produce written work, or asked to peer review the work of other students. This can be quite anxiety-provoking, in our experience: as a student receiving feedback, you may be anxious about criticism. As a student giving feedback, you may be anxious not to offend your fellow student. If you are required to give or receive peer feedback, here are some tips you might find helpful:

- *Talk about what is on the page*. Be specific and don't generalise; that is, rather than saying an essay is disorganised, point to a specific example ('in the second paragraph on page 2, I don't understand how the reason connects to the evidence').
- *Ask very specific questions about the argument*:
  - What are you claiming?
  - What are your reasons?
  - What evidence do you have to base these reasons on?
  - What justification connects your claims and your reasons?
  - Have you thought of this alternative (or objection)?
- *Phrase your criticism in terms of your response as a reader*. Your colleague is less likely to get defensive if you follow this rule. So, rather than saying, 'This point is confusing', it is better to say, 'When I read this point, I was confused'.
- *Offer a principle and show how it relates to what is on the page*. Thus, rather than saying 'every claim needs evidence to back it up', you can say 'This claim would be more convincing to me if it had evidence to support it'.[44]

---

44 Joseph M Williams and Gregory G Columb, *The Craft of Argument* (Longman, 2nd ed, 2003).

## III EDITING AND PROOFREADING

As we noted earlier, you may have to go through the drafting cycle a number of times. Once you have a final draft, you will move on to the all-important editing and proofreading processes (Figure 4.2).

FIGURE 4.2

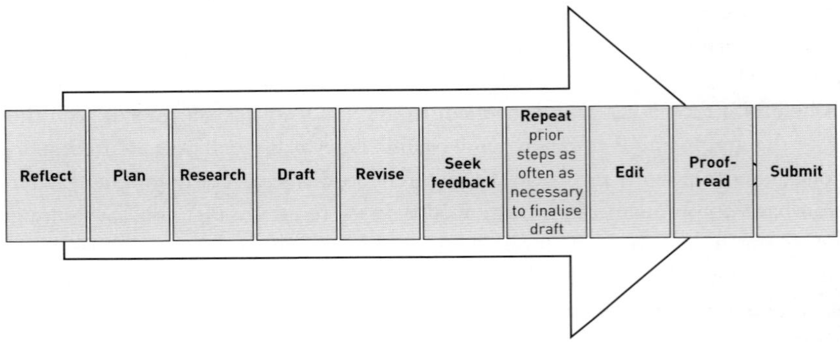


Rowe observes that '[w]riting in the legal context must be edited to perfection'.[45] Novice legal writers often neglect the editing and proofreading stages but these stages are fundamental: a lack of polish can undermine your attempts to engage with the reader and convince them you are worth listening to.[46] For a lawyer, care with presentation can be particularly important professionally: errors in the text suggest the writer is sloppy and careless, qualities that are not associated with good lawyers.[47] An important aspect of planning and time management is to leave yourself enough time to edit your document: James[48] suggests you should allocate as much time to editing as to drafting.

So, before printing the document:

- run a spell-checker over it;
- ensure it is double-spaced so you can see mistakes and have room for corrections and insertions;[49]
- verify the spellings of names and addresses;[50]
- read through the draft carefully. James provides a helpful checklist for this stage of the process:[51]

---

45 Rowe, above n 7, 1208.
46 Sonia Von Matt Stoddard, 'Proofreading for Perfection' (1997) 14(4) *Paralegal Today* 84, 84.
47 Osbeck, above n 13, 428 n 35.
48 Neil James, *Writing at Work* (Allen and Unwin, 2007) 300.
49 Stoddard, above n 46, 84.
50 Ibid.
51 James, above n 48, 301.

| Editing stage | Check | | Assess |
|---|---|---|---|
| Content | 1 | Clarity | Are message and purpose clear to the reader? |
| | 2 | Accuracy | Are facts and figures correct? |
| | 3 | Objectivity | Are opinions supported? |
| | 4 | Logic | Is the argument effective? |
| | 5 | Completeness | Are depth and breadth sufficient? |
| Structure | 6 | Focus | Is the level of detail appropriate? |
| | 7 | Structure | Are design, balance and navigation effective? |
| | 8 | Coherence | Is there a unified purpose and are transitions smooth? |
| | 9 | Design | Do the visual elements reinforce content? |
| Expression | 10 | Tone | Have you used the right level of formality? |
| | 11 | Word choice | Have you minimised jargon, complexity and abstraction? |
| | 12 | Mechanics | Do you have good average sentence length, structure and variation? |
| | 13 | Verbs | Are verbs mostly in the active voice? |
| | 14 | Efficiency | Have you used concise expression? |
| | 15 | Grammar | Have you used correct pronoun references, modifiers, verb agreement, verb tenses and word order? |
| Style | 16 | Formatting | Have you used a consistent layout or correct use of a template? |
| | 17 | Language | Have you checked spelling, capitals and shortened forms? |
| | 18 | Numbering | Have you checked accuracy of dates, time, money and numerals? |
| | 19 | Punctuation | Is punctuation consistent and correct? |
| | 20 | Sourcing | Is referencing accurate, consistent and complete? |

James recommends that you start at the top of the table and work down. This provides you with a descending order of focus. If time is limited, do two edits: one for content and structure, and one for expression and style.[52]

Once the document is printed:

- *Proofread it carefully*, preferably at different sittings so you don't miss the same errors.[53] James provides a 'top ten' list of proofreading tips:
  1. 'Read against the original copy.
  2. Read aloud.
  3. Force yourself to read word by word, using card, pen or ruler.
  4. Read text backwards.
  5. Be aware of your blind spots.
  6. Re-check the early pages of text.
  7. Never trust a machine.
  8. Assess the flow-on impact of any changes.
  9. Read in short bursts, rather than marathon sessions.
  10. Check everything.'[54]
- *Mark corrections and insertions in coloured pen.* It is helpful to learn to use proofreading marks. You can find tables of these on the internet.
- *Flag lines where corrections are to be made*, particularly if they are minor and so easily overlooked.[55]

## IV CONSIDERATION OF THE SOURCES: REFERENCING AND CITATION

In the study and practice of law, it is vital to acknowledge the sources of your information. Acknowledgment of your sources provides a number of functions: validation of your research (that is, substantiating your claims by showing your work is based on decided cases, legislation and published authorities); demonstrating the breadth and depth of your research;[56] enabling readers to locate your sources should they wish to find out more on a particular matter; situating your work in the discipline (research builds upon work that has been done previously), and, of course avoiding plagiarism.

---

52 Ibid.

53 Stoddard, above n 46, 84.

54 James above n 48, 323.

55 Stoddard, above n 46, 85.

56 Becky Batogal and Melissa Castan 'Citations, Sources and References' (2012) 37(1) *Alternative Law Journal* 50, 50.

Legal writing, particularly academic legal writing, often makes extensive use of footnotes:

> Footnotes are used to indicate the source of an idea relied upon, to acknowledge the relevance of a source to an argument and, occasionally, to provide additional information that is not suitable to include in the main text. A footnote should always follow a paraphrase or a quotation.[57]

As a student, you should never use footnotes to avoid word count limits![58] In fact footnotes are now generally counted in doctoral theses.

Generally, you will cite your sources in the text of the document but you may also be required to provide a reference list, case list or list of legislation.

## *Style guides*

Style guides provide standards for matters such as language, spelling, formatting and punctuation, and often strict rules for the presentation of citations, references and bibliographies. Style guides are used by students, academics, publishers, and those who work in specialised fields including law and journalism. They are always helpful for writers, but in some cases they are mandatory. In Australia, the AGLC is commonly used, but some law schools encourage the use of the *Harvard Guide to Legal Citation* and a number of law journals have their own, unique style guides. Other disciplines, such as psychology, also have their own style guides. You can find the AGLC on the internet,[59] along with a 'Quick Guide' to the style.

The purpose of style guides is consistency: they give uniformity both within a document and across multiple documents. They also streamline the author's work by providing a consistent approach to, say, footnotes. After a while, using a particular style guide, such as the AGLC, becomes almost second nature.

## *Plagiarism and academic integrity*

Plagiarism has been defined as 'the act of representing someone's words or ideas as being of one's own'.[60] Law students are generally warned in their first year about the potential consequences of plagiarism which can have an impact on admission

57 Ibid 50.

58 Ibid 50.

59 The AGLC is available for download at: http://law.unimelb.edu.au/mulr/aglc; the Quick Guide can be found at http://law.unimelb.edu.au/mulr/submissions/quick-aglc.

60 Joe Mirarchi, 'Plagiarism: What is it? How to Avoid it? and Why?' (2000–2001) 4 *Thomas M Cooley Journal of Practical and Clinical Law* 382, 383. For an interesting discussion of notions of plagiarism as being culturally-specific, see Alastair Pennycook, 'Borrowing Others' Words: Text, Ownership, Memory and Plagiarism' (1996) 30(2) *TESOL Quarterly* 201.

to the profession.[61] Plagiarism is an important aspect of the ethics of legal writing: '[It] touches not only on the matter of originality and thoroughness in research and scholarship but on the matter of integrity of those producing works of scholarship'.[62]

Plagiarism may be intentional or it may be negligent. Intentional plagiarism is when an individual knowingly and willingly misappropriates another's words and ideas as their own.[63] As teachers, we have seen instances where students have cut and pasted whole paragraphs, and even whole articles, into their assessable work, and presented it as their own. This is clearly dishonest. Negligent plagiarism is where the individual is careless about documenting their sources.[64] This commonly is the case where students are under pressure and their work becomes slapdash. Collusion is also considered a breach of academic integrity. This is where two or more students work together on a piece of assessable work, but each presents it as their own, individual effort.

How do you avoid plagiarism? Mirarchi[65] provides some helpful instructions:

- Provide a source for EVERY assertion of fact or law.
- Where you use the actual words from a source, always format as a quote.
- Try to avoid quoting material in one source that is a quote of another source, which raises the possibility of double-plagiarism. Verify your sources back to the original author.

We also discuss plagiarism in relation to academic work in Chapter 6, 'Research Essays, Theses and Dissertations'; and in relation to legal practice in Chapter 9, 'Form Writing, Standard Forms and Use of Precedents'.

## V CONCLUSION

In this chapter, we have considered the second part of the writing cycle - drafting, revising and seeking feedback; and then the processes of editing and proofreading once that cycle is complete. We provided checklists for editing and proof reading and introduced the fundamentals of referencing and citation. In Chapter 5 we turn to consider specific genres of academic writing.

---

61 See further Lillian Corbin and Justin Carter, 'Is Plagiarism Indicative of Prospective Legal Practice?' (2007) 17 *Legal Education Review* 53.
62 Mirarchi, above n 60, 383, quoting Mawdsley.
63 Ibid 383.
64 Ibid 383.
65 Ibid 384–5.

# REVIEW MATERIALS

## SUMMARY

This chapter focused on drafting and revising for accuracy, brevity and clarity, and giving and receiving feedback. It explained systematic editing and proofreading, and the academic writing requirements of referencing to acknowledge sources and avoid plagiarism.

## KEY POINTS

1. The process of writing is recursive, not linear. You will thus often return to the pre-writing tasks of reflecting on your purpose and audience, planning and research a number of times in order to refine your work;
2. Not only your writing, but your understanding of the issues and the law will improve with successive drafts;
3. You can make your writing more engaging by paying attention to variation, voice, tone and presentation;
4. Don't be afraid of giving or receiving feedback. Both activities will develop you as a writer;
5. Legal writing imposes high standards of presentation. You thus need to edit and proof read carefully, and pay attention to matters of style, presentation and citation.

## REFLECTIVE QUESTIONS

1. What is the difference between revising, editing and proofreading?
2. Do you ordinarily build in time to edit and proofread your assignments? If not, why is this the case?
3. What is 'legalese'? Are there any circumstances in which it is acceptable to use 'legalese'?
4. Do you become anxious at the idea of peer feedback on your writing? If so, why is this the case? What can you do to alleviate that anxiety?
5. Why is it important to acknowledge your sources accurately?

## EXERCISES

1. Revision exercise

   Take a draft assignment, or one of your old completed assignments, and revise it:

   a. Using the following **FACT** structure. **FACT** is an acronym for a process that leads to holistic essay revision:

      **F** Does the whole essay **FIT** together, presenting a central point? Do all parts connect to the thesis?

      **A** What do you need to **ADD**? Where does the reader need more info or examples to understand the paper's message? What major ideas have been left out?

      **C** What do you need to **CUT**? Where is there repetition? What doesn't contribute to the essay?

      **T** Carefully **TEST** the organisation of the essay. Does the text flow smoothly from point to point with clear transitions between the various ideas? Is the organisation logical?[66]

   b. Using the following points to make your sentences come alive or more specifically to have an effect on the reader.

      - Use words that evoke the reader's emotions. For instance, 'Those on the beach were horrified to see the child being swept away by the waves.'
      - Use the active voice as much as possible. Compare the passive: 'The child was watched as she was swept away', with the active voice: 'The group on the beach watched as the waves swept the child away'.
      - The addition of adjectives and adverbs can strengthen the emotional effect of the words on the reader, although their over-use can tend to make the text 'flowery'. They can add colour and detail. For instance, 'The elderly group on the beach watched powerlessly as the waves swept the young child away'.
      - Vary the length of your sentences, and avoid using the same word multiple times. This provides a sense of anticipation. 'As the group on the beach watched, the huge waves swept the very young child out to sea. Those watching were horrified. They feared that the little girl would drown.'[67]

---

66 From http://iws.collin.edu/asjohnson/Planning,%20Drafting,%20Revising,%20and%20Editing%20(Day1and2presentation)%20PDF.pdf.

67 The Writing Center at Chapel Hill, 'Revising Drafts', available at http://writingcenter.unc.edu/handouts/revising-drafts/.

2. Some grammar exercises[68]

   Before undertaking these, you might like to look over the Grammar Primer we have provided.

   a. Rewrite the following sentences to ensure gender neutrality:

      Common sense suggests that when a student is injured at the university, he should immediately notify his lawyer. He, in turn, should consider whether there is a basis for legal action.

   b. Correct these sentences (dangling/misplaced modifiers)
      - Applying this test to the facts of the case, the defendant's argument is considered inadequate.
      - The defendant had a tattoo on his right shoulder that depicted a panda bear.
      - We accept arguments as legitimate in part because lawyers are trained in rhetoric.

   c. Rewrite (nominalisations):
      - The legislature has given no indication that a universal identification document is constitutional.

   d. Rewrite (parallelism):
      - Reasonable efforts to maintain secrecy include putting the document in a locked safe, storing pages of the document in separate locations or a continuing course of conduct that creates a confidential relationship.
      - Part II of this note will discuss the historical background of agreements leading up to this TRIPS agreement, the scope of other agreements and lay out reasons for limiting geographical protection.

   e. Rewrite (split infinitives):
      - To accurately assess the situation you have to carefully weigh up all the factors and you need to sensibly think about the consequences.

   f. Who or whom?
      - Rhetorical analysis asks 'For ______ is this document intended?'
      - The Committee decides ______ should be nominated for a scholarship.
      - The defendant, ______ they knew, was convicted of fraud.
      - Is there no one ______ we can trust?

---

68 These are adapted from Elizabeth Fajans and Mary R Falk, *Scholarly Writing for Law Students* (4th ed, West, 2011).

3. Plain language exercises

   Rewrite each of the following in concise and plain language:

   a. I am writing to advise that this firm, and in particular, the writer (who has been given carriage of this matter) has received instructions from Mr. John Bloggs to pursue an interest he maintains he has in your client's business. During our initial appointment with him, he provided us with correspondence he has received from you regarding your client's view on the matter.
      At this point in time our purpose in writing is to simply alert you to the above facts. Once we have reviewed the document and considered our clients instructions more carefully, we will revert to you by way of further correspondence.

      Yours very sincerely

   b. The mortgage documents relating to the business located at Brisbane Road, Labrador are returned herewith having been duly executed by my client who has signed as the borrower.

   c. If an application is made to a court any competent jurisdiction, and that court finds any term, provision, Section, or portion of this Agreement to be invalid, void, or unenforceable, this will not necessarily have any effect on the enforceability and effect of the remaining terms, provisions, Sections, and portions of this Agreement.

## FURTHER RESOURCES

1. Active/passive voice:
   http://www.yourdictionary.com/index.php/pdf/articles/43.activevspassive voice.pdf
   https://owl.english.purdue.edu/owl/owlprint/539/
2. Variety in tone:
   http://literarydevices.net/tone/
   http://examples.yourdictionary.com/examples-of-tone-in-a-story.html
   http://valenciacollege.edu/east/academicsuccess/eap/documents/tonewords.pdf
3. Is your work clear and concise?
   https://owl.english.purdue.edu/exercises/2/
4. Plain language and law:
   http://www.lawfoundation.net.au/ljf/app/&id=/2FD34F71BE2A0155CA257 14C001739DA
5. Quick guide AGLC:
   http://law.unimelb.edu.au/mulr/submissions/quick-aglc

# CHAPTER 5

# CASE NOTES AND PROBLEM QUESTIONS

## I INTRODUCTION

In this chapter, we outline methodologies for completing case notes (sometimes referred to as case briefs or case analyses) and problem questions (often termed **hypotheticals**). The ability to master these genres is closely linked to the ethical obligations of lawyers. For instance, the Australian Solicitors Conduct Rules require solicitors to 'give clear and timely advice to assist a client to understand relevant legal issues and to make informed choices' (ASCR r 7.1); 'act in the best interests of a client' (ASCR r 4.1.1); act with competence (ASCR r 4.1.3); and refrain from acting as the mere mouthpiece of the client (ASCR r 17.1). Lawyers thus have an obligation to ensure that they know and understand the law and can communicate it objectively and accurately to their clients, to the court and to others on behalf of the clients.

The ability to master these genres is also closely linked to learning to 'think like a lawyer'. It is common in the first year of legal education to teach the writing of case notes and introducing students to the method of solving problem questions. This serves as an introduction to mastering the skills of legal analysis and 'learning a method of argument',[1] that is, using legal reasoning 'to persuade others to accept a particular interpretation of the law'.[2]

The methodologies introduced in this chapter are both '**schemas**' that provide the writer with a learning context and ways of thinking to solve problems.[3]

1 James Boyle, 'The Anatomy of a Torts Class' (1985) 34 *American University Law Review* 1003, 1051.
2 Wilson R Huhn, 'Teaching Legal Analysis Using a Pluralistic Model of Law' (2000–2001) 36 *Gonzaga Law Review* 433, 457.
3 Paula Lustbader, 'Construction Sites, Building Types, and Bridging Gaps: A Cognitive Theory of the Learning Progression of Law Students' (1997) 33 *Willamette Law Review* 315, 326.

These schemas[4] can both familiarise you with the legal landscape and provide you with the means to reflect on new information and evaluate its worth. Indeed, we would suggest that it is possible to include aspects of your 'voice and values'.[5] This is important because, whether entering university straight from school or retraining after working for a number of years in another career, you may be overwhelmed by your introduction to law school. Pommersheim makes the following observation about the experience of law students:

> The gulf between law school and life widens daily… Their common language of discourse is stripped away and replaced with the baffling lexicon of case analysis – facts, issues, rules, holdings, reasons. It is a puzzling vocabulary unhinged from any apparently meaningful connection with ordinary experience.[6]

He goes on to say:

> This environment demands – often without saying so – that students not only learn but also change. Change not only their ways of thinking, but also their understanding of their values, their sense of what is meaningful, and the social obstacles that limit what is possible.[7]

This is an issue also taken up by Mertz, who refers to the strategies adopted to help novice writers 'think like a lawyer' as dehumanising. He suggests that novice writers are 'abruptly forced to set aside their sense of morality, fairness, and sensitivity to human suffering … Fluidity of position, to enable arguing either side of an issue, is encouraged and further promotes an instrumental, amoral mindset'.[8] Krieger suggests that this approach is 'very damaging … [as] it is usually conveyed, and understood, as a new and superior way of thinking, rather than an important but strictly limited legal tool'.[9] It is our view that the narrow paradigm for legal practice needs to be expanded to allow you, as a legal writer, to accommodate your own moral sensitivities by analysing and evaluating legal decisions in order to develop your own 'critical voice'.

---

4 Leah M Christensen, 'The Psychology Behind Case Briefing: A Powerful Cognitive Schema' (2006) 29 (1) *Campbell Law Review* 5, 5.

5 Frank Pommersheim, 'Voice, Values, and Community: Some Reflections on Legal Writing' (1988) XII (4) *Legal Studies Forum* 477, 480.

6 Ibid 477.

7 Ibid 480.

8 Elizabeth Mertz, *The Language of Law School: Learning to 'Think Like a Lawyer'* (Oxford University Press, 2007) 95, 98 cited in Lawrence S Krieger, 'Human Nature as a Guiding Philosophy for Legal Education and the Profession' (2008) 47 *Washburn Law Journal* 247, 265.

9 Lawrence S Krieger, 'Institutional Denial About the Dark Side of Law School, and Fresh Empirical Guidance for Constructively Breaking the Silence' (2002) 52 *Journal of Legal Education* 112, 117.

Before we look at case notes, we would first like to point out that the structure of both a case note and an answer to a problem question have much in common. Ordinarily, both are organised using a method such as IRAC (you may recall from our earlier discussion, that IRAC stands for Issue, Rule, Application, Conclusion)[10] or an adaptation of that method;[11] and both require you to analyse the legal reasoning that underlies the decisions of judges.

## II THE CASE NOTE

It is generally understood that one of the first skills introduced to the commencing legal writer is how to write a case note (or case brief). This is a written summary of the case, preferably using your own words. Yet, this seemingly simple task can present as a complex challenge to novice writers, who are yet to make the transition 'from being non-law students to law students'.[12] At this stage, as a novice writer, you are generally not familiar with the structure of the legal system, its conventions and its values.[13] As a result, unsurprisingly, you may struggle with the legal terms and the unique organisational text structure, and consequently you may have difficulty comprehending what you are reading.[14] This tends to lead to a mechanical approach of inserting information under the relevant headings that are usually included in a case note, and ultimately to the abandonment of the case note as a learning tool.[15]

Yet if you are encouraged throughout your degree and beyond graduation to continue to use case notes to conduct a detailed analysis of cases, this will increase your understanding of the art of legal reasoning. This, in turn, can help you to better construct your legal arguments. In other words, knowing how to summarise a case has the potential to provide novice and more sophisticated legal writers with much more than knowledge of the formal writing requirements. It can also develop a deep understanding of legal reasoning and serve to develop your own legal voice. We turn now to consider the value of the case note.

---

10 Generally understood to be '(1) state the legal issue on which each section of a memo is based; (2) extrapolate a set of rules from several cases and explain how they were used to decide those cases; (3) synthesize those rules in to a theory of law; (4) apply that rule to the set of facts using analogy and distinction; and (5) state the conclusion reached through that application': Soma R Kedia, 'Redirecting the Scope of First-Year Writing Courses: Toward a New Paradigm of Teaching Legal Writing' (2009–2010) 87 *University of Detroit Mercy Law Review* 147, 169.

11 For an overview of the many related methods, see Troy Simpson, 'The Art of Written Persuasion: From IRAC to FAILSAFE – A Compilation of Legal Problem-Solving Models' (2008), available at http://www.llrx.com/columns/persuasion3.htm.

12 Lustbader, above n 3, 330.

13 Ibid 330.

14 Christensen, above n 4, 8.

15 Ibid 14.

## *The value of the case note*

A case note provides a 'schema'. Derived from the discipline of cognitive science, a schema is a cognitive framework or concept that helps to organise and interpret information. Utilising a schema can enable you to understand your environment, deal with new information and recognise gaps in your understanding.[16] This strategy provides the writer with 'both a context and a method to process what they learn'.[17]

More specifically, case noting can introduce you to the structure of your future community of practice, that is, learning about the court hierarchy and the doctrine of **precedent**; and its language. The language of law is distinctive in the way it converses and communicates. Case noting encourages you to identify the *stare decisis* and distinguish it from *obiter dicta*. It teaches you to consider the legal practitioner's 'special responsibility in society'[18] by including an element of analysis, that is, considering the decision of the court through the perspective of public policy and other relevant theories. Treating a case note as a stand-alone task has some value as an organising note for one case, yet it truly becomes legal analysis in the sense of an examination of the judges' legal reasoning, when the creator of the brief evaluates the case.

Completing a case note can encourage the development of critical thinking. As one commentator puts it, it is important for legal writers to '"talk back" to the text':[19] 'To be effective counsellors and advocates, lawyers cannot take legal documents at their word. They ought to be able to read between the lines and to link texts to larger contexts'.[20] As a novice writer, you thus need to develop your 'own thoughts and reactions to the case'.[21] Taking this approach, you may want to think about incorporating comparisons of other cases and consider whether the judges have employed public policies or theories to support their decisions. For example, it is a useful exercise to examine critically the individual judgments of the case through the perspective of, for example, the different versions of liberalism, or feminism, or economic theory and consider whether the judges' reasons refer to policy arguments.

Encouraging you, as a legal writer, to undertake this kind of analysis also provides you with the opportunity to practise your legal writing and express your own 'voice', your opinions based on your own values,[22] and helps you retain your individuality and 'sense of what is meaningful'.[23] More pragmatically, case note also provide you,

---

16 Ibid 11.

17 Lustbader, above n 3, 320.

18 Pommersheim, above n 5, 478.

19 Elizabeth Fajans and Mary Falk, 'Against the Tyranny of Paraphrase: Talking Back to the Texts' (1993) 78 *Cornell Law Review* 163.

20 Ibid 163.

21 Christensen, above n 4, 17.

22 Pommersheim, above n 5, 481–5.

23 Ibid 480. While this article was written in 1988, it seems to suggest an approach to teaching law students that is currently being advocated by Mary C Gentile in her book *Giving Voice to Values: How to Speak Your Mind When you Know What's Right* (Yale University Press, 2010).

as a student, with an invaluable study aid for answering problem questions and preparing for assignments and examinations.

Cases are, of course, often intricate and can be hard to follow. Facts, timelines, parties and reasoning can be complex. Before putting the case into words, it often helps to use diagrams and images to 'sketch out' the case. As Rosman points out, '[w]ords may be a lawyer's primary tool, but they're not the only tool'.[24] We turn now to the case note schema.

## *The case note schema*

In what follows, we explain Figure 5.1, and highlight the elements of IRAC as they apply to case notes.

FIGURE 5.1

| | |
|---|---|
| **Citatation** | • Who were the parties? How do you locate the case? In which court was the matter heard? What is the date of hearing? Which judge or judges handed down judgments? |
| **Facts** | • What facts were material to the dispute? |
| **Procedural history** | • How did the case come before the court? If this is an appeal, record the decisions and reasoning of the earlier courts. |
| **Issue** | • What was the legal issue (or issues) in this case? |
| **Arguments** | • What arguments were put forward on behalf of the parties? |
| **Decision** | • What was the court's decision? |
| **Ratio (rule)** | • What is the legal rule essential to the decision in this case? |
| **Obiter** | • Were comments made by the judge that are not directly related to the decision in this case, but may be important to issues raised in other cases? |
| **Dissent** | • Were there important dissenting judgments? |
| **Evaluation** | • Provide your own analysis of the decision, *in your own words.* |

24 Adam L Rosman, 'Visualizing the Law: Using Charts, Diagrams, and Other Images to Improve Legal Briefs' (2013) 63(1) *Journal of Legal Education* 70, 70.

### Citation

The citation includes information on the parties and how to locate the case. You may also want to note whether the parties to a civil matter are plaintiffs or defendants, or appellants or respondents. Alternatively, you might find it helpful to use more generic terms, such as buyer and seller. You also need to record the relevant court; the date of hearing; and the judge(s) involved.

### Facts

Here, you need to be as concise as possible. You need to record the *relevant* facts. Facts are only relevant if they are needed to discuss a legal issue – a legal question.

### Procedural history

This sets out what has happened before the matter reached the court which handed down the decision you are currently reading. For example, one of the parties may have initiated a matter in a lower court, a decision was made and then one of the parties appealed that decision. When referring to the earlier courts, record what each decided, and make a note of the reasons why a party appealed the decision.

### Issue

State the issue in dispute as a question: for example, has a contract been formed? Has the defendant breached his duty of care to the plaintiff? This is the 'I' in IRAC.

### The arguments

Provide a summary of the arguments made on behalf of the parties.

### Decision

Note the court's decision, that is, its conclusion. This is the 'C' in IRAC. This decision should explain how the court applied the rules to the facts relating to the issue. This is the 'A' in IRAC.

Note how many judges were in the majority and whose decision forms part of the majority.

### The rationale (ratio decidendi)

The *ratio decidendi* is the legal principle upon which the decision is founded – the fundamental propositions of law and legal reasoning that were essential to the court's decision. The ratio contains the legal rule that binds future courts. This is the 'R' in IRAC.

### *Comments 'by the by' (*obiter dicta*)*

*'Obiter dicta'* translates to 'said in passing'. Sometimes, judges will make comments that are not directly related to the issue, but which may be important to issues raised in other cases. This is the case even though the facts are not exactly the same. Under the doctrine of precedent, such statements are not binding, but may be of persuasive value.

### *Dissenting opinions*

Note any dissenting opinions and the reasons for the dissent. These are often important in later cases or on appeal.

### *Analysis and evaluation*

Here is where you start developing your own 'critical voice'. In analysing the case, you may find the following prompts to be helpful:

- What is your assessment of the court's decision? Do you find the reasons given in the dissenting opinions to be more persuasive? Why?
- Can you identify influences on the court's decision, such as a strong policy issue or particular values?
- Do certain legal/political theories account for the reasons for the decision? If one applied a different theory, would the result differ? For an interesting example of this, see *Australian Feminist Judgments: Righting and Re-Writing Law*[25] where decided cases were rewritten from a feminist perspective.
- What are the political, economic or social impacts of the decision?
- Are these favourable for society?
- Does this decision achieve justice?
- Has the decision been made for policy reasons? Acknowledging that a policy argument relies on an assumption that a particular decision will bring about certain consequences, is that interpretation justified? Is there empirical evidence for this assumption?

This approach requires a considerable amount of work, but the benefits in understanding not only the case, but the nature of legal reasoning are considerable. By articulating and arranging the information contained in cases in this way the writer can influence or persuade others to think in a more detailed way about the legal reasoning process.[26] A critical approach is also recommended for answering problem questions.

---

25 Heather Douglas, Francesca Bartlett, Trish Luker, Rosemary Hunter (eds), *Australian Feminist Judgments: Righting and Re-Writing Law* (Hart Publishing, 2014).

26 George D Gopen, 'IRAC, REA, Where We are Now, and Where We Should be Going in the Teaching of Legal Writing' (2011) 17 *Legal Writing Journal of the Legal Writing Institute* xvii, xxii.

## III PROBLEM QUESTIONS

In conjunction with case noting, legal writers at all stages of their professional career are required to answer problem questions. IRAC is again useful as a way of organising and structuring a response. It calls for the writer to state the issue, identify the rules (the applicable principles extracted from cases), apply those rules to the relevant facts; and generate a logical conclusion. This structure has been recommended to students by many law schools, although there are now a number of variants of this schema.[27]

> When using these analytical formats law students will begin by breaking down the legal rule into elements and then organising the legal writing accordingly. Students then analyze each individual element separately, stating a conclusion, discussing the law, explaining relevant case precedent and then applying the law to the client's case facts, before restating the conclusion for each. Approaching legal analysis in this manner can provide students with a process for organizing a legal issue and isolating its various parts.[28]

This task also requires legal writers to both analyse the legal reasoning of the judiciary and utilise their own legal reasoning to predict the likely outcome of a dispute or to persuade others to a particular view on a matter[29] on behalf of their clients.

This exercise, too, presents you, as a novice writer, with a challenge you may not have previously encountered. While you may come to law school knowing what it means to write academic papers, this task requires you to write for a totally different audience – that is, for professionals such as the senior partner in a law firm, or for clients, each of whom are hypothetically relying on your work to provide solutions.[30] This can be quite daunting, especially when you are required to cover arguments both for and against a course of action.

Maclean calls this a transition in identity and a need to come to terms with a new 'positioning', moving from 'academic' to 'practitioner'.[31] In this process, you must

---

27 See further Margaret Liddle, 'The Varied Landscape of Legal Problem Solving' (2004) 38(1) *The Law Teacher* 55. For an example of the application of an alternative, but similar schema, see Michelle Backstrom and Donna Maree Cooper, 'Hiring a Nashville Sensation': Using Narrative Learning to Develop the Problem Solving Skills of Contract Law Students' (2014) 7(1&2) *Journal of the Australasian Law Teachers Association* 51.

28 Sherri Lee Keene 'One Small Step for Legal Writing, One Giant Leap for Legal Education: Making the Case for More Writing Opportunities in the "Practice Ready" Law School Curriculum' (2014) 65 *Mercer Law Review* 467, 483 n 65.

29 Wilson R Huhn, 'Teaching Legal Analysis Using a Pluralistic Model of Law' (2000–2001) 36 *Gonzaga Law Review* 433, 457.

30 Kedia, above n 10, 156.

31 Rod Maclean, 'First-year Law Students' Constructions of Professional Identity Through Writing' (2010) 12(2) *Discourse Studies* 177, 179.

learn that, instead of directing your writing to academic scholars, you are required to add a 'practical, client-oriented focus on the law'.[32] The writing of novice writers initially evidences several different voices, whereas professional lawyers manage to conceal 'the tensions by foregrounding one position and allowing others to retreat to the background'.[33]

While it is generally recognised that problem-solving exercises, or hypotheticals, are a good way to teach substantive law and the necessary analytical and organisational skills,[34] we suggest that the following model, based on that recommended by Kedia, extends IRAC somewhat. It has, however, an added advantage in that it 'guides the student learning process'.[35] This schema includes some statements from Kedia that both explain what is required and show how novice writers learn.[36]

## *An IRAC-based schema*

FIGURE 5.2

| | |
|---|---|
| **Facts** | • State the material facts as succintly as possible. |
| **Issue** | • State the relevant legal issue(s) as a question (or questions). |
| **Rule/research** | • Identify and state the law relevant to the issue. |
| **Application/analysis** | • Apply the relevant law to the facts. Ensure you address any counterarguments. |
| **Conclusion** | • State your conclusion as to the likely outcome, based on your analysis. |

### *Facts*

Clearly and concisely state the facts that relate to the issue and have given rise to the dispute. A thorough understanding of the facts includes the client's goals, which help to guide the rest of the legal reasoning process, as well as an understanding of the client interviewing process. Of course, it is often the case that facts are incomplete or simply not available. Where there are gaps in the facts, these should be acknowledged.

---

32 Ibid 192.

33 Ibid.

34 Sherran Clarence, Latiefa Albertus, and Lea Mwambene, 'Building an Evolving Method and Materials for Teaching Legal Writing in Large Classes' (2014) 67 *Higher Education* 839, 844.

35 Kedia, above n 10, 172.

36 Ibid 173–177.

### *Issue*

Identify the issue or issues that are key to the dispute. Once you have identified the legal issues, phrase them as questions. These are the questions that, in effect, a judge might be asked to answer. Novice writers often find issue identification difficult. At its base, issue identification is about understanding the possible legal implications of the facts of the case. Although it may initially be difficult for you to spot issues without substantive knowledge of the doctrinal law in the area, with knowledge of a client's goals you should still be capable of identifying potential controversies. These can be affirmed through later research and thinking critically about potential problems arising from those controversies. In other words, you should learn to initially identify issues *and* later revise that assessment through careful research.

### *Research (or rule)*

The next step is to identify the relevant law. If the area is familiar, you may already know the relevant law (that is, the relevant legislation or seminal cases). In most cases, however, this step involves research to find the relevant authorities that support arguments for and *against* what the client wishes to achieve. You will see that ASCR r 19.6 requires solicitors to advise the court of any binding authority, even those that go against the client's case. In this step, you may find it helpful to brainstorm search terms with specific facts and issues in mind.

It is vital that any claim that you make is supported by evidence derived from primary sources (cases and legislation). You need to be very specific when stating the relevant law and always make sure you support each legal proposition you make. You will need to also identify any exceptions, limitations or defences that might apply. Higgins and Tatham[37] observe that, in legal argument:

- An assertion or proposition of law needs a primary source (case or legislation) as authority.
- An assertion of fact needs a secondary source as authority.
- An assertion which is common knowledge or common legal knowledge does not need an authority.

The rule will generally need to be broken down into its component parts. Whether your rule is derived from a judicial decision or a statute, it can generally be framed as a conditional statement: 'If … then …'. (If [the required factual conditions exist] then [the specified legal consequences follow].) You need to separate out these

---

37 Edwina Higgins and Laura Tatham, *Successful Legal Writing* (Sweet and Maxwell, 2nd ed, 2011) 107.

factual conditions from the legal consequences.[38] Where there are multiple elements, you will need to ascertain whether they are conjunctive (indicated by the word 'and'); disjunctive or alternative (indicated by the word 'or'); aggregate (are enough factors present to justify the legal consequences?); or balancing (do you have to balance factors favouring one outcome against those favouring another in order to determine whether legal consequences follow?).[39]

When focusing on the Rule provision of IRAC, Schmedemann and Kunz[40] advise:

- 'If the rule is derived from a single case, you should present the court's statement of the rule from the case, along with a summary of the facts and the holding, if the facts are similar enough to merit a comparison with your client's situation.'
- If the rule is derived from a set of cases, state the rule as fused from those cases and reference them. You might summarise a case that is factually similar to that of your client, or briefly present two cases with different facts and outcomes.
- 'If your rule is derived from a statute or rule supplemented by case law or other materials, you will first quote the statute or rule and then present the supplementary material.'
- Whether your rule is from a statute or case law, if it would assist the reader to understand the rule's underlying policy at this point, state the policy also, ordinarily placing it at the end of the rule section.

Not all rules are of equal merit. Certain factors can influence the strength of the rule. Under the rule of *stare decisis*, a decision made by a superior court, or the same court in an earlier decision will be strong. Thus, you need to look to the rank of the court: a High Court decision trumps a decision of a state Supreme Court, for example. Other factors may also influence the strength of the precedent: the age of the decision may be relevant, for example, or whether the decision had a particularly strong dissent.

## 4 *Analysis (or application)*

Apply the law to the facts methodically. At each step, you need to consider any counter-arguments. If you are seeking to persuade readers of your client's case, you need to find ways of distinguishing authorities that go against your client's case or overcoming their authority.

---

38 Deborah A Schmedemann and Christina L Kunz, *Synthesis: Legal Reading, Reasoning and Writing* (Wolters Kluwer, 4th ed, 2014) 12.

39 Ibid 15.

40 Schmedemann and Kunz, above n 38, 99.

In his book *The Art of Argument*,[41] Klee recommends that, in developing your legal argument, you:

- Read the facts carefully.
- Identify who it is you represent.
- Compile a list of arguments.
- Imagine you represent the other side of the dispute and respond to your arguments.
- *Repeat the last two steps five times.*

Although repeating those steps five times may feel excessive, the process will certainly draw out and develop your arguments!

## 5 *Conclusion*

It has been said that a good conclusion in legal writing performs four functions: summation, evaluation, prediction and recommendation.[42] State your conclusion as to the likely outcome. Summarise your arguments to suggest an answer to the issues that translates to what the audience, the judge or the client, would consider to be an appropriate solution. In legal analysis, there is generally no right or wrong answer. Rather, your aim is to provide a reasonable conclusion that follows a logical analysis based in the relevant law.

Legal problem solving does not end when a lawyer arrives at a legal conclusion regarding an unresolved legal issue: the lawyer must then translate those conclusions into client solutions by thinking about the multiple ways the issue could be resolved, whether through negotiation, settlement, mediation, litigation, or other methods. Legal issues do not end once the 'right' result is found. Rather, academic, intellectual, and analytical work needs to be translated into a practical solution for a client. A conclusion may thus include a recommendation, for example, that ADR methods might be an appropriate course of action (see ASCR r 7.2).

Writing an IRAC analysis in a prose form will then look something like this:

- Paragraph 1: Introduction
- Paragraph 2: Rule from case or statute (with any judicial interpretation of that statute)
- Paragraph 3: Application highlighting similarities between authority and client situation
- Paragraph 4: Application highlighting differences between authority and client situation

---

41 Christopher Kee, *The Art of Argument: A Guide to Mooting* (Cambridge University Press, 2006) 18.

42 Lucy Katz, *Winning Words: A Guide to Persuasive Writing for Lawyers* (Law and Business, 1986) 118.

- Paragraph 5: Policy analysis (where appropriate)
- Paragraph 6: Conclusion.[43]

## *IRAC and its debates*

Although IRAC is quite commonly recommended as a problem-solving device, there are debates about its use. Generally IRAC utilises deductive reasoning, that is, the process of logically reasoning from one or more premises to reach a conclusion. More specifically, it is characterised as 'classical **syllogism**', a methodology which uses the rule as the major premise and the application to the facts as the minor premise.[44] Cornwell, however, provides an example of an IRAC-type syllogism to make the point that ultimately the construction of the minor premise, which deals with the facts, may be just an observation, rather than a verifiable fact, and the reasoning is therefore flawed:

> Issue: Does an interstate carrier violate a statutory requirement by failing to obtain an **ICC** permit before transporting frozen eviscerated chickens across state lines? Rule (major premise): Objects that are not manufactured products do not require ICC permits. Application (minor premise): Frozen eviscerated chickens **are or are not** manufactured products. Conclusion: Therefore, the carrier **did or did not** violate the statute.[45]

This shows that the statement of the minor premise depends on a decision or a value judgment being made – in this case, whether frozen eviscerated chickens resemble 'items that in past cases have been deemed manufactured products or agricultural goods'.[46]

Thus, when you are answering problem questions, you need to recognise that the legal reasoning you are reading in cases is the result of ethical decisions by those involved. You, in turn, need to make choices regarding your interpretations of the law: '[t]he critical analysis of any legal problem must accordingly focus in large measure upon the operative prejudices of the analyst'.[47]

While the preceding discussion might suggest that the IRAC method is flawed when it uses a deductive process – where a conclusion is thought to arise 'naturally from the marriage of a rule and a set of facts', it may be very effective as an inductive

43 Schmedemann and Kunz, above n 38, 101.
44 Joel R Cornwell, 'Legal Writing as a King of Philosophy' (1996-1997) 48 *Mercer Law Review* 1091, 1113.
45 Ibid 1114. We have bolded the words that are important – showing that the writer has a choice to make.
46 Ibid.
47 Ibid 1115.

process that focuses on an 'outcome-oriented rather than rule-oriented'[48] approach to writing. This model can include deductive reasoning, and the use of analogies,[49] but it includes reasoning, based on policy judgments or 'natural reasoning' which aims to find a resolution for the client.[50] Therefore in this model 'legal reasoning is about the interdependent relationship of the facts, legal issues, and legal rules in a case or scenario'.[51] Before deciding which facts should be considered in light of the applicable law, the writer considers carefully 'what types of legal and practical consequences or implications some facts might have'.[52] In other words, the writer uses the legal rules to argue for the desired client outcome, rather than being restricted by the legal rules.[53] In this way the writer 'is arguing about the implications of the law in proscribing client conduct,'[54] also using this method to consider counter-arguments.

IRAC has also been criticised for the fact that, although it may be suited to analysis of problems in domestic legal systems, it is ultimately insufficient in a global context.[55] Whalen-Bridge argues:

> IRAC is a didactic device, which in the beginning stage of legal education quite helpfully tells students how to categorise legal knowledge (issues, rules, analysis) and how to present the solution to a legal issue in a manner that is recognised by professionals as logicl... IRAC is a template designed to give certainty and structure to legal analysis by limiting the information that is considered relevant. However, in unfamiliar environments, the knowledge acquired by students is necessarily tentative.[56]

Whalen-Bridge goes on to suggest that IRAC tends to shut down possibilities when what is needed in the global context is a method that expands on possibilities: 'Students in a more global legal context need a tool that intelligently prompts them to expand the ways in which to engage with an unfamiliar legal environment'.[57]

---

48 Kedia, above n 10, 151.
49 'Reasoning by analogy is nothing more than A is *like* B, so the same conclusion should attach to both': Nelson P Miller and Bradley J Charles, 'Meeting the Carnegie Report's Challenge to Make Legal Analysis Explicit – Subsidiary Skills to the IRAC Framework' (2009-2010) 59 *Journal of Legal Education* 192, 209.
50 Kedia, above n 10, 160.
51 Ibid 161.
52 Ibid.
53 Ibid 171.
54 Ibid 161.
55 Helena Whalen-Bridge, 'We Don't Need Another IRAC: Identifying Global Legal Skills' (2014) (10) *International Journal of Law in Context*, 315, 317.
56 Ibid 328–9.
57 Ibid 329.

In sum, IRAC should not be used without reflection and consideration of whether there are more appropriate alternatives. Where its use is appropriate, IRAC should be used thoughtfully.

## IV CONCLUSION

In this chapter, we have outlined two schemas, one for case notes and one to structure legal problem solving. Two points need to be made before concluding. The first is that the schemas may give rise to the perception that legal problem solving is the task of the individual. In fact,

> [r]eal world problem solving, however, involves multi-party, multi-issue, multi-jurisdictional and multi-cultural inputs, and lawyers are increasingly working in more complex groups of individuals who may come from a variety of different domains. Working collaboratively (rather than exclusively competitively or cooperatively, in that false dichotomy of the negotiation literature) is an important element of legal problem solving.[58]

Second, although these schemas are helpful, and tend to be used mechanically in the early stages of legal study, they should not become 'straitjackets'. As your legal writing and analysis grow in sophistication, you will develop your own voice and the process will become increasingly creative. Creativity is not necessarily something we immediately connect with the study of law – certainly not in the way that we link critical thinking with legal education. But we would argue that the best lawyers are also creative thinkers and creative problem-solvers. As Menkel-Meadow reminds us:

> [C]reatively solving problems in the legal domain implicates the development of creative faculties, exercised within some constraints of law and legal principle. The creative legal problem solver, then, must learn to navigate within the seas of optimistic creativity, the swells of dynamic interaction with others (client and other counsel and parties) and the oceans of realistic legal possibility.[59]

---

58 Carrie Menkel-Meadow, 'Aha? Is Creativity Possible in Legal Problem Solving and Teachable in Legal Education?' (2001) 6 *Harvard Negotiation Law Review* 97, 141.

59 Ibid 103.

# REVIEW MATERIALS

## SUMMARY

In this chapter, we outlined methodologies for completing case briefs and problem questions. We introduced the concept of a 'schema', a cognitive framework or concept that helps to organise and interpret information. We emphasised that case briefs, although generally used as an introduction to legal reasoning, can be a valuable tool that can assist your development as a legal writer and professional. In regard to problem questions, we highlighted the pros and cons of the IRAC method.

## KEY POINTS

1. Mastering the techniques for case briefs and hypotheticals is important for learning the fundamentals of lawyering.
2. A schema can be a valuable way of learning how to structure and organise a response.
3. Schemas are generally used fairly 'mechanically' at the beginning, but as you master the structure you will develop your own technique.
4. In all legal writing, a key aspect of technique is the use of evidence. Generally, in answering hypotheticals, your evidence will be drawn from primary sources: legislation and judicial decisions.
5. Although case briefing is often abandoned after the initial years of legal study, its ongoing use can be valuable in understanding, analysing and applying the law.

## QUESTIONS FOR REFLECTION

1. What does it mean to 'think like a lawyer'?
2. What is the difference between critical thinking and creative thinking? In what ways can legal analysis be considered creative?
3. What is a professional 'voice'? Can you think of writers (in the law or otherwise) whose voice is 'distinct'? Why is that voice so distinctive?
4. Why is it said that good legal writing is 'tentative'?
5. Why is use of evidence so fundamental to legal method?

## EXERCISES

1. Distinguishing questions of fact from questions of law[60]
   Two steps required in both a case brief and answering a hypothetical are identifying questions of fact and questions of law. You need to establish the relevant facts in order to be able to deal with the appropriate legal issues. However, distinguishing between the facts and the issues is a skill.
   The following statements are either questions of fact or questions of law. Can an answer be found in the law alone, or are the facts required?
   a. Is the client's claim for compensation reasonable in terms of her injuries?
   b. Can the client's claim for compensation include future medical bills?
   c. Did the client contribute to her own injuries?
2. Stating the issues
   Legal issues are generally written as questions. Frame the following legal issues as questions. In writing the legal issue as a question, you might like to think about what appears to be the problem or what has gone wrong between the parties.
   a. A builder agreed to build a deck onto his brother's house. However, after a year he had not even started the construction.
   b. John, the owner of a set of flats, had a number of applications, but all from potential Sudanese tenants. He did not accept any of them. Instead, he advertised the flats again the following week.
   c. Penelope worked for a national company for 12 years, but when she applied for maternity leave, she was asked to leave.
3. Evaluating judicial decisions
   Choose a decided case and analyse it using the following questions as prompts:
   - What is your opinion of the court's decision? Do you prefer a dissenting opinion? Why?
   - Can you identify influences on the court's decision, such as a strong policy issue or particular values?
   - Do certain legal/political theories account for the reasons for the decision?
   - What are the political, economic or social impacts of the decision?
   - Are these favourable for society?
   - Does this decision achieve justice?

---

60 Georgia State University School of Accountancy, 'Lesson 1: Facts and Legal Issues', available at http://www2.gsu.edu/~wwwerl/iid/lessons/FactandLegal.htm.

- Has the decision been made for policy reasons? Acknowledging that a policy argument relies on an assumption that a particular decision will bring about certain consequences, is that interpretation justified? Is there empirical evidence for this assumption?

## FURTHER RESOURCES

1. Identifying the ratio of a decision:
   Alisdair Gillespie, 'Identifying the Ratio', available at Oxford Online Resources, http://global.oup.com/uk/orc/law/els/gillespie4e/student/activities/identifying/
   Routledge, 'Case Examples', available at *The English Legal System* Companion Website, http://cw.routledge.com/textbooks/9780415639989/downloads/update1.pdf

# CHAPTER 6

# RESEARCH ESSAYS, THESES AND DISSERTATIONS

## I INTRODUCTION

In this chapter, we examine the writing of research essays, theses and **dissertations**. The fundamental principles are the same, though the writing of theses and dissertations is generally a great deal more stressful. These forms of academic writing require the skills of critical analysis, persuasion, sound research skills, good organisation and, importantly, sound time management.

## II RESEARCH ESSAYS

Legal research essays are often considered a form of persuasive writing (see Chapter 8) and are a common form of assessment in many law schools. The purpose of writing a legal essay is to advance understanding, interpretation, application and/or reform of the law. In writing a legal essay, you will generally be expected to develop coherent, sophisticated and often creative arguments.

To construct a good legal essay you need an understanding of the conventions of legal essay writing. You may have written academic research essays in other disciplines. Like essays in other disciplines, legal essays should be written in an objective and formal tone, and have a clear structure with a strong introduction and conclusion.

Essays for law have certain distinctive characteristics, however, when compared with essays in other disciplines. First, they require a strong central argument, based on logical reasoning; second, they should be based on a critical analysis of the issues and the materials; third, the arguments and assertions should be backed by evidence (this often results in a higher number of references than is common in essays in other disciplines); fourth, the use of headings and subheadings is generally encouraged; and last, legal essays will generally be expected to conform to a particular style guide.

The best way to become familiar with the expectations of a good legal research essay is to read some articles in legal journals, taking note of style, tone and citation.

In examining research essays, we consider audience and purpose, critical analysis, argument and evidence, the writing process, and the ethical obligation to avoid plagiarism. These elements are summarised in Figure 6.1.

FIGURE 6.1

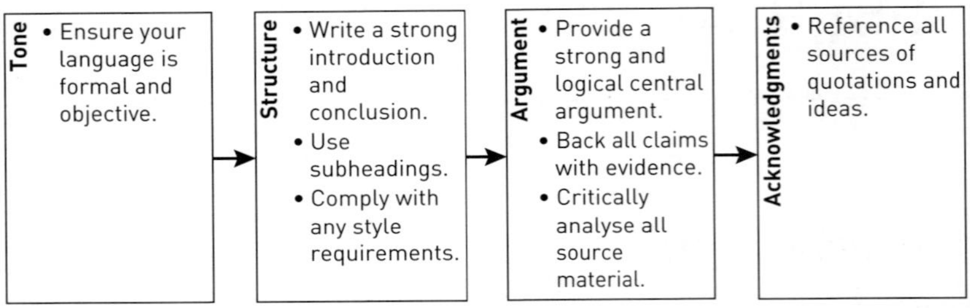


## *Audience and purpose*

In practical terms, the audience for your essay is going to be your lecturer (or whoever is marking your work). But in more general terms, the imagined reader is a member of the legal community, such as a lawyer, a policy maker, a judge or an academic researcher. You can thus assume some familiarity on the part of the reader with basic aspects of law and its institutions. Your tone should be objective and respectful and you should be careful to use gender-neutral language (we discuss gender-neutral language in the Grammar Primer in the Learning Materials section at the back of the book).

Legal essays usually ask you to demonstrate not only your familiarity with course content, but the ability to think independently beyond the limits of class content. Your purpose as a legal essay writer is (ordinarily) to persuade your readers to a particular view. This is done through a critical examination of principle, authority, evidence and argument.

Where you have been given a topic, it is important to read it carefully and analyse the words within it to ensure you understand what is being asked of you. You will see that we have provided a list of commonly used directions in essays, with their meanings, later in this chapter. If you don't understand your writing task, seek clarification from your lecturer or course coordinator. It is a common problem with research essays that the specified question goes answered or a key part of the question is neglected or misunderstood.

## *Critical analysis, argument and evidence*

You will generally be expected to provide a 'critical analysis' of the topic. 'Critical analysis' and 'critical thinking' are umbrella terms used to describe certain 'higher order' thinking activities. Critical thinking has been defined as:

> the intellectually disciplined process of actively and skillfully conceptualizing, applying, analyzing, synthesizing, and/or evaluating information gathered from, or generated by, observation, experience, reflection, reasoning, or communication, as a guide to belief and action. In its exemplary form, it is based on universal intellectual values that transcend subject matter divisions: clarity, accuracy, precision, consistency, relevance, sound evidence, good reasons, depth, breadth, and fairness.[1]

Critical thinking is thus often contrasted with description – a critical analysis goes well beyond reproduction of information. At the same time, it is important to realise that critical analysis is not the same as criticism and is not, therefore, inherently negative. Rather, a critical analysis will define terms, question assumptions, use logical reasoning, support all claims with evidence and extend existing knowledge.

As noted earlier, your essay will be expected to put forward an argument. An 'argument' in common language means a disagreement. However, in law it is a representation of your position or 'point of view' on the topic under consideration, based on your research, your reasoning and the available evidence. An argument needs to have a central thesis (also called a central contention or proposition), which is developed and supported throughout the paper by reasons: 'A thesis sentence is not a statement of accepted fact; it is the position that needs the proof you will provide in your argument'.[2] If your thesis is something that is generally agreed upon or accepted as fact then there is no reason to try to persuade the reader to your way of thinking! This central contention should be stated clearly in your introduction: you tell the reader what you are going to argue before you do so. In turn, your reasons should be accurate, relevant and based on evidence.[3]

Because you are presenting an argument, you must acknowledge views that oppose your own – you cannot simply ignore them. As a legal writer, your task is to deal with these opposing arguments in a reasoned and persuasive manner.

Evidence should be distinguished from assumption and opinion. Evidence is something that you can prove. Assumption is something that one can safely infer

---

1 Michael Scriven and Richard Paul, 'Critical Thinking as Defined by the National Council for Excellence in Critical Thinking' (1987), available at https://www.criticalthinking.org/pages/defining-critical-thinking/766.

2 Sharon Williams and Laura Reidy, 'Introductions and Thesis Statements' Hamilton College, Nesbitt-Johnson Writing Center [Online], available at http://www.hamilton.edu/academics/Resource/WC/Intro_Thesis.html.

3 Edwina Higgins and Laura Tatham, *Successful Legal Writing* (Sweet and Maxwell, 2nd ed, 2011) 104.

from the evidence at hand. Opinion is your own (or someone else's) particular interpretation of the evidence.[4]

Do you have sufficient evidence to support your ideas? You need to think carefully about what evidence you need to persuade the reader that your view is justified. A common error in undergraduate law essays is the making of assertions with no evidence provided by way of support. Throughout this book you will notice that we make certain claims, and when we do we include references to support this claim – you might like to note, particularly, how this is done in Chapter 1. Use of authority is one kind of evidence.

## *The process of writing your research essay*

### *Considering a given topic*

In many academic situations where you are asked to write an essay, you will be given a topic or a choice of topics. If this is the case, as we noted above, read the wording of the topic(s) carefully to ensure you understand the parameters of the paper and how you will be graded. Often, the assessor will use key words that require you to undertake specific tasks. It is important that you understand what is being asked of you. Such key words, and their meanings, include:[5]

- *Analyse:* Separate the issue into its constituent parts in order to discover its function, characteristics, relationship etc. Look in depth at each part using supporting arguments and evidence for and against as well as how these interrelate to one another. Focus on the 'how' and 'why'. Do not simply describe or summarise.
- *Argue:* Make a case, based on appropriate evidence for and/or against some given point of view.
- *Assess:* Weigh up to what extent something is true. Persuade the reader of your view but also acknowledge flaws and counter-arguments. Support your view with evidence. Conclude by stating succinctly how far you are in agreement with the original proposition.
- *Clarify:* Make something clearer and, where appropriate, simplify it.
- *Compare:* Identify the similarities and differences between two or more phenomena, such as ideas, events or interpretations. Identify whether any of

---

4 Dartmouth, Institute for Writing and Rhetoric, 'What is an Academic Paper?', available at https://writing-speech.dartmouth.edu/learning/materials/materials-first-year-writers/what-academic-paper.

5 Adapted from: University of Leicester, 'Essay Terms Explained', available at http://www2.le.ac.uk/offices/ld/resources/writing/writing-resources/essay-terms; University of New England, 'Analysing the Question'; Unilearning Essay Writing Identifying Instructional Terms, available at http://unilearning.uow.edu.au/essay/2c.html.

the shared similarities or differences are particularly significant. 'Compare' and 'contrast' will often feature together in an essay question.

- *Contrast:* Similar to compare but here you are being asked to emphasise the dissimilarities between two or more phenomena. Point out any differences which are particularly significant.
- *Comment:* Make critical observations, even if they are fairly open-ended. Go beyond criticism or summary. Generally implies 'analyse' or 'assess'.
- *Critically evaluate* or *Evaluate:* Provide a judgment as to what extent a statement or research findings are true, or to what extent you agree with them. Provide evidence from a range of sources. Acknowledge evidence that contradicts your argument. Provide a succinct conclusion, basing your decision on what you judge to be the most important factors and justify how you have made your choice.
- *Criticise:* Examine the topic or argument in terms of its strengths and weaknesses.
- *Define:* Provide concise and clear meanings. Cite the boundaries or limitations of the definition. Identify the 'class' to which a thing belongs and what may serve to differentiate the thing from others in that class.
- *Demonstrate:* Show how, with examples to illustrate.
- *Describe:* Provide a detailed explanation of the phenomenon in question. Be precise and thorough. Examples may be helpful in some cases.
- *Discuss:* Present a point of view after considering both sides of an issue or question. Your opinion should be based in logical reasoning and supported by evidence. Remember to arrive at a conclusion.
- *Elaborate:* Provide more detail about, or provide more information in relation to the topic, issue, event or phenomenon under discussion.
- *Enumerate:* Provide a list or outline form of reply. Recount, individually and concisely, the points required.
- *Examine:* Critically consider in close detail and establish the key facts and important issues surrounding a topic. Highlight the implications.
- *Explain:* Focus on the 'why' of a particular issue, or on the 'how' seeking to clarify reasons, causes and effects or on what is meant by the use of a term in a particular context.
- *Explore:* Adopt a questioning approach and consider a variety of different viewpoints.
- *Give an account of:* Give a detailed description of something.
- *Identify:* Identify the key features of something and the implications of these.
- *Illustrate:* A similar instruction to 'explain', making use of definite examples.
- *Interpret:* Explain the meaning of something and give your own judgment of the situation. Demonstrate your understanding of an issue or topic.
- *Justify:* Make a case for something by providing evidence to support your ideas and points of view. Consider evidence and opinions which may oppose your view.

- *List:* Write your answer as an itemised or tabulated series which may be in point form.
- *Outline:* Provide an organised description that conveys the main points. Emphasise global structures and interrelationships rather than minute detail.
- *Prove:* Provide factual evidence, examples or clear logical reasons which verify or confirm a statement or idea.
- *Relate:* Demonstrate how things are connected or similar to each other.
- *Review:* Critically re-examine, analyse and comment on the major points of an issue.
- *Show how:* Present, in a logical order, and with reference to relevant evidence the stages and combination of factors that give rise to something.
- *State:* Specify clearly the key aspects of a topic. Refer to evidence and examples where appropriate. Present the main points in brief, clear sequence.
- *Summarise:* Give a condensed version drawing out the main facts. Omit superfluous information.
- *To what extent:* Explore the case for a stated proposition or explanation. Provide a thorough assessment of the evidence, both for and against.
- *Trace:* Provide an account of the development, progress or history of a thing, event or idea. Often proceeds from the latest to the earliest evidence.

## Generating your own topic

In some cases, however, you will be asked to develop your own topic. In our experience, this can often throw students into a frenzy of indecision and procrastination. There are two key considerations in choosing a topic: first, the topic has to be one that enables you to develop an argument. And second, the topic has to be one where that argument can be made successfully within the given word length. You may want to revisit the thoughts on choosing a research topic set out in Chapter 3 (Research for Writing). In addition, you might find the following prompts for developing a topic helpful, from the Institute for Writing and Rhetoric at Dartmouth:

- 'Have you formed an intellectual question? In other words, have you constructed a question that will require a complex, thoughtful answer?
- Is the question provocative? Startling? Controversial? Fresh?
- Will you be able to answer this question adequately in a few pages? Or is the question impossibly broad?
- If the question seems broad, how might you narrow it?

...

- Will your reader care about this question? Or will [they] say, "So what?"'[6]

---

6 Dartmouth, Institute for Writing and Rhetoric, above n 4

## Researching and note-taking

Be discriminating in your research. Don't make the mistake of thinking that because something is in print (or on the web!) it has cornered the market on truth.[7] Neither should you become too attached to your research. Regardless of how interesting the information you source may be, only use it if it supports your thesis or directly challenges opposing arguments. Don't try to cram all your research into your essay.

Along with critical analysis, you need to read critically. Some tips for critical reading include:

- *Read with the topic or essay question in mind.* As you read, refer back to the topic or question and think about your emerging answers to it.[8]
- *Skim all parts of the reading to begin.* Sometimes the abstract, footnotes, table of content and introduction can provide you with valuable information and can narrow the reading down.
- *Read with a friend.* Set reading goals together and plan to share your reactions to sections of the reading.

As you take notes, ask yourself:

- Why are you writing this information down?
- What is especially interesting about this particular information?
- What is the relationship between this information and what you have already written down and learned?[9]
- What is missing in the reading? Issues, events or ideas that are missing, left out, avoided, or not discussed/addressed in the book might be important. Thinking about these omissions can give you a critical perspective on the reading by showing you what the author (consciously or unconsciously) doesn't want to deal with.

## Sketching and note-taking

Your thesis gives your paper's general direction, but you need to organise the argument. It may be helpful to begin by 'sketching' your argument:

> In sketching your argument your goal is to fill the page with your ideas. Begin by writing your thesis. Put it where your instincts tell you to: at the top of the page, in the center, at the bottom. Around the thesis, cluster the points you want to make. Under each of these points, note the observations you've made and the evidence you'll use. Don't get nervous when your sketch starts

---

7 Ibid.

8 Villanova University Writing Centre, 'How to Write a College Paper' (2011), available at https://www1.villanova.edu/villanova/artsci/acsp/writingcenter/guide.html.

9 Jan A Pechenik, *A Short Guide to Writing about Biology* (5th ed, Pearson Longman, 2004) 126.

> to look like a mess. Use arrows. Draw circles. Take up colored pens. Any of these methods can help you to find connections between your ideas that otherwise might go unseen. Working from your sketch, try to see the line of reasoning that is evolving. Sketching is an important step in the writing process because it allows you to explore visually the connections between your ideas. If you outline a paper too early in the writing process, you risk missing these connections. You line up your argument - A. B. C. - without fully understanding why. Sketching your argument helps you to see, for example, that points A and C really overlap and need to be thought through more carefully.[10]

Once you have your sketch, it is easier to outline your argument. The purpose of outlining is to determine the best, most logical structure for your argument. As we noted in Chapter 4, the process of writing is recursive. Your outline will guide you, but don't remain too attached to this original structure. Often, writing is actually a way of thinking through the issues and it may be that your structure changes as you write. Stay flexible.

## Introductions and conclusions

Your introduction should explain what the answer is going to do. Thus, you should declare your argument (your thesis), place your argument within the larger, ongoing conversation about your topic which usually identifies why the topic is significant,[11] define your key terms, and provide the reader with a 'road map' of the article itself, that is, an outline of how you have structured your discussion.

In a law essay, the introduction is generally entitled, simply, 'Introduction', signalling that it is a functional rather than substantive section of the paper.[12] In length, as a rough guide, an introduction should be no more than about 10 per cent of the total length of the paper. It is often helpful to write the introduction *after* you have written the body of your essay. In our experience, it is very common for students to get stuck on the introduction if they attempt to write the introduction before the body of the paper.

Your conclusion should restate your central argument and the main supporting reasons for your view; and restate the conclusions that you reach. It is important that you synthesise, rather than summarise: by all means, include a brief summary of the paper's main points, but go on to demonstrate how the points you made

---

10 Dartmouth Institute for Writing and Rhetoric, 'Considering Structure and Organisation', available at http://writing-speech.dartmouth.edu/learning/materials-first-year-writers/considering-structure-and-organization.

11 Ibid.

12 Melbourne Law School, 'LAWresources, Research Essays, Introductions', available at http://www.law.unimelb.edu.au/lawresources/research-essays/structures/introductions.

and evidence you used fit together. Just as the introduction sought to place the paper in the larger, ongoing conversation about the topic, so should the conclusion, emphasising your contribution to that conversation. This is often described as the 'so what' factor:

> Just as your introduction acts as a bridge that transports your readers from their own lives into the 'place' of your analysis, your conclusion can provide a bridge to help your readers make the transition back to their daily lives. Such a conclusion will help them see why all your analysis and information should matter to them after they put the paper down.[13]

It is a convention that you do not introduce new material into the conclusion. In length, the conclusion is generally 5 to 10 per cent of the total word length and is usually simply headed 'Conclusion'.[14] Higgins and Tatham[15] provide some tips for conclusions:

- ensure the conclusion is brief and to the point;
- answer the core question;
- do not introduce new ideas;
- do not conclude with a cliché;
- do not apologise;
- do not contradict yourself;
- do not merely summarise.

## Time management

Essays are not projects to be begun the night before submission! Generally, a 2000–3000 word essay should be started about three or four weeks before the due date. This allows time for topic analysis, planning and research, writing the first draft, revision and proofreading.

In our experience, the most common error students make, apart from leaving the project until the last minute, is to spend too much time in the research phase, leaving insufficient time for revising, editing, referencing and proofreading. As a rule of thumb, revising should take up about 20–25 per cent of your total time; 50 per cent of your time should be spent on analysis and research; and 25 per cent on developing your first draft.

---

13 UNC College of Arts and Sciences, The Writing Centre, 'Conclusions', available at http://writingcenter.unc.edu/handouts/conclusions/.

14 Melbourne Law School, above n 12.

15 Higgins and Tatham, above n 3, 144.

## Revising, editing and proofreading

Writing a research essay often involves multiple drafts and it is likely that the text will be cut and pasted a number of times. You need to be aware that this often results in errors within the paper: inconsistent referencing, changes in font size and type, and even potential plagiarism.

Editing can be a difficult task. If you have the time, put the essay away for a day after you have drafted it. It is then easier to see errors. It is often easier to see errors, too, if the paper is printed, rather than trying to edit it on screen. When you come to edit, try reading the paper aloud: this is often the best way of ensuring the arguments are coherent, logical and concise and that the text flows. You can also ask a family member or friend if they will read through the edited paper. Often someone unfamiliar with the text will pick up errors you do not see. As you edit your paper, you may find the following prompts helpful:

- 'What is the main point of your paper?
- Does the introduction clearly introduce the point?
- Is there a thesis statement near the beginning (in the introduction or the first or second paragraph of the text) that clearly and concisely asserts the main point?
- Does each paragraph help to advance your main line of thought? Does any paragraph digress from that line of thought? Does each paragraph fit in with the other paragraphs surrounding it?
- Is your tone – your attitude towards the subject – consistent? (If not, you may want to re-examine your attitude towards the topic.)
- Does the conclusion show that the essay has reached its goal?'[16]
- Have you overused quotations? Check to see that you have limited the length of your quotes, that you have not started a paragraph with a quote; and that where you have used a quote, you have explained its significance to the reader.

## Referencing and avoiding plagiarism

Correct referencing is an important aspect of law essays. You must ensure that your citations are correct and complete and that they conform to any style guide that may be specified in the essay instructions.

You will have received warnings against plagiarism and the potential for academic misconduct to potentially impact on the admission process. But the point of documenting sources in academic papers is not just to avoid disciplinary proceedings. Referencing demonstrates that you are aware of what has been written in your field of study; acknowledges the work of those that have come before you (the ethical

16 Villanova Writing Centre above n 8.

component); and is a courtesy to your readers because it enables them to find the material you have cited. It is always safer to over-reference than to under-reference.

In terms of form, ensure that direct quotations are enclosed in quotation marks; and that the ideas you take from others, even where paraphrased, are acknowledged. Generally, in a research essay you will also need to create a reference list or **bibliography**. Bibliographies should be double-spaced and arranged alphabetically by author, or if no author is disclosed, by title.

We turn now to consider the writing of theses and dissertations which, as we mentioned in the introduction to this chapter, have much in common with writing essays, but are usually only required for postgraduate or upper year level students, for example, those completing honours degrees.

## III THESES AND DISSERTATIONS

There are varying definitions of thesis. For instance, a thesis has been defined as: 'a formal document whose sole purpose is to prove that you have made an original contribution to knowledge'.[17] A thesis consists of an argument or a series of arguments combined with the description and discussion of research you have undertaken. Its purpose is to prepare you to be a professional in your discipline, successfully demonstrating that you can undertake a significant research project and bring it to a reasoned conclusion. Following from this proposition, a thesis has also been defined as: 'a written record of the work that has been undertaken by a candidate. It constitutes objective *evidence* of the author's *knowledge* and *capabilities* in the field of interest and is therefore a fair means to *gauge* them'.[18] Sometimes the word 'thesis' is used in relation to Honours or Masters work; and 'dissertation' in relation to doctoral work. In this chapter, we use 'thesis' to apply to a major research project, generally a PhD or Masters by research, thus including dissertations.

Undertaking a thesis is a type of research apprenticeship. It is thus not just about the research outcome, but how the process affects personal and professional learning.[19] In reality, the principles for writing a thesis are little different from those for writing a critical essay. As has been pointed out, '[t]he difference between the undergraduate and postgraduate theses is one of *degree* rather than *kind*'.[20]

Writing a thesis or dissertation is at once more demanding and more rewarding than other academic requirements.[21] It is rewarding because you have the freedom

---

17 Mark C Griffin, 'Writing the Thesis' (2011) 1, available at http://online.sfsu.edu/mgriffin/WritingTheThesis.pdf.

18 R (Chandra) Chandrasekhar, 'How to Write a Thesis: A Working Guide' (2008) [1.1], available at ciips.ee.uwa.edu.au/pub/HowToWriteAThesis.pdf.

19 G Shacklock and J Smyth, *Being Reflexive in Critical Educational and Social Research* (Falmer, 1998).

20 Chandrasekhar, above n 18 [1.2].

21 Charles Lipson, *How to Write a BA Thesis* (University of Chicago Press, 2005) 9.

to explore issues that interest you deeply; and, as you progress in your thesis, you can develop a sense of mastery and your own, distinctive writing voice. But a thesis is also demanding: the project is large and sustaining coherence throughout the writing can be a challenge. Also, the relative freedom to manage your time can create difficulties. The deadline, when starting a thesis, seems a long way off and, because there is little short-term pressure, it is easy to be distracted, or to put off writing until it is too late. Thesis students thus tend to find themselves very stressed indeed in the writing of a thesis, particularly as the submission date draws near. But, as we will see, some simple measures can do much to alleviate this stress.

In this section, we begin by briefly outlining the conventions of a thesis before considering the expectations of your audience: the thesis examiners. In this section we consider, in particular, the notions of 'originality' and 'significance' as they apply to a thesis, as well as the concept of argument and the thesis statement. We then consider preliminary matters, such as developing a thesis topic and a thesis proposal; and some matters you might consider before you start the thesis in earnest. We consider the role of the supervisor, then provide some insights on managing your time; researching your thesis; and on writing your thesis.

### *Thesis conventions*

Conventions are the standardised rules you need to follow in your thesis regarding referencing and citations, bibliographies, style, and presentation requirements such as page setup.[22] In general, a thesis generally has a standard form, which tends to be similar in most institutions, with relatively minor variations:[23] it consists of an abstract; acknowledgments; table of contents; an introduction, stating the problem, argument, purpose and significance of the study; a **literature review**; a methodology chapter; results; discussion; conclusion; appendices and references.

Beyond this very general format, the thesis will need to comply with both university and discipline-specific conventions. Each university has its own rules and regulations regarding the thesis and may have further guidelines on writing up – these may be very specific and even extend to font size, type and pagination. Regulations and guidance notes are most often found in the student course handbook or on the institution's website. It is also worth checking the exact word count, as some institutions allow a 10 per cent leeway. Remember to check whether appendices and references fall within the word count.[24]

---

22 Monash University, 'Writing a Thesis in Education' (2014), available at https://www.monash.edu/__data/assets/pdf_file/0007/145816/booklet-writing-a-thesis-in-education.pdf.

23 SJ Cunningham, 'How to Write a Thesis' (2004) 31 *Journal of Orthodontics* 144, 144.

24 Sally Hardy and Janet Ramjeet, 'Reflections on How to Write a Research Thesis' (2005) 13(2) *Nurse Researcher* 27.

But there are also disciplinary conventions in thesis writing. Murray[25] recommends that the thesis writer ask such questions as: '[w]hat language – nouns, verbs, links, etc. – do writers [in this discipline] use? How are debates represented? How is the researcher represented, if at all? How is structure revealed? What are the options in style and structure?' To get a sense of these disciplinary conventions, it is helpful to read other law theses, particularly those from your own institution.

## *Your audience: examiners and their expectations*

There may be many audiences for your thesis, but the key audience will be your examiners, so it is helpful to understand their expectations. In general, examiners will look for:

- the candidate's ability to identify or define a problem;
- their ability to generate questions and arguments;
- an original contribution to knowledge (in the case of a Masters by research or PhD thesis);
- a coherent argument which is sustained from beginning to the end of the thesis;
- evidence of critical thinking;
- evidence that the candidate has read and understood the relevant literature;
- an appropriate methodology; and
- a considered conclusion.

Examiners are experts in the field, but candidates sometimes forget that, like all readers, examiners need to be assisted in their reading by the use of clear and concise writing, appropriate signposting, logical structure, good presentation and the absence of excessive repetition.[26] Three specific points in relation to examiners' expectations are worth elaborating on here: significance, originality and the thesis statement.

### *What does 'significance' mean in relation to a thesis?*

In the case of a PhD, and to a lesser extent, a Masters research thesis, the research is expected to make a 'significant contribution to the chosen field'.[27] So-called 'minor theses' (such as those written for Honours or coursework Masters programs) may also contribute to the knowledge in the field, though the expectation is lower: the main requirement is that they provide evidence of an understanding of the field.[28]

---

25 Rowena Murray, *How to Write a Thesis* (3rd ed, Open University Press, 2011) 12.

26 Learning Centre, UNSW, 'From Finish to Start: Writing your Thesis with the End in View' (2006), available at www.lc.unsw.edu.au/dload/thesis_pres2006.pdf.

27 Estelle Phillips and Derek Pugh, *How to get a PhD: A Handbook for Students and Their Supervisors* (McGraw-Hill International, 1994) 23.

28 Monash University, above n 22.

'Significance' in relation to the contribution of a thesis means that the thesis should add something to the state of expert knowledge about the field.[29] This might be by way of:

- 'a nontrivial to very important breakthrough at the empirical, conceptual, theoretical, or policy level;
- being useful and having impact;
- leading those inside (and possibly those outside) the community of practice to see things differently;
- influencing the conversation, research, and teaching in the discipline;
- having implications for, and advances the field, the discipline, other disciplines, or society'.[30]

## *What does 'originality' mean in relation to a thesis?*

A research thesis is generally expected to make an original contribution to knowledge. 'Originality' in this context does not necessarily mean that the thesis has to be something no one else has ever thought of before. Rather, the thesis should add new insights, new directions or new ideas to what is already known. This is one reason why a literature review (discussed in more detail below) is essential: it is here that the thesis writer not only acknowledges and critically evaluates the work that already exists, it is where they show that their thesis fills a gap in existing knowledge, moves existing knowledge forward in some significant way, or contributes a greater understanding to what is already known.

Originality may be manifested in different ways. Murray provides a helpful list of different potential forms of originality, based on work by Phillips and Pugh.[31] You might:

- 'say something no one has said before;
- do empirical work that has not been done before;
- synthesise things that have not been put together before;
- make a new interpretation of someone else's material/ideas;
- do something in this country that has only been done elsewhere;
- take an existing technique and apply it to a new area;
- work across disciplines, using different methodologies;
- look at topics that people in your discipline have not looked at;
- test existing knowledge in an original way;

---

29 Eugene Volokh, 'Academic Legal Writing: Law Review Articles, Student Notes, Seminar Papers and Getting on Law Review' (Foundation Press, 2007) 15.

30 Yale University, 'Writing a Thesis or Dissertation' (2009), available at https://web.archive.org/web/20150204000052/http://www.yale.edu/graduateschool/writing/forms/Writing%20Theses%20and%20Dissertations.pdf.

31 Philips and Pugh, above n 364, 63–4.

- add to knowledge in a way that has not been done before;
- write down a new piece of information for the first time;
- give a good exposition of someone else's idea;
- continue an original piece of work'.

In addition to surveying the existing literature to see whether your work is sufficiently original, it is helpful to speak to your supervisor and other experts working in the area.[32]

### *What is a thesis statement?*

Examiners will expect to see a core argument sustained throughout the thesis. At the heart of the argument is the thesis statement, 'an original, supportable hypothesis or assertion about a topic'. The thesis targets a specific point or aspect of the law, articulates a problem, and ideally attempts to resolve it. In short, your thesis statement embodies your argument'.[33]

However, before we move on to discuss the process of developing an argument, we should note that the definition of a thesis statement that we have quoted mentions a 'hypothesis'. This raises a question that is often asked: do all research questions test a hypothesis? The answer is that it depends on the questions you are researching. If you are dealing with a topic that questions a grand theory in the pure sciences or researching an interdisciplinary topic involving science, the approach taken usually includes testing a hypothesis (a predictive statement). However, law topics are usually about the effectiveness or the interpretation of law or law's effect on society, and so research questions more appropriately outline the approach to be taken, and frame the arguments that will be made.

To develop an argument, you must first identify a problem. This may be doctrinal, empirical, or historical. The argument will then be your proposed solution to that problem.[34] It may be helpful to try to capture your claim in a single sentence to help focus your discussion and help you communicate your core point to the readers.[35] Position this statement somewhere that you can see at all times (for example, on a whiteboard). It will help you to focus your reading and thoughts on what you want to achieve.

Arguments may be developed from particular perspectives: *Arguments from precedent* assert that precedent is binding or should be extended, adopted, or overruled;

---

32 A related issue on originality is whether to publish from your thesis prior to completion. Again, it is best to ask your supervisor's advice on this point.

33 The Writing Center at GULC, 'Developing a Thesis Statement' (2003), available at http://www.law.georgetown.edu/academics/academic-programs/legal-writing-scholarship/writing-center/upload/thesis.pdf.

34 Volokh, above n 29, 12.

35 Ibid.

*interpretive arguments* examine the language of constitutions, statutes, and regulations; *normative arguments* assert that a certain rule or result is good, justified by morality, social policy, economics, or justice between the parties; *institutional arguments* examine the appropriateness of the roles of the judiciary, legislature, or executive or address the administrative impact of a certain result. Alternatively, you may want to reflect on the following, based on the suggestions published on the Georgetown University Law Centre's Legal Writing website:

- identify and resolve inconsistencies, logical errors, and omissions in the arguments of others. You might wish to examine issues a writer omits, logical fallacies, false dichotomies, unsupported empirical claims, claims not supported by cited authorities, or a court's unstated reasons for a decision;
- identify and question jurisprudential approaches; or examine the approach a judge takes in a decision, and imagine the outcome from another perspective (such as Formalism, Legal Realism, Law and Economics, Feminism or Critical Legal Studies);
- examine the context of a decision, law, statute or issue;
- consider a decision's place in a larger social or historical context; or
- undertake an interdisciplinary comparison.[36]

An important point to note is that, when told to 'develop an argument', some students misunderstand the nature of the task. Murray[37] advises:

> [W]hen you write for your thesis you are joining a debate. Anything you write can be challenged, not because your argument is weak or your writing is poor – although they may be – but because that is the nature of the context. Entering the debate tentatively is probably a sound strategy. See yourself participating in, rather than 'winning' or 'losing', the debate. See yourself making your point clearly, rather than demolishing – or impressing – the opposition.

This advice also fits well with the point made earlier in this book that expert legal writing tends to be tentative.

## *Choosing a thesis topic*

The fact that you can choose your own topic makes the thesis different from the vast majority of undergraduate subjects you may have taken.[38] This freedom can be a blessing and a curse. Many students become bogged down in finding the

---

36 The Writing Centre at GULC, above n 33.
37 Murray, above n 25, 40.
38 Lipson, above n 21, 16.

'perfect' topic but there is no 'Right Topic':[39] what is topical today may no longer be particularly topical by the time you finish. You may thus find it helpful to develop three or four topics to discuss with your supervisor.[40]

Some prompts[41] may help you develop your potential thesis topics:

- 'Is there current interest in this topic in your field or in a closely related field?
- Is there a gap in knowledge that work on this topic could help to fill or a controversy that it might help to resolve?
- Is it possible to focus on a small enough segment of the topic to make a manageable thesis project?
- Can you envisage a way to study the topic that will allow conclusions to be drawn with substantial objectivity? Is the data collection approach (eg questionnaire, interview) acceptable in your school or department?
- Is there a body of literature available relevant to the topic? Is a search manageable?
- Are there large problems (egoistic, attitudinal) to be surmounted in working in this topic? Do you have the means to handle them?
- Does the topic relate reasonably well to others done in your department? If not, do you have any information about its acceptability?
- Would financial assistance be required? If yes, is it available?
- Are the needed data easily accessible? Will you have control of the data?
- Do you have a clear statement of the purpose, scope, objectives, procedures, and limitations of the study? Do you have a tentative table of contents? Are any of the skills called on by the study skills that you have yet to acquire?'[42]

Preliminary discussions with your supervisor about potential topics can be helpful, particularly in honing a general topic down to a manageable size.[43]

Most people who advise in this area concur that, ultimately, the primary factor in deciding on a topic should be interest: you have to live with the thesis for a long time and it is important that the topic is one that is capable of sustaining your interest for that period: 'if you care about the subject, you will pursue interesting questions because you want to know the answers. That, more than anything else, will draw you

---

39 Mickie Edwardson, 'How To Make a Thesis Less Painful and More Satisfying' 8 in *Guidelines for Writing a Thesis or Dissertation* (2008), available at http://www.jou.ufl.edu/grad/forms/Guidelines-for-writing-thesis-or-dissertation.pdf.

40 Lipson, above n 21, 23.

41 Also refer back to the thoughts included on choosing a research topic set out in Chapter 3, Research for Writing.

42 University of Sydney Learning Centre, 'Writing a Thesis Proposal' (2012), available at http://sydney.edu.au/stuserv/documents/learning_centre/Thesis_Proposal_2012.pdf.

43 Lipson, above n 21, 9.

into the subject, enrich your work, and sustain you for the long haul'.[44] Thus, we would suggest that although the thesis writer should listen to the supervisor's advice in relation to the thesis topic, it is often unwise to take on a topic recommended by a supervisor if you have no interest in it.

## *Developing a research proposal*

In Chapter 3 we discussed constructing a research proposal, although in that instance we wrote more generally as research proposals can be required for students completing a legal methodology and theory unit or an honours thesis. The following relates more specifically to those who are proposing a PhD topic, but again, it can also be relevant to those seeking research funding.

A thesis proposal has been defined as 'a document that presents a case for an idea and the action one proposes with respect to it'.[45] Its purpose is 'to justify what you plan to do in order to gain approval for it'.[46] Most institutions require a thesis proposal[47] either prior to candidature or in the very early stages of the candidature. To this end, the thesis proposal should contain: a rationale for the research; a statement as to why the research is significant; the aim of the research and what the anticipated results will be, in terms of practical benefit and/or contribution to knowledge; the hypothesis; a brief indication of previous research on the topic; the intended research methodology; and a proposed timetable for the research.[48]

Because the thesis proposal is primarily written to obtain approval for candidature, it is often underrated and seen only as a compliance document. But it can be a valuable tool that helps you write the thesis: a good thesis proposal provides the background to the problem or issue to be discussed, an outline of the relevant literature, a statement of the argument and the methodology. For this reason, the proposal can serve as the core of the thesis, so that all you need to do is expand upon it to develop the thesis. Having said that, a thesis proposal is not set in stone, and it is often the case that the direction of the thesis changes as the writer becomes an expert on the particular subject.

---

44 Ibid 11.

45 University of Sydney Learning Centre, above n 42 quoting Krathwohl (1988) 12.

46 Ibid quoting Thornquist (1986) 3.

47 You might also want to revisit what was discussed about research proposals in Chapter 3, 'Researching for Writing'.

48 Barry Witcher and Adrian Wilkinson, 'Guideline for a PhD Thesis' (2000), available at http://www.griffith.edu.au/__data/assets/pdf_file/0008/137771/Guidelines_For_Phd.pdf.

## *Ready, set, go!*

There are a few things you need to do before starting your thesis. Most importantly, you need to understand your university's expectations and understand your role as a researcher. Your university will generally have published guidelines on the expectations and responsibilities of thesis students. Be sure you are familiar with these. You will also need an initial meeting with your supervisor to discuss their expectations and to develop a writing process.

You need to have in place a good system of backup for your work. You need to back up your thesis regularly – at least on a weekly basis. Some academics advise that you keep two backup copies and utilise external hard drives rather than memory sticks (the rationale being that memory sticks are relatively easy to lose).

You will need to have an appropriate style manual. Putting your draft work into style saves huge amounts of work in the long run and will make it easier for your supervisor to read your work.

You will need an appropriate referencing system, such as Endnote. You might find it helpful to set up a research diary. This is discussed below.[49]

## *The role of the supervisor*

Your supervisor should be your first point of contact for any and all questions related to your research throughout your candidature. In some situations you will have the ability to choose your supervisor. Lipson[50] advises that you should 'pick an adviser who is comfortable for you to work with and an expert in your area of interest'. It is normal for you to have two supervisors, one of whom is usually the principal supervisor. Both of these could be experts in your area of interest, but there are variations. For instance, you may be undertaking comparative work across two jurisdictions, and have a supervisor from each jurisdiction. Alternatively, you may have a content expert as principal supervisor and another supervisor who specialises in the structural organisation and writing of a thesis.

You may have a choice of supervisor. If this is the case, Lipson[51] advises that, in your first meeting with a supervisor, you want to establish rapport, determine whether your interests fit well with theirs, and ultimately decide whether you want to work together. The best way to do that is to discuss possible thesis topics and get some concrete advice about how to approach the project.

In other cases, your supervisor will be assigned to you by the university. The first meeting will thus be aimed at establishing rapport and clarifying expectations in

---

49 These principles are adapted from Murray, above n 25.

50 Lipson, above n 21, 17.

51 Ibid 19.

terms of submission deadlines and the form of written work the supervisor wants in order to give feedback.

Meetings during the writing of the thesis are essential to keep on track and to overcome any procrastination or writers block. It is helpful to come to your thesis meetings well prepared, either with questions you have written down, or with written work on which you seek feedback. Lipson[52] advises that at the end of *each* meeting with your adviser, you should set a date for your next meeting (if this is not already in place) and agree on the specific tasks that you wish to accomplish for that meeting. He also advises that you should proofread everything you turn in to your supervisor:

> Nothing says 'I really can't be bothered about this project' like a few dreadful typos. Everybody goofs up; the point is to catch these errors before you inflict them on your adviser. Obviously, you will run spell-check. Do that *each time* you turn in a draft, even if the draft is brief and informal. Informal [is not equivalent to] sloppy.[53]

A note about supervisor avoidance: students are often reluctant to contact their supervisor because they feel they should be working 'independently' and it is true that the notion of independent study is at the core of thesis writing. But independence grows over time with experience and as expertise develops. Students can also fall into the trap of 'supervisor avoidance' if they feel they are not making progress, their work is not good enough, or they are overwhelmed by the research. But avoiding the supervisor will only make the problem worse. You need to initiate and maintain regular contact with your supervisor and talk about these issues if they arise.

## *Managing time and keeping on track*

The key to a thesis is learning to be an independent researcher and writer. As noted in the introduction, the thesis is a large and often unwieldy piece of work that requires good project management skills. Time is a particular issue for at least two reasons. First, time is unstructured. As Bloom[54] points out, the nature of thesis writing time 'may be too unstructured for the students' own good. Most writers work more efficiently with clear goals and time deadlines than without'. Second, the thesis is generally written over a very long period of some years. This means that the writer may tend to suffer:

> a discontinuity of perspective as advisors go on leave, change jobs, or retire. New advisors may make now demands, require new methodology, question

52 Ibid 25.

53 Ibid 68.

54 Lynn Z Bloom, 'Why Graduate Students Can't Write: Research on Writing for Graduate Education', Paper presented at the Annual Meeting of the Conference on College Composition: and Communication (32nd, Dallas. TX, March 26–28, 1981), 6.

> previously accepted research results and interpretations. The longer the writing period extends, the more likely such problems are to appear.[55]

You can take a number of steps to alleviate the problem of unstructured time: First, planning is essential to the success of the thesis. Writing is easier and faster if you know what it is you need to write and why. Griffin[56] recommends that you create a timetable and plan when you will have each phase of your project finished in order to help you to budget your time. The rationale is that '[o]therwise, the temptation is to set a date when the final draft is due and turn in the draft at the last minute. Drafts prepared in this manner are generally horribly disorganized and hopelessly incomplete'. Work backwards from the intended submission date. You can ask your supervisor if they are willing to set deadlines or you can impose them yourself. If imposing your own deadlines, it is often helpful to check with the supervisor or a mentor whether the deadlines you have set yourself are realistic. Research students often feel disappointed with the amount of work they achieve in a given time, because their aims are overambitious, or because they do not realise how complicated a task is.[57]

Second, the adage 'write early, write often and seek feedback' is good advice.[58] The writing process inevitably takes more time than you might imagine; and writing up the thesis often takes longer than the research process:

> writing-up is part of the intellectual discipline of a thesis and is an integral part not separate. It is often only when you start expressing your ideas in writing that complex ideas suddenly click into place and their true meaning and the contribution of your own research, become apparent.[59]

Third, setting daily targets can be helpful. Working every day to achieve a modest and achievable target is preferable to 'binge' working.[60] You might choose to set targets by the number of words written: setting a modest target of about 500 words a day, and ensuring that you meet that target will keep your work progressing well. Five hundred words a day mounts up quickly. Alternatively, you might want to set a target of time spent on task. It can be helpful to break up your time into 25 minute intervals (set a timer) with five-minute breaks in between (the so-called 'Pomodoro Technique').[61] Alternatively, you may find it helpful to break the thesis into small,

---

55 Ibid 7-8.
56 Griffin, above n 17, 4–5.
57 Phillips and Pugh, above n 27, 8.
58 Learning Centre, UNSW, above n 26.
59 Witcher and Wilkinson, above n 46.
60 Lipson, above n 21, 27.
61 Francesco Cirillo, 'The Pomodoro Technique', available at http://baomee.info/pdf/technique/1.pdf.

manageable chunks (one task per chunk) and complete a task a day. These tasks could include:

- putting together a reading list;
- creating your cover page or acknowledgment page;
- adding five citations to your bibliography;
- writing an introduction for each chapter;
- downloading important deadlines and putting them into your calendar;
- downloading your university's dissertation or thesis template or creating your own with the correct margins, font size, etc;
- creating a table and write one paragraph which explains the table;
- creating a figure and write one paragraph which explains the figure;
- outlining the chapter;
- creating a table of contents;
- summarising a journal article or book;
- making a case note.

Murray observes:

> It does not matter too much which method you choose for defining your writing targets. Do the best you can. Counting words, setting goals and acknowledging increments are ways of recognizing your progress. The beauty of counting is that it is simple and concrete.[62]

Fourth, minimise distractions. Ideally, work at a computer with no internet connection. Otherwise, turn off all automatic email notifications and social networking programs.

Lastly, the use of a thesis diary can help to keep you on track, document your progress, provide a place for your ideas and discoveries and can be a valuable basis for the writing process.[63] It is also a way of ameliorating the issue of discontinuity of perspective that arises from the long-term nature of thesis writing.

## *Tips on researching the thesis*

We have discussed the fundamentals of researching for writing and choosing your methodology in Chapter 3, but some key tips for researching for theses and dissertations are as follows:

- As soon as you have worked out what you wish to do, you should establish whether or not you will need to apply to your university ethics committee

---

62 Murray, above n 25, 19.

63 See further H Altrichter and ML Holly, 'Research Diaries', in B Somekh and C Lewon (eds) *Research Methods in the Social Sciences* (Sage, 2005).

for approval of your research. As a general rule, you need ethics approval if you intend to observe, talk to, consult or deal with living human beings or animals. Applications involve detailed explanation of what you will do, so it is important to think about your methods at an early stage, and in particular to think about how any participants you work with will be protected from harm.[64]

- Electronic databases are invaluable and you should ensure that you contact your university library to see what is available and for classes on their efficient use.
- Free writing (discussed below) can be a help in research. Often the research task seems huge: starting by writing what you already know about the subject can help you identify areas where there are gaps in your knowledge.
- Lipson argues that, in research by reading you need to be discriminating in your work: 'Your goal is to extract what you need without getting bogged down in the rest. Remember: *You are reading to write*'.[65]
- Ensure you take bibliographic details as you go: 'Begin your notes for each new book, article, and web site by writing down the author, title, and other essential data'.[66] From the first day of your thesis, you need a database of complete references, kept in a consistent citation style. Tools such as EndNote or ProCite can be invaluable here. You need to pay attention to the details of your references, ensuring the spelling is correct and the references are complete – there is nothing worse than having to trawl through information at the end to find a page number. Ensure, as noted above, that you are familiar with any citation style that may be dictated by the university or your discipline.
- Research by reading can be a means of avoiding writing! Even when it is not, it is important to know when you have done enough research. Generally, your research is sufficient when you reach what is known as 'saturation point', that is, you are hearing or reading the same ideas repeatedly.

## The literature review

A literature review is often a stand-alone chapter in a thesis, but some writers prefer to integrate the literature into the arguments, incorporating it in several chapters. Murray[67] cites a number of definitions of a literature review: as '[a]n interpretation and synthesis of published research';[68] as a 'research project in its own right';[69] as '[a]

---

64 Monash University, above n 22.
65 Lipson, above n 21, 41.
66 Ibid 41.
67 Murray, above n 25, 123.
68 SB Merriam, *Case Study Research in Education: A Qualitative Approach* (Jossey-Bass, 1988) 6.
69 EE Brent, 'The Computer-assisted Literature Review' (1986) 2 *Computers and the Social Sciences* 137, 137.

task that continues throughout the duration of the thesis ... shows how the problem under investigation relates to previous research';[70] and as '[an opportunity to] look again at the literature ... in ... an area not necessarily identical with, but collateral to, your own area of study'.[71] One reason for the multitude of definitions is that the literature review is both process and product:

> The process involves the researcher in exploring the literature to establish the status quo, formulate a problem or research enquiry, to defend the value of pursuing the line of enquiry established, and to compare the findings and ideas of others with his or her own. The product involves the synthesis of the work of others in a form which demonstrates the accomplishment of the exploratory process.[72]

However you choose to define it, the literature review is essential: 'a researcher cannot perform significant research without first understanding the literature in the field'.[73] As noted above, a literature review shows the examiner that you can effectively research secondary sources; and that your project is original in that it fills a gap in existing knowledge or adds to what is already known in some significant way. Indeed, it has been noted that:

> Examiners typically started reviewing a dissertation with the expectation that it would pass; but a poorly conceptualized or written literature review often indicated for them that the rest of the dissertation might have problems. On encountering an inadequate literature review, examiners would proceed to look at the methods of data collection, the analysis, and the conclusions more carefully.[74]

Your literature review is thus not merely a list of sources, but, more importantly, a critical evaluation of the work that has already been done in and around your topic. Cunningham advises that the literature review should be 'as comprehensive as possible in the space available'.[75] He also advises discrimination in that you should ensure the literature you use gives an appropriate background to your study and does

---

70 J Anderson, B Durston and M Poole, *Thesis and Assignment Writing* (Wiley, 1970) 17.
71 P Leedy, *Practical Research: Planning and Design* (Macmillan, 4th edn,1989) 66.
72 CS Bruce Research students' early experiences of the dissertation literature Review (1994) 19(2) *Studies in Higher Education*, 217, 218.
73 David N Boote and Penny Beile, 'Scholars Before Researchers: On the Centrality of the Dissertation Literature Review in Research Preparation' (2005) 34(6) *Educational Researcher* 3, 3.
74 Ibid 6.
75 Cunningham, above n 23, 135.

not include everything you have ever read on the subject. Murray[76] provides some helpful prompts, maintaining that a literature review should answer the following questions:

- 'Why is this subject important?
- Who else thinks it's important?
- Who has worked on this subject before?
- Who has done something similar to what I will be doing?
- What can be adapted to my own study?
- What are the gaps in the research?
- Who is going to use my material?
- What use will my project be?
- What will my contribution be?
- What specific questions will I answer?'

Preparing a literature review is often advocated as the first task in your thesis. Lipson provides some helpful ways to begin. He suggests: ask your supervisor to suggest a few good books and articles to get you started, then follow the footnotes in these to other readings; identify the leading scholarly journals in your field and thumb through the past few years, looking for articles on your topic; supplement that by searching your library's database; do a general web search (but be wary of the quality of what you find); and consult your library's reference librarians.[77]

## *Tips on writing the thesis*

### *The benefits of 'freewriting'*

As we noted earlier, writing early is often the key to completing the thesis in a timely (and relatively stress-free) fashion. It is very common, however, for thesis writers to put off writing as long as they can; or to suffer from writer's block. Indeed, many thesis writers become paralysed with anxiety at putting words to paper – even to develop an outline. This is often because they are worried that once they commit something to writing it is set in stone. But you should never be afraid to change your mind. In fact, it is inevitable that your work will change through the period of the thesis because, as you research and write, you own ideas will evolve. The key is to remain flexible.

The problems of procrastination and writer's block can often be addressed by what is called 'freewriting'. This is simply writing for a predetermined amount of time (5 minutes or 20 minutes, for example) without stopping. You write in

76 Murray, above n 25, 128.
77 Lipson, above n 21, 29–30.

sentences, but there is no structure required and the writing is, at least in the first instance, private, that is, only for your own use.

Freewriting can be used in different ways: for instance, it can be used as a 'warm-up' to actual writing; or it can be used after you have done some reading to get your ideas on paper. Murray, an advocate of freewriting, observes that you can use freewriting, among other things: as a warm-up for writing; to clarify topics; to get into the writing habit; to develop fluency; to clarify your understanding; to increase confidence in your writing; to overcome obstacles by articulating them; and to put the 'personal' voice into impersonal research.[78] In particular, she recommends alternating freewriting and note-taking as an effective means of developing understanding and ensuring that your writing progresses.[79]

### *The inevitability of redrafting*

Thesis writers often imagine that their work will be ready for submission (or nearly ready) on completion of the first draft. They often thus underestimate two things: first, the amount of time necessary to redraft. On this point, Griffin cautions that 'you should count on ***at least*** five or six drafts (many of them swimming in red) before the final draft';[80] second, the amount of time necessary to set aside for the final editing and proofreading process, which can be very time consuming. You will generally need to set aside at least three months to finish off any last things that may be necessary.

It is very important that, during the process of writing, you share your work: do not be afraid to submit your written work to your supervisor for feedback; and take every opportunity to present your work orally at postgraduate forums and at appropriate conferences and to publish during your thesis. Even if you do not get your work published, you will receive valuable feedback from the expert reviewers which will help you refine your ideas and your writing.

### *Introductions and conclusions*

Some examiners will start by reading the introduction and the conclusion of the thesis to determine whether the argument is viable and has been sustained. The introduction is thus extremely important for indicating to your examiners the quality of your work, persuading your examiner that the thesis is useful and interesting, and by providing a frame within which the reader reads the rest of the thesis. Generally, an introduction:

- provides background information related to the *need* for the research;
- identifies the problem or issue;

---

78 Murray, above n 25, 108.
79 Ibid 128.
80 Griffin, above n 17, 11.

- builds an argument for the research (rationale);
- presents research question(s) and aims;
- indicates the significance and original contribution of the thesis;
- defines key terms;
- states any limitations or caveats on the thesis;
- may present personal motivations behind research;
- may present a theoretical starting point;
- gives an outline of subsequent chapters.[81]

The conclusion should mirror the introduction, reiterating the aims of the thesis, the results, its significance and implications. Generally, you will restate the arguments and evidence for your point of view and identify any further areas for research or, in some theses, make recommendations for future practice.

### *The abstract*

The abstract is an important element of the thesis. It is normally a page or so of double-spaced text though some institutions specify a word limit for the abstract, so check this beforehand. It should offer a succinct overview of the entire thesis, including a statement about findings and main results. It also offers you an opportunity to capture the reader and engage them in the topic.[82] It is normally written last when all these matters are finalised (though you may have a working abstract early on).

### *Editing, more editing and proofreading*

Good editing is essential for your thesis. As a researcher, you need to be able to communicate your findings effectively. The reader is unlikely to be persuaded by your thesis if they cannot understand it; and even if your work is important, poor writing may lead an examiner to give up on the paper.[83]

As has been pointed out, 'all readers [including examiners] require assistance to understand the work, … they feel distracted and irritated by poorly presented work, and … they appreciate well-written, interesting and logically presented arguments'.[84] Because a thesis is a substantial amount of reading, a thesis writer needs to assist the reader ensure that the writing is clear, concise and free from grammatical and spelling errors. The presentation, too, is important. A good page layout with appropriate white space and referencing that conforms to the norms

81 Monash, above n 22.
82 Hardy and Ramjeet, above n 24.
83 Don Davis, 'PhD Thesis – Where do I Start?' (2009), available at www.columbia.edu/~drd28/Thesis%20Research.pdf.
84 S Johnston, 'Examining the Examiners: an analysis of examiners' reports on doctoral theses' (1997) 22(3) *Studies in Higher Education* 333, 340.

of the discipline are essential. And the reader needs to provide good signposting to facilitate the reader's understanding: in the thesis as a whole, you will have an introduction, a body and a conclusion. Similarly, within each chapter, you will start by saying what this section is about; then give the details in the body of the chapter; before concluding and linking to the next chapter. Each paragraph should describe a single idea, the first sentence introducing the idea and linking it to the previous paragraph, the last sentence concluding the idea and linking to the next paragraph. Remember to break up large amounts of text with headings and subheadings.

In the editing process, therefore, you need to review, first, the overall *structure* of the thesis to ensure it is logical and that the argument is sustained from beginning to end and that the argument is carefully signposted throughout. Second, you need to review the text, editing and proofreading carefully. One means of editing is to number your paragraphs from the beginning to the conclusion, then, paragraph by paragraph, edit them *in reverse order*, not only checking on grammar and spelling but ensuring that the paragraph follows on logically from the previous paragraph. Third, you should review all citations to ensure that they are complete and in the correct style; and lastly, you should review the thesis to ensure that your work demonstrates academic integrity, that is, it must be free of plagiarism or the misuse of data. We have discussed the ethics of research in Chapter 3. Plagiarism is a serious violation of academic rules; quotations, data, experiments, and the ideas of others should never be falsified or distorted.[85] Lipson's rules for writing with academic integrity are:

- 'You are responsible for your written work, including the ideas, facts, and interpretations you include.
- Unless you say otherwise, every word you write is assumed to be your own.
- When you rely on others' work or ideas, acknowledge it openly:
  - When you use their ideas or data, give them credit.
  - When you use their exact words, use quotation marks plus a citation.
  - When you paraphrase, use your own distinctive voice and cite the original source. Make sure your language doesn't mimic the original. If it still does after rewriting, then use direct quotes.
  - When you rely heavily on an author for part of your paper, say so.
- When you draw on others' work, present it fairly. No distortions. No straw men.
- When you present empirical material, show where you acquired it so others can check the data for themselves (the exception is commonly known material, which does not need to be cited).'[86]

---

85 Lipson, above n 21, 46.
86 Ibid 57.

## IV CONCLUSION

In this chapter, we have considered the processes for writing research essays, theses and dissertations. Although a thesis or dissertation is a much larger and more complex piece of work, the fundamental processes are very similar to writing research essays. All require critical thinking, a core argument, logical reasoning and good use of evidence. All require good planning, careful time management, good organisational skills and careful attention to writing, editing and proofreading. And all start with a consideration of audience and purpose. The core ethical obligations for these forms of writing are originality and careful acknowledgment of sources.

# REVIEW MATERIALS

## SUMMARY

This chapter focused on research essays, theses and dissertations, and the techniques of critical analysis required for these forms of academic writing. It included tips for essay writing, including choosing topics, interpreting topics, time-management and writing effective introduction and conclusions. For theses and dissertations, it identified key factors such as originality and significance, and discussed concepts such as the thesis statement and the literature review, as well as outlining various aspects of the writing process including the technique of free-writing to overcome writer's block and procrastination.

## KEY POINTS

1. Research essays, theses and dissertations are forms of persuasive writing (you may thus also find Chapter 8 helpful).
2. Research essays, theses and dissertations present an argument, that is, a representation of your position or 'point of view' on the topic under consideration, based on your research, your reasoning and the available evidence.
3. If undertaking a thesis or dissertation, ensure you understand the relevance and fundamentals of the literature review.
4. Writing an essay, dissertation or thesis requires careful time management. If you tend to procrastinate, have difficulty meeting deadlines or suffer from writer's block, put in place some strategies to keep your work moving.
5. Plagiarism is a serious violation of academic rules. Quotations, data, experiments, and the ideas of others should always be acknowledged, and never falsified or distorted.

## QUESTIONS FOR REFLECTION

1. The next time you find yourself in a disagreement, spend a few minutes asking the other person questions to help you clarify their argument. Ask about general principles. Offer alternatives in the form of questions (eg 'How would you respond to someone who said ...?'). Do some questions elicit more heated responses than others? How do you feel about asking them?[87]

87 Adapted from Joseph M Williams and Gregory G Clomb, *The Craft of Argument* (2nd ed, Longman, 2003) 58.

2. Are advertisements arguments? They will rarely say so explicitly, but most give reasons and present an image which seems to constitute evidence. Try reflecting on, and analysing, three or four advertisements as arguments.[88] How is the argument presented? What evidence (if any!) is given in support of the argument? How are images used to support or present the argument?
3. What are the differences between critical and creative thinking?
4. At university, plagiarism is often viewed only as a compliance issue, but why is it important to the reader that the writer avoids plagiarism?
5. Do you find it easier to write in response to a given topic, or do you prefer to generate your own topic? Why?

## EXERCISES

1. Which one of the following is a thesis statement? Justify your answer:
   a. Reasons why Australia has a common law system.
   b. The common law system was inherited from England.
   c. The common law system is superior to the civil law system.
   d. While the common law system does not have codified laws governing all aspects of citizens' lives, the judicial precedent system is very effective.
2. Assume the following is your topic. What research questions might you propose to fully address the topic?
   Sanctions in criminal law are important to society as they have the potential to alter the behaviour of both the person found guilty of a crime and that of other potential offenders.
3. Choose a portion of an article from a legal journal and provide both a criticism and a critique of it. Identify their points of difference, and consider what response from the original author each might provoke, and draw some conclusions about why it is important to critique rather than to criticise others' work.

## FURTHER RESOURCES

1. Argumentative writing and the Toulmin Method[89]
   The Toulmin Method of logic is a common and easy to use formula for organising an argument. The basic format for the Toulmin Method is as follows:

---

88 Ibid.

89 OWL Perdue Online Writing Lab, 'Organizing your Argument', available at https://owl.english.purdue.edu/owl/resource/588/03/. See also http://www.rohan.sdsu.edu/~digger/305/toulmin_model.htm.

**Claim:** The overall thesis the writer will argue for.
**Data:** Evidence gathered to support the claim.
**Warrant (also referred to as a bridge):** Explanation of why or how the data supports the claim, the underlying assumption that connects your data to your claim.
**Backing (also referred to as the foundation):** Additional logic or reasoning that may be necessary to support the warrant.
**Counterclaim:** A claim that negates or disagrees with the thesis/claim.
**Rebuttal:** Evidence that negates or disagrees with the counterclaim.

Thus, by way of example:

**Claim:** The element of 'intention' must be present to make a finding of plagiarism.
**Data 1:** Many universities include the word 'intention' in their definition of plagiarism.
**Warrant 1:** Many instances of plagiarism are the result of a lack of education or understanding what constitutes plagiarism.
**Data 2:** Plagiarism can often result from a lack of attention.
**Warrant 2:** Students may simply be careless when they are under pressure from work, family obligations or study more generally.
**Data 3:** A finding of plagiarism has serious consequences for law students applying for admission as a lawyer.
**Warrant 3:** Universities should be careful not to impede a student's career possibilities because they fail to understand that other people's work should be cited or that they mistakenly fail to do so.
**Counterclaim:** Since a reader assumes that what s/he is reading is the work of the author, there should not be a requirement for 'intention' to be present to make a finding of plagiarism.
**Rebuttal:** While a consideration of whether a student intended to pass off work of others as his own or not is important, it should only be a factor in determining the penalty awarded against a student who has plagiarised.

2. Persuasion map
Go to: http://www.readwritethink.org/files/resources/interactives/persuasion_map/
You can use this tool to map out your thesis and supporting arguments. It can be completed online or you can print the document and fill it out. If you wish to save the document choose 'CutePDF Writer'.

3. Critical thinking[90]

   The following phrases may be useful for your critique:

   **'Introducing questions, problems and limitations: theory or argument**

   - The main weakness with this theory is that …
   - The key problem with this explanation is that …
   - However, this theory does not fully explain why …
   - One criticism of much of the literature on X is that …
   - However, there is an inconsistency with this argument.
   - A serious weakness with this argument, however, is that …
   - One question that needs to be asked, however, is whether …
   - Smith's argument relies too heavily on qualitative analysis of …
   - Smith's interpretation overlooks much of the historical research …
   - Many writers have challenged Smith's claim on the grounds that …
   - Smith's analysis does not take account of X, nor does he examine …
   - It seems that Jones' understanding of the X framework is questionable.
   - The existing accounts fail to resolve the contradiction between X and Y.
   - One of the limitations with this explanation is that it does not explain why …

   **Introducing questions, problems and limitations: method or practice**

   - One major drawback of this approach is that …
   - Selection bias is another potential concern because …
   - Perhaps the most serious disadvantage of this method is that …
   - The main limitation of biosynthetic incorporation, however, is …
   - All the studies reviewed so far, however, suffer from the fact that …
   - Another problem with this approach is that it fails to take X into account.
   - Difficulties arise, however, when an attempt is made to implement the policy.
   - Nevertheless, the strategy has not escaped criticism from governments, agencies and academics.'

90 From Manchester University, 'Academic Phrasebank', available at http://www.phrasebank.manchester.ac.uk/being-critical/.

PART 2

# PROFESSIONAL WRITING

# CHAPTER 7

# BALANCED WRITING: THE MEMORANDUM AND CLIENT LETTER

## I INTRODUCTION

Generally, legal documents can be divided into two types: objective and persuasive.[1] Objective legal documents seek to inform, advise, and counsel. Examples include office memos, judicial opinions, and advice emails.[2] These documents must be 'scrupulous, balanced, and reliable'.[3] A persuasive document, on the other hand, seeks to argue, convince, and induce action. Examples include appellate briefs, responses and replies.[4] These documents must be 'logical, credible, and compelling'.[5] Both forms of document drafting constitute 'a professional skill, or "craft," that is acquired through both study and experience'.[6]

Balanced writing, sometimes called analytical, objective or argumentative writing, requires the development of *both* sides of an issue or problem, offering both claims and counterclaims. Balanced writing is not about persuading the reader to your view, but rather presenting the reader with a reasoned conclusion on the strengths and weaknesses of the client's position or a particular legal issue. In this

1 Jill Barton and Rachel H Smith, *The Handbook for the New Legal Writer* (Wolters Kluwer Law & Business, 2014) 1. Indeed, in the US, many law schools teaching objective and persuasive writing in different semesters: Suzanne E Rowe, 'Legal Research, Legal Writing and Legal Analysis: Putting Law School into Practice' (2009) *Stetson Law Review* 10.

2 Ibid 1.

3 Ibid.

4 Ibid.

5 Ibid.

6 Ibid 260.

chapter, we focus on two particular instances of balanced legal writing: client letters and internal memoranda.

There is another meaning of 'balanced writing' that is relevant to this discussion: that is, the need for the lawyer to stay balanced, to 'stay poised' and 'keep steady', rather than be caught up in the emotion of a client's matter. Of course, this applies to both balanced and persuasive writing. The ASCR 34 (specifically r 34.1.1) expresses the kind of behaviour expected of a lawyer. It requires lawyers to refrain from making 'any statement which grossly exceeds the legitimate assertion of the rights or entitlements of the solicitor's client, and which misleads or intimidates the other person'. Rules ASCR 34.1.2 and 34.1.3 go on to warn against threatening legal proceedings or using tactics 'that go beyond' those that are considered to be legitimate in terms of a solicitor's advocacy for a client.

Since this rule is couched in terms of what a lawyer should *not* do, it is useful to provide a recent example of behaviour that would be covered by the rule. In *Legal Services Commissioner v Sampson (Legal Practice)*,[7] Sampson, a Victorian lawyer, was found guilty of two counts of professional misconduct. Sampson was a debt-collection lawyer who acted for two prominent DVD hire chains whose activities consisted predominantly of sending letters of demand and what were described by the Victorian Legal Services Commissioner, as 'official-looking notices'[8] to those who owed money to the video stores. In 2013, Sampson was found guilty of claiming legal costs from the debtors. There was no provision in the contract consumers signed with the video stores that they would be 'charged legal costs on top of the debt if they failed to pay'.[9] Therefore they were not her clients, or those of the firm for which she worked.[10] Additionally, it was found that the notices were 'designed to look like official court documents'[11] and therefore held to be misleading. The gravity of Sampson's behaviour was exacerbated by the fact that she had personally been warned in 2009 by the office of the Legal Services Commissioner[12] and would have been a recipient of a warning sent to all Victorian debt-collection lawyers in June 2011, alerting them to the fact that lawyers were now required 'to meet higher standards of ethical conduct'.[13] Thus, Sampson, as a lawyer, could legitimately send letters of demand to debtors, but she transgressed the conduct provisions by creating

---

7 *Legal Services Commissioner v Sampson (Legal Practice)* [2013] VCAT 1177 (10 July 2013).

8 Michael McGarvie, 'Misconduct Findings for Video Debt Lawyer' 11 July 2013 Media Release, available at http://lsbc.vic.gov.au/documents/2013-07-11_MR_Misconduct_findings_for_video_debt_lawyer.pdf.

9 Ibid.

10 *Legal Services Commissioner v Sampson (Legal Practice)* [2013] VCAT 1177 (10 July 2013) paras 17 and 35. Sampson had no contractual entitlement.

11 McGarvie, above n 8.

12 *Legal Services Commissioner v Sampson (Legal Practice)* [2013] VCAT 1177 (10 July 2013) para 37.

13 McGarvie, above n 8.

look-alike court documents to bring pressure on the debtors – and further, charged her own services to those debtors.

While keeping the ramifications of a breach of ASCR r 34 in mind, other rules are relevant to the content of this chapter. These will be discussed in relation to two routine practices for lawyers: writing client letters and writing memoranda. We discuss the processes involved in writing each of these forms of communication, and the ethical issues involved, before considering the increasing use of email in relation to these sorts of communications (and the particular ethical issues this may raise).

## II CLIENT LETTERS

### *The process of writing client letters*

Although students of legal writing are generally encouraged to use IRAC or some similar schema[14] for organising their analysis, such schemas do not work for advising a client. Although an IRAC style analysis may form the basis of your advice to a client, the written advice needs to be crafted to the client's needs.

The first step, as in all writing, is reflection on purpose and audience. You need to be clear on your instructions – whether those of your senior or of the client. Letters to clients may serve a variety of purposes: they may communicate advice or information, convey details of required actions or constitute a record of some kind. Think about what question or questions the client needs answered or what information they need. Sophisticated commercial clients may be very clear on their needs. Other clients, particularly those with little or no prior engagement with the law, may not be. It may thus be necessary to seek clarification of the client's instructions.

Similarly, consideration of audience is important because this will guide your use of tone and language. If your client is, for instance, a corporation and you are writing to in-house counsel, your tone, language and the complexity of your discussion will be very different from those used to write to, for instance, an elderly man for whom English is not his first language, seeking advice on a neighbourhood dispute (indeed, in such cases, you may need to have your letter translated). In-house counsel are likely to need a formal legal analysis and full case or legislative details. At the same time, a sophisticated client will often have a level of understanding which means you do not have to outline the basics. Non-legally trained clients need information, but may not understand technicalities and may need more fundamental information about concepts and processes.

You should then start to plan: brainstorm or write a rough outline of the information you need to include in the letter and how it will be presented before

---

14 See further Chapter 6.

you draft the letter. Generally, your firm will have a letter template to guide your drafting. This will commonly include the firm's reference number for the matter, and a heading that provides the parties' names and a description of the matter. When you write, you should also note any reference number and heading of the recipient, and if you are responding to their letter, refer to the date of that letter.

When drafting, keep in mind that client letters should be carefully structured, with an emphasis on clear and concise language. The purpose of the letter, and any action required by the recipient, should be stated up front. Don't be afraid to use headings and summaries to clarify the information and provide a 'road map' for the reader. If the advice in the letter is particularly lengthy, it may be helpful to provide a summary at the beginning.

In addition, these communications must, in keeping with the ethical obligations discussed below, be accurate and up to date in their use of the law. The tone of all client letters, regardless of the recipient's background, should be balanced, objective and professional, but also appropriate relative to purpose (for example, some letters need to convey a sense of urgency; others a sense of sympathy). The letter is a permanent record, so do not joke or make inappropriate remarks, and avoid ambiguities.

Don't neglect the feedback stage of the drafting cycle. Once drafted, consider sharing your draft with a colleague, particularly if you are relatively inexperienced. In particular, you should ask your colleague to consider how the reader may interpret what you have written and ensure that you are conveying the message you need to convey.

Presentation should be impeccable: client letters should be carefully proofread and free of substantive and presentation errors. This step includes double checking dates, names, addresses, references and enclosures (these are documents or other items you send with the letter).

## *Parts of a letter*

Client letters should contain each of the following elements.

- *Date:* Always date your letter and try to send it on the same day. Dating your letter enables you to keep a clear paper trail in relation to a matter. It also establishes a time line for any proposed action (eg, where you ask the recipient to respond within two weeks of receipt).
- *Return address:* this is generally in your office letterhead, so does not need to be repeated.
- *Recipient address:* check and double check that you have the correct recipient, address details are right and that you have spelled the recipient's name correctly.
- *Subject line:* provide a specific, one phrase statement. In some cases, you may include the client and matter numbers.

- *Salutation:* keep your salutation formal and ensure you use the correct salutation (eg the recipient may be Doctor or Professor, rather than Ms).
- *Body of the letter:* use plain language and simple organisation. State the purpose of the letter up front; provide any necessary context; and state the bottom line conclusion if there is one. Make explicit any assumptions you may be making. After your analysis, provide a statement of available options and provide advice as to the best course of action. Advise of any next steps, specifically and directly. Generally in a letter you will not need to provide full citations to cases.
- *Closing:* Close with 'sincerely' or some other appropriate, formal expression and type your full name under your signature. Indicate whether there are any enclosures.

We have included a sample letter, with the parts of the letter identified, at the end of this chapter.

## *Ethical obligations in writing client letters*

The legislation governing lawyers requires lawyers to disclose the basis upon which costs will be charged to clients,[15] but there is no requirement for lawyers to enter into a written retainer. Yet it is normal practice for lawyers, after having interviewed their client for the first time, to write to clients. This letter is usually referred to as an 'engagement letter',[16] and in fact serves a number of purposes, some of which it will be noted, can clarify issues that often form the basis of litigation alleging that lawyers have breached their contract or been negligent.

### *Scope of the retainer*

The engagement letter is an opportunity to provide an early response to the client setting out the lawyer's understanding of the client's instructions. This is the first step towards complying with ASCR r 8 – to follow a client's lawful, proper and competent instructions. This letter sets out what the lawyer believes are the client's objectives and the lawyer's role in achieving those objectives. It provides an opportunity for a client to correct or confirm the lawyer's understanding of what the client wants.[17]

### *Who is the client?*

This question may seem strange, yet it is a question that often comes before a court to decide. For instance, it is important for a lawyer to clearly identify whether she is acting for a director of a company personally, or for the company as a separate entity.

---

15 *Legal Profession Uniform Law* s 174.

16 Karen Sneddon and David Hricik, 'Improving Routine Documents Part 1: Engagement Letters' (2012) 18(2) *Georgia Bar Journal* 54, 55.

17 Ibid 55.

Similarly, confusion can arise with respect to partnerships.[18] A clear statement in an engagement letter that identifies the client makes it clear as to whose instructions the lawyer is obeying, and with whom she will correspond.[19]

### *Plain language*

In recent years there has been much written about the importance of writing in plain language. You will find the fundamentals of plain language in the Grammar Primer in our Learning Materials. Written letters should use clear and understandable terms, rather than using legalistic terminology. This applies to communications with the public[20] (implicitly this includes clients) and other members of the legal profession, including the judiciary.[21] Lawyer communications should be reader-friendly. Legal writing should accurately convey information without including superfluous words,[22] and attention should be paid to the way in which the letter is formatted, to promote a client's comprehension of the message being conveyed.[23] In fact, to do otherwise, may breach ASCR r 7.1, which requires lawyers to give 'clear … advice to assist a client to understand relevant legal issues and to make informed choices … consistent with the terms of the engagement'.

### *Informing and managing client communication expectations*

The ASCR makes another point with respect to a lawyer's communications. It talks about providing timely advice (ASCR r 7.1). Yet there can be different perspectives on what it means to be 'timely'. This is particularly the case that we are mostly dealing with instantaneous communication technologies, which gives rise to an expectation of an immediate response, as is the case with emails. It is therefore wise for a lawyer to include a sentence or two in the engagement letter outlining the probable timeframe within which she will answer emails in order to avoid client frustration and the receipt of difficult (and frustrated) client phone calls.[24]

While the above discussion has been couched in terms of the engagement letter, much of what was discussed should be applied to letter writing generally (whether that letter is sent by email or snail mail). It should also be noted that a number of

---

18 For a more detailed discussion, see 'Identifying the Client: To Whom is the Duty Owed?' in Paula Baron and Lillian Corbin, *Ethics and Legal Professionalism in Australia* (2014, Oxford University Press) 122–7.

19 Sneddon and Hricik, above n 16, 55.

20 Christopher R Trudeau, 'The Public Speaks: An Empirical Study of Legal Communication' (2011–2012) 14 *The Scribes Journal of Legal Writing* 121.

21 Sean Flammer, 'Persuading Judges: An Empirical Analysis of Writing Style, Persuasion, and the Use of Plain English' (2010) 18 *Legal Writing Journal of the Legal Writing Institute* 183.

22 Ibid 184.

23 Sneddon and Hricik, above n 16, 55.

24 Betty Adams, 'Client Communication and Contact' (2008) January/February *GP Solo* 18, 19.

other rules can apply to a lawyer's letter writing. Perhaps the most important of these is ASCR r 4.1.3 – that is, the obligation to deliver legal services competently. While this rule does not mention writing specifically, it is obvious that a client would expect a lawyer's writing to be competent. Competency, from the client's perspective, is something more than just describing the relevant law and applying it to the client's matter. A client questions a lawyer's competency if the letter contains spelling mistakes and other errors. Such errors may cause the client to lose confidence in the lawyer's ability. The legal writer should therefore plan carefully to ensure that their letters meet the client's needs. In particular, the writer should consider potential courses of action or suggest solutions for a client's concerns, and carefully review all correspondence to ensure that it is free of grammatical and spelling errors. Also, in order to guard against breaching a client's confidentiality (ASCR r 9), it is important to ensure that communications are correctly addressed. This is particularly the case with email, discussed below.

## III INTERNAL MEMORANDA

### *The process of writing internal memoranda*

Another important part of a lawyer's role is to compose internal memoranda, of which there are two main types: a memorandum to file (also called a 'note to file' or 'file note') and a memorandum prepared by a junior member of staff after conducting legal research for a master or a senior member of the firm. The latter may be used for a number of purposes: for instance, as a basis on which to prepare a letter of advice to a client; to decide whether to take a case; or as a brief for a barrister. But at its core, the internal memorandum is written in order to enable someone else to make a decision.[25] In both cases, the exercise is practical (not focused, for instance, on legal theory) and time-scripted.[26]

As for other forms of legal writing, you need to start by reflecting on your audience and purpose. What is the purpose of this document and what does the reader need?

### Memorandum to file

All interactions between a lawyer (or her support staff) and clients; a lawyer and colleagues; and a lawyer with third parties that relate to client matters, have the potential to be important.[27] Therefore these interactions should be formally

---

25 Terry Hutchinson, *Researching and Writing in Law* (Thomson Reuters, 3rd ed, 2010) 205.

26 Ibid.

27 Karen Sneddon and David Hricik, 'Improving Routine Documents Part 2: Memo to File' (2012) *Georgia Bar Journal* 70, 70.

documented as they may later serve one or more purposes. These include (1) ensuring that the lawyer does not mistakenly recollect facts or events; (2) reminding the lawyer to take a certain course of action at a later time; (3) serving as a primer for other members of the firm to identify what needs to be done on the file;[28] and (4) as a protection against negligence claims and to support preparation of bills of cost in detailed form for taxation.

For these reasons, and to ensure that the matter is recorded accurately, you should complete a memo to file 'as soon as practicable'.[29] In practice, the memo to file should include the following elements:

**Memorandum to file:**

**From:** **[The author]**

**Re:** **[The file number and name]**

**Date:** **[The date of the interaction or event, and some firms include the time]**

It is also usual to record the nature of the interaction, that is, whether it was a phone call, a personal attendance by the client at the office, or an attendance outside the office by the solicitor. Take care to provide the relevant detail that describes the interaction as often these are client instructions that must be followed (ASCR r 8). Depending on the seniority of the person creating the memorandum, a proposed action dealing with the interaction might also be included.

Since the memorandum could potentially become part of a court document, you should couch the tone of the writing in professional terms and follow grammatical and punctuation conventions.[30]

## *Internal memoranda*

As always, start by considering purpose and audience. It is common for junior lawyers to be expected to prepare memoranda for senior members of their firm. This has at least three audience-related implications: first, the reader is someone who is experienced in law. Thus, you need not explain very basic ideas relating to law or the legal system. Second, the reader will have expectations about the organisation, analysis and presentation of the document. And third, the reader is likely to be time-poor, which means they need a document that is clear and concise. The task requires the junior lawyer to craft quality arguments based on detailed legal research, but

28 Ibid.
29 Ibid.
30 Ibid.

these ought to be presented with 'clarity and concision'.[31] You need to balance the need to be concise with the need to provide the reader with the information they need. The elements of the process are summarised in Figure 7.1.

FIGURE 7.1

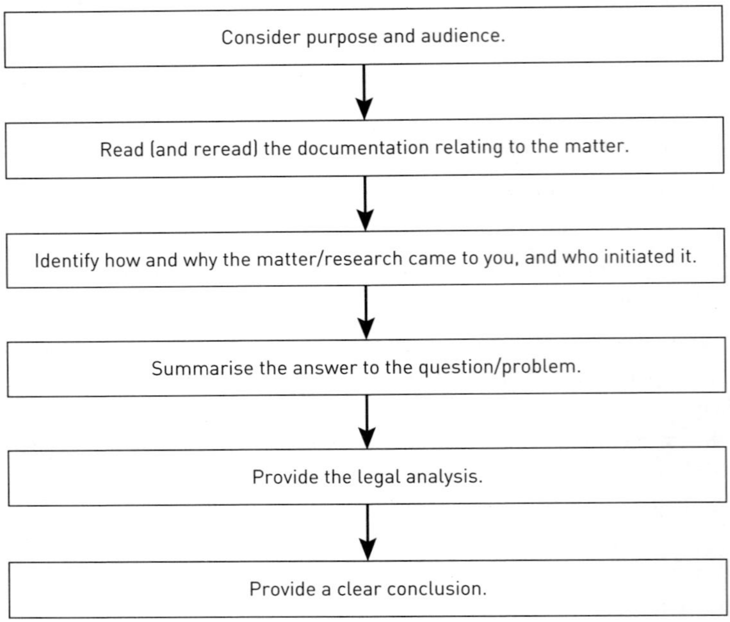


The first step is to read and reread any documentation relating to the matter. Outline the issues and the facts, and then research the relevant law. Do not just search for law that supports the client's position. You need to ascertain any law that goes against the client's case. Chart the law against the facts, identify the issues, then sketch an outline of the memo.

Generally, the memorandum follows a standard format:

**MEMORANDUM**

**TO: [name of recipient]**

**FROM: [name of author]**

**DATE: [date]**

**RE: [subject of memo]**

---

31 Andrey Spektor and Michael A Zuckerman, 'Legal Writing as Good Writing: Tips from the Trenches' (2013) 14(2) *Journal of Appellate Practice and Process* 303, 304.

Start by identifying how and why the matter or research came to you, and who initiated it. Clearly state the issue (that is, the legal question the memorandum seeks to address). The memorandum should then provide a summary of the answer to this issue. In most cases it is appropriate to outline the facts giving rise to the issue in the next section. Here, you need to identify the material facts (that is, those that affect the outcome), both procedural and substantive. Thus ensure the accuracy of dates, times, places and parties. Identify any disputed facts (eg X 'alleged' or 'stated').

The core of the memorandum is then devoted to legal analysis of the issue, applying the law to the facts and critically analysing relevant authorities. It is essential that the memorandum canvass all aspects of the issue, including discussion of any opposing authority.

Generally, the discussion will use an IRAC approach or some variation of IRAC. That is, each paragraph addresses one issue (I). It starts by stating this point, then states the relevant legal rule (R). The rule, and the application of the rule to the facts, are then critically analysed (A). You cannot assume that the meaning and application of the rule are obvious. The analysis needs to go beyond a mere statement of the rule to explanation of its interpretation and application (eg identify any ambiguities in the rule, explain the underlying policy or judicial interpretation and application of the rule). You should then provide a conclusion (C) for that issue. All authorities should be cited in full. Use headings and numbering systems so the structure of the document is clear and the logic easy to follow.

The last section of the memorandum should provide an overview that clearly states the conclusion and what actions should follow from the advice. Keep in mind that the purpose of the memorandum is to inform, rather than persuade. Your goal is to provide an objective and realistic analysis of the legal issue at hand. The memorandum may later be used to prepare a persuasive case, but at this stage it seeks to predict the likely outcome of the issue in an impartial way. One difficult part of writing the conclusion is to reach a conclusion where the law is uncertain. In some cases, you may find a practical solution to the problem that avoids this uncertainty. But overall, you need to decide what outcome a court would be likely to come to, should the matter be litigated.

Of course, edit and proofread your document. In the interests of clarity and credibility, Spektor and Zuckermann suggest some ground rules for the writing of memoranda. For instance, they stress that you should guard against grammatical errors as these may undermine your credibility.[32] They also recommend that you should be careful not to let quotes intrude on the message. For instance, they suggest that you should avoid inserting block quotes as these imply that you lack confidence

32 Ibid 311.

in your own 'voice' or your own understanding of the authority.[33] They recommend a writer should 'paraphrase when the source's exact language is not critical and quote only when it is'.[34] These authors also warn against including a 'marginal argument' in a footnote as this tends to indicate that it is not important.[35]

### *Ethical obligations in writing memoranda*

It is difficult to see that internal memoranda would ever be the subject of breaches of ethical rules, as they are created by staff members for staff members. In addition, making an ethical complaint relating to internal memoranda would ultimately draw attention to a senior staff member's supervisory methods. However, internal memoranda are primarily created for the purpose of advising clients, so it is important to at least refer to the basic rules that should be considered.

The most obvious ethical obligation is that of competency (ASCR r 4.1.3). It is also important that the detail of the client's matter is recorded accurately, as there would be a breach of ASCR r 19 ('frankness in court') if misleading statements were made. There are also some other rules that may be applicable to the writing of memoranda. For instance, ASCR r 7.1 implies that the information contained in these memoranda should be set out clearly at a level that a client would understand. ASCR r 8 reminds the writer that they are writing for a client in obedience to their instructions, but that practitioners must remain independent (ASCR r 17), and make sure that they draw the writer's attention to the fact that litigation is not the only option for a client (ASCR r 7.2).

The writer must also take care to ensure that their advice is balanced. In other words, the writer of a memorandum would be expected to canvass the applicability of case law that both supports and challenges the arguments their client wishes to make. It is a breach of ASCR r 19.6 if the court is not informed of case law or legislation that is relevant, even that that goes against the client's case.

## IV THE MOVE TO 'SUBSTANTIVE EMAIL'

In a study in 2008 in the US,[36] law school graduates reported using substantive email as their primary means of communication with a client and partners. Substantive email ranked first as the graduates' preferred method for communicating research results and advice to clients.[37] This was not to say that learning the traditional form

33 Ibid 305.

34 Ibid 306.

35 Ibid 312–13.

36 Kristen Konrad Robbins-Tiscione, 'From Snail Mail to E-mail: The Traditional Legal Memorandum in the Twenty-first Century' (2008) 58 *Journal of Legal Education* 32.

37 Ibid 48.

of memoranda was unhelpful. They considered it a good basis for the analysis, but observed it was necessary to be able to adapt the form to new technologies. Generally, their substantive email began with a statement of the issue and a recommendation, followed by the legal analysis, often divided into headings.[38]

The graduates reported that this form of communication generally looked 'like a letter' but that the medium had its dangers. They warned that, although email is perceived to be informal, it should not be taken as a more casual form of communication than a memo to another lawyer. One graduate observed that emails containing research need 'a beginning, middle and end so they make sense for posterity'. Another cautioned that, as a new graduate, one had to be conscious of the differences between emailing friends and emailing clients, ensure that the presentation of the email was professional, and to be aware how easy it is for emails to be forwarded to third parties.[39]

These comments accord with the observation that, although technological means of client communications are ordinarily faster and more convenient than traditional modes of communication, a lawyer's choices of whether and how to use technology are dictated by three fundamental ethical obligations: to communicate with the client, preserve the confidentiality of that communication and to provide competent representation.[40]

Thus, although the use of new technologies for client communication is ubiquitous, this does not mean their use is always appropriate.[41] Hazelwood lists a number of circumstances where the appropriateness of technological means of communication may be called into question. Her list includes:

- 'using technology to communicate regarding extremely sensitive matters;
- using technology to communicate with the client who does not use technology effectively;
- using technology to communicate with a client who uses a device or system that third parties can access;
- using technology carelessly, such as by not scrutinising the recipient list or not checking the document carefully for metadata;
- using technology without understanding the service provider's policies regarding confidentiality and data retention;
- using unsecure mobile devices or public internet connections when communicating with a client or working on confidential client information;

38 Ibid 48–9.

39 Ibid.

40 Kristin J Hazelwood, 'Technology and Client Communications: Preparing Law Students and New Lawyers to Make Choices That Comply with the Ethical Duties of Confidentiality, Competence, and Communication' (2014) 83 *Mississippi Law Journal* 245, 247.

41 Ibid.

- continuing to use technology to communicate with a client even when the electronic communication is not producing the information the lawyer needs in order to provide competent representation;
- recognising client expectations for the lawyer's responsiveness for communications sent through an instantaneous technology like email; and
- evaluating risks associated with new or developing technologies or new risks of interception for established technologies.'[42]

Following on from Hazelwood's advice, Coughlin et al[43] say that although email is very convenient, it may be more appropriate to send a letter in the following circumstances:

- 'if you want to signal to the recipient that the information is important, or you wish to formalise your advice';
- 'if you would like the letter to become a part of your client's permanent file';
- 'if the communication contains highly sensitive or highly confidential material, and you are concerned that the material may be inappropriately shared';
- if the recipient is likely to be technically unsophisticated, or for some other reason likely to be unwilling or unable to use email.

Finally, if you are unsure whether to send a letter or an email, err on the side of formality and send a letter.[44]

Of course, if you do choose to use email, you should take the same care as you would with a letter, considering tone, content and format. Emails should be kept relatively short. If you need to communicate a lengthy legal analysis, provide it in a separate attachment. Remember to title all attachments appropriately and always use the same confidentiality warnings you would use on a letter.[45] The medium used for communication thus requires some careful reflection and you may wish to read Chapter 12 on 'Reflective Practices and Everyday Writing'.

## V CONCLUSION

In this chapter, we have outlined the process and ethics of balanced writing, expressed commonly through the genres of client letters and memoranda. We have noted the move to substantive email, and observed the ethical issues this may entail. Lawyers cannot always resolve a client's problem, but achieving client satisfaction

---

42 Ibid 288.

43 Christine Coughlin, Joan Malmud Rocklin and Sandy Patrick, *A Lawyer Writes: A Practical Guide to Legal Analysis* (2nd ed, Carolina Academic Press, 2013) 292.

44 Ibid.

45 Ibid.

by 'effort, attitude, and communication is attainable',[46] through implementing some very simple procedures. Writing client letters and memoranda require thought to the audience and purpose. Although the legal analysis will often utilise IRAC or a similar schema, the writing will require careful crafting for the particular audience. Writing client letters and memoranda also raise issues of professional obligations, particularly the obligations of competency and honesty. We now turn, in Chapter 8, to consider persuasive writing.

46 Adams, above n 24, 18.

# REVIEW MATERIALS

## SUMMARY

This chapter discussed professional writing. It introduced the concept of balanced writing, which seeks to inform, advise, and counsel and is utilised in client letters and memoranda. It set out content requirements, argument claims and counterclaims, and the process and ethics of writing client letters and memoranda, and also discussed issues raised by the use of substantive email.

## KEY POINTS

1. Generally, legal professional writing can be classified as *balanced* or *persuasive*. Balanced writing seeks to inform and advise, and should be reliable and objective.
2. Good client letters rely on a clear understanding of the needs, background and expectations of the intended audience.
3. When preparing internal memoranda, the writer needs to balance the need to be comprehensive with the fact that the reader is likely to be time-poor.
4. Email is rapidly increasing in usage by lawyers, but its use does entail potential ethical and substantive issues and it should therefore be used thoughtfully.
5. Plain language writing is fundamental to good client letters.

## QUESTIONS FOR REFLECTION

1. Why is it important for lawyers to remain dispassionate in their dealings with others? Is it ever justifiable for a lawyer to express anger?
2. In what situations might it be difficult to identify your client?
3. When you have little time to read and understand something (this might be pre-reading for a class, or report reading for work) what strategies do you employ, as a reader, to digest the information quickly? How might these strategies influence your writing?
4. How can you protect confidentiality in email communications?
5. Have you ever sent an email to an unintended recipient? If so, what did you do to rectify the situation? If not, what steps do you take to ensure your email always goes to the intended recipient?

## EXERCISES

1. Rewrite the following to eliminate letter 'legalese'.[47]

   Dear Chaplain Smith

   Enclosed herein find for your perusal documentation relating to your establishment of the Circle of Friends Foundation. Time is of the essence, so please provide your signature on the documents and return them to my office as soon as permitted by your schedule. Pursuant to the by-laws of your diocese, we are obligated to provide a copy of the documents to Bishop John Peters within thirty days of the official formation of the foundation. I have appended a copy of the proposed letter to the said Bishop Peters herein. Please review the letter and return it along with the aforementioned documents. I am cognizant of the fact that you wish to get the foundation running at utmost haste and I am at the present moment finishing the remaining paperwork. I will alert you when the loose ends are tied.
2. Explain what these mean in plain language:
   - Re: instruction letter:
     - In order to pursue this case I will be requesting a police report, doctors' reports and other material to be able to prepare a Statement of Claim.
   - Re: advanced litigation letter:
     - This denial means your lawsuit continues, and we can either attempt to settle your suit with the defendant or go forward with a jury trial.

## FURTHER RESOURCES

1. Writing client letters[48]

   *Who is the client?*
   - Is the client an individual or a company? If individual, is the recipient a professional?

   *How often should you write?*
   - This may depend on the type of matter; and the purpose of the letter and how much the client wants to be involved. Individuals may want to limit the number of letters you write for cost reasons. Corporate clients may want you to report periodically, for instance, at certain points in the litigation.

---

47 Adapted from Coughlin et al, above n 43, 290.

48 This exercise has been adapted from Megan E Boyd, Lady (Legal) Writer, available at http://ladylegalwriter.blogspot.com/2014/05/tips-for-client-letters.html. If you use such material as inspiration, be careful. Much law-related content on the web is US-based, and reflects practices that are different from Australian ones.

*How detailed should the letter should be?*

- Unsophisticated clients may need to have certain legal terms and concepts explained.
- You would not have to explain industry terms to professionals.
- Use short sentences – avoid the use of 'and'.
- Case citations should sometimes be included, but use your judgement. They can be a distraction in a letter.

*Introduction of the letter*

Summarise what has happened. Both of the examples used below assume unsophisticated clients, but they deal with litigation at different stages.[49]

- Re: instruction letter (plaintiff client):
  - At our meeting on March 21 you attended my office and gave me instructions. It is my understanding that you wish me to represent you in your claim against the Eggs-ce-lent Restaurant for your long-term illness following food poisoning from tainted eggs.
- Re: advanced litigation letter (defendant client):
  - As you know, today I attended the preliminary hearing on your behalf, to argue that the plaintiff's application for summary judgment should not be granted. I'm pleased to say the judge has made the order we requested, and the application was dismissed. We now resume preparation for the trial, as discussed last week.

*Tell the client what to expect*

Advise the client about what will happen in response to your actions (or the court's orders, if appropriate). This includes advising on time frames, as many clients do not appreciate how long it takes to gather facts or engage in court processes.

- Re: instruction letter:
  - Gathering this information will take some time. The information will then be used to prepare a Statement of Claim. Once this is prepared we will contact you to make an appointment.
- Re: advanced litigation letter:[50]
  - The next step in the litigation process will be discovery. This means you have to disclose to the other side all documents that relate to the case, and they have to do the same with their own documents. All relevant documents have to be listed, and most have to be shown to the other side, but we will advise you about this when we discuss the contents of your

49 The content of the advanced litigation letter has been adapted from Tips for Lawyers, available at http://www.tipsforlawyers.com/legal-drafting-writing-for-lawyers/.

50 The content of the advanced litigation letter has been adapted from http://www.tipsforlawyers.com/legal-drafting-writing-for-lawyers/. If you use such material as inspiration, be careful, as with any material from the web, that it does not reflect practices (particularly US practices) that are different from Australian ones.

list. The list will be attached to an affidavit, which you will need to swear or affirm. We then exchange affidavits with the other side, and arrange to inspect the other side's documents, and show them yours. Please start getting your list together now, and make an appointment to bring in the documents and discuss the list in the next few days.

*Invite questions*

Even though you feel you have given full explanations, it is wise to assure the client that they can contact you if they have any questions about the letter or the litigation in general.

- Re: instruction letter:
  - I realise that pursuing a claim in court is new to you, and that it probably adds to the stress you are feeling as a result of your illness, but I want to assure you that I am happy for you to contact me if you have any questions about this letter or the litigation in general.
- Re: advanced litigation letter:
  - The application to rule the plaintiff's expert affidavit inadmissible has been set down for hearing on 21 June. I will let you know what the ruling is. In the meantime, if you have any questions about your case, or the contents of this letter, please feel free to call or email me.

*Letter to a sophisticated recipient*

This letter is written to the instructing client's regular medical practitioner. Similar letters would be sent to specialists examining the client for the purpose of preparing a medical report.

I act for John Harm, who is bringing a legal claim for damages as a result of food poisoning on March 21 this year.

I understand that you have been his general practitioner for several years and treated him at the time. John has an appointment with you on November 20 for a medical examination and review to enable you to formally report on the food poisoning from your perspective, being familiar with his prior health status, his suffering during the acute phase and the longer-term changes brought about by the poisoning. In particular, we ask you to give full details of the treatment given, including samples taken, and to consider the temporary and permanent effects, such as his ability to work and undertake other activities, as obviously this will determine the size of the claim.

There is some urgency in getting the claim filed, so it would be appreciated if you would forward your report (and your account for your services) within a month of the appointment.

Please do not hesitate to contact me if you require any further details about the matter generally.

2. A sample letter[51]
   This sample letter below relates to a consumer contract matter. We have identified the parts of the letter.

Butterfield and Butterfield
65-21 High Street
Northcote, VIC
(03) 340 4200

October 23, 2010

Willi Loman
Loman's Fashions
885 Swanston St
Melbourne VIC 3000

Dear Dr Loman

Re: Contract Dispute, Loman's Fashions

Recently you wrote to us that Loman's Fashions had been sued by a shopper in the Melbourne Magistrates Court for a breach of contract. As you've described it, the shopper claims that she responded to an ad for the sale of a 'manufacturer's discontinued line' of designer leather coats; the ad stated that the 'early' shopper would 'get a bargain'. The shopper complains that Loman's failed to have enough stock for the consumers who responded to the advertisement. Specifically, you have asked for advice on the question whether Loman's breached a contract with the shopper under the circumstances. I note that you have specifically asked us to advise only on the contract law relating to such incidents, and not to address matters of consumer protection law, which would also have direct bearing on the problem.

After researching the issue, and based on the facts set out below, I believe that a court would be likely to conclude that Loman's did not enter into a contract with this shopper because the advertisement was not an offer to sell the coats; thus, there was no contract that Loman's could breach. I will explain this conclusion more fully below after first setting out the facts as I understand them.[a]

Loman's Fashions, a retailer of women's and men's coats, distributed a circular last July advertising designer leather coats at a reduced price of $59.99 that regularly

---

51 Adapted from a letter from Cuny School of Law, 'Drafting a Client Letter', available at http://www.law.cuny.edu/legal-writing/students/client-letter.html, with minor changes to reflect Australian legal practice.

sold for $300.00, since the manufacturer of the coats had discontinued making them. The ad announced that the store would open at 7 a.m. on Friday, July 21, and stated that those who arrived early would secure a bargain. After about fifteen minutes, all the advertised coats had been sold. At 7:30 a.m., a shopper inquired about the coats and was told that there was no stock left. She then complained that Loman's was obligated to sell her a comparably valued designer leather coat at the advertised price. The store manager declined, and the shopper filed a complaint in the Melbourne Magistrates Court, claiming that Loman's had breached a contract by failing to sell the advertised leather coats at the advertised price.

You mentioned to me that the store occasionally gives rain checks when it is possible to replenish supplies of an item that Loman's can purchase at a discount. In this case, the manufacturer had discontinued the line of coats and Loman's was not willing to sell other, designer leather coats at such a drastic markdown. You are concerned that, if the shopper's interpretation were to be honoured, Loman's would have to reconsider its marketing strategies. Although you had assumed that the advertised terms applied only while supplies lasted, your ad had not included language to that effect.b You have asked for this law firm's opinion whether this shopper could succeed on her breach of contract claim.

Under these facts, a court would likely apply the well-settled law that a general advertisement that merely lists items for sale is at best an invitation to negotiate, not an offer to form a contract.[c] The courts that have considered this question focus on two related considerations.[d] The first is whether the advertisement is complete and definite in its terms. For example, where an advertisement containing terms for sale was missing the amount of goods available for sale, a court held that the seller had not made an offer that was complete and definite in all material terms. Thus, no contract was ever made between the seller and a person who submitted a purchase order.[e]

The second consideration is whether an advertisement promises to sell an item in return for something requested, for example, if a storeowner promised to sell an item for a specified price to anyone who came to the store ready to pay that amount.[f] Where such a promise was lacking, a court held that an advertisement by a department store was not an offer but an invitation to all persons that the advertiser was ready to receive offers for the goods upon the stated terms.[g] Even if a person's willingness to purchase the advertised item could be thought to turn the offer into a contract, that court ruled that a purchaser did not have the right to select the item that a seller did not have in stock or was not willing to sell at a reduced price.[h]

Applying these legal rules to Loman's advertisement supports the conclusion that the ad was not an offer to enter into a contract of sale and created no contractual duty in Loman's.[i] Here, the advertisement did not specify the amount of coats to sell, but rather described the leather coats as a 'manufacturer's discontinued line': selling at a substantially reduced price.[j] In addition, the advertisement did not contain a promise to sell the leather coats in exchange for some requested act or promise.[k] Furthermore, the ad did not give the public the right to choose any comparably priced leather coat if the advertised coats were no longer available.[l] Although the shopper here might argue that the advertisement did not contain limiting language, for example, that the coats were for sale while supplies lasted,[m] the ad did state that the store, opening for business on the day of the sale at 7 a.m., was catering to early morning shoppers. By announcing that those who arrived early would secure a bargain, implied that the supplies would run out.[n]

To sum up, based on the facts as I have recited them in this letter, I believe that a court would conclude that Loman's ad did not make an offer to sell leather coats that a purchaser could accept, but that it was at best an invitation to negotiate. Thus, no contract came into existence from this transaction.o To avoid the possibility that Loman's will face future claims on this same point, I would recommend that, going forward, Loman's ads include language such as 'while supplies last', 'first come, first served', or 'quantities limited – no substitutes permitted'. In this way, Loman's would communicate to shoppers that there were no guarantees that they could purchase an advertised item, or a substitute. Although the additional text might increase the cost of advertising, in the long run inserting this additional language in the ads could save you time and the costs involved in defending claims such as this one.[p]

I hope this is helpful, and would be happy to discuss this matter with you further. Please feel free to call my office if you have questions, or would like to set up a time to meet.[q]

Sincerely,
Madala King

a. The opening paragraph states the client's problem and specifies the legal issue on which the client seeks advice. To protect herself against any later claim that she has failed to advise fully, the writer carefully excludes an important and clearly relevant area that is not being discussed. The second paragraph, stating the writer's conclusion, could form part of the first paragraph, but it has been set out by itself for easier reading.
b. This paragraph and the preceding paragraph set out legally significant facts – facts upon which the writer will base her analysis. The factual criteria of the rule for offers under contract law, discussed in the following paragraph of the letter, are the source of the legally significant facts.
c. The writer here restates her conclusion.
d. The writer begins translating the law into relatively straightforward language, without naming specific cases.
e. The writer here offers an example of how the rule would operate and then explains the implication of this analysis: that no contract was formed.
f. The writer explains part of the rule by providing an example.

g. The writer illustrates the point of law by discussing the facts and ruling in a similar case.
h. The writer refers to an alternative holding in the case.
i. The writer restates her conclusion as she moves to an analysis of her client's facts.
j. The writer applies the first part of the rule – relating to definiteness and completeness of material terms – to Loman's facts.
k. The writer now turns to the second part of the rule, requiring a promise in exchange for a requested act or promise, and applies it to Loman's facts.
l. The writer points to facts (specifically, the absence of facts) in Loman's that provide an alternative basis for the writer's conclusion.
m. The writer introduces a possible counterargument.
n. The writer resolves the counterargument in favour of her original conclusion.
o. The writer summarises and restates her conclusion.
p. The writer offers some preventive advice that addresses the possibility of future legal claims and also addresses extra-legal factors – cost and time.
q. The writer invites a follow-up conversation with the client.

3. Resources for Writing Memoranda

Best Guide to Canadian Research, 'Preparing a Legal Memorandum', available at http://legalresearch.org/writing-analysis/legal-memorandum/

Monash University, 'Writing Legal Memos', available at http://guides.lib.monash.edu/law/legalmemos

# CHAPTER 8

# PERSUASIVE WRITING

## I INTRODUCTION

> *The details of legal discourse matter. First and foremost, the details of legal discourse matter because language is the essential mechanism through which the power of the law is realized, exercised, reproduced, and occasionally challenged and subverted.*[1]

As we noted in the previous chapter, legal documents can generally be divided into two types: objective and persuasive.[2] Objective legal documents seek to inform, advise, and counsel. The examples we looked at in the previous chapter included client letters and office memoranda.[3] We emphasised that these documents must be 'scrupulous, balanced, and reliable'.[4] A persuasive document, on the other hand, seeks to argue, convince, and induce action. Examples include appellate briefs, responses and replies.[5] These documents must be 'logical, credible, and compelling'.[6]

'Persuasion' has been defined as 'an attempt to change the beliefs, emotions and behaviours (including language) of others'.[7] Persuasive writing is ubiquitous in contemporary culture: found in advertising, newspaper editorials, blogs, and political speeches.[8] In attempting change, persuasive writing is also educative

1 John M Conley and William M O'Barr, *Just Words: Law, Language, and Power* (2nd ed, University of Chicago Press, 2005) 129.
2 Suzanne E Rowe, 'Legal Research, Legal Writing, and Legal Analysis: Putting Law School into Practice' (1999) 29 *Stetson Law Review* 1193, 1202.
3 Barton and Smith, above n 2, 1.
4 Ibid.
5 Ibid.
6 Ibid.
7 John Wade, 'Persuasion in Negotiation and Mediation' (2008) 8(2) *QUT Law Journal* 253, 253.
8 Time4Writing.com, 'Tips on Writing a Persuasive Essay', available at http://www.time4writing.com/writing-resources/writing-resourcespersuasive-essay/.

writing,[9] so it requires good research, awareness of the reader's biases, and a sound understanding of both sides of the issue. Good persuasive writing demonstrates not only why the writer's opinion is correct, but also why the opposing view is incorrect.[10]

Persuasion is said to be at the heart of the lawyer's craft[11] and ubiquitous in the practice of law:[12]

> [a] lawyer's professional day is largely made up of conversations, oral and written, in which the object is to persuade another to a particular view. In this sense [the lawyer] is a professional rhetorician, and must be concerned with the possibilities of rhetoric as a way of life.[13]

Similarly, Stanchi claims: [w]hether you are a litigator, transactional lawyer, or trial lawyer, part of your job is to persuade people to make decisions, or do things, that they may not have chosen to do but for your intervention'.[14] Flammer claims that, for a litigator, 'persuasiveness of your writing is ... paramount to your success'.[15] This is because of the decrease in oral argument and fewer full trials. Rappaport frames persuasion as something of an ethical obligation: '[l]awyers, as advocates for a client's cause, have an obligation to make their writing not only accessible and understandable, but interesting'. Similarly, Younger stresses the need to ensure that a particular form of persuasive writing, the appellate brief, is written with a view to making it interesting to the court.[16]

Increasingly, persuasive writing takes place in an electronic environment. The electronic platform is becoming, increasingly, the media of choice for persuasive documentation:

> As the judicial community becomes more acclimated to this electronic platform, the legal community must respond with electronic submissions that effectively tap into their sources of the technology and meet the needs of

9 Maria Perez Crist, 'The E-Brief: Legal Writing for an Online World' (2003) 33 *New Mexico Law Review* 49, 67–8.

10 Time4Writing.com, above n 8

11 Kathryn Stanchi 'Persuasion: An Annotated Bibliography' (2009) 6 *Journal of the Association of Legal Writing Directors* 75, 75.

12 Mark DeForrest 'Introducing Persuasive Legal Argument via the Letter from a Birmingham City Jail' (2009) 15 *The Journal of the Legal Writing Institute* 109, 109.

13 James Boyd White, *Heracles' Bow: Essays on the Rhetoric and Poetics of Law* (University of Wisconsin Press, 1985) 4.

14 Stanchi, above n 11, 75.

15 Sean Flammer, 'Persuading Judges: An Empirical Analysis of Writing Style, Persuasion and the use of Plain English' (2010) 16 *Journal of the Legal Writing Institute* 183, 183.

16 Irving Younger, 'Persuasive Writing: Ready, Set, Wait' (1988) *ABA Journal* 122, 122.

> the judicial reader. This means providing a clear and pervasive organizational blueprint for the brief. It means using hypertext effectively to aid both in navigation and to access materials outside the document as needed. It means writing in a style that understands both the constraints and the possibilities inherent in the technology.[17]

## II REFLECT ON THE TASK

### *Purpose and audience*

As in other genres of writing, the advice is to begin by considering purpose and audience. An understanding of both will guide your choices through the writing process, from choosing content, strategy, and organisation to revising. The persuasive writer needs to know at least three things before they begin: the message that needs to be conveyed; the way in which that message will be conveyed; and what the particular audience will do with the message.[18] Indeed, it has been suggested that '[p]ersuasion by written communication depends on the fragile relationship between writers and readers'.[19] Much has been written, in particular, on writing persuasive documentation for busy, time-poor judges and the need to make material concise and interesting.

### *The particulars of the genre*

It has been suggested that all legal writing is persuasive to the extent that the writer is trying to convince the reader that they have a competent command of the subject.[20] Indeed, you will recall that competence is a fundamental professional obligation (ASCR r 4.1.3). But persuasive writing requires a certain approach and particular skills.[21] Meehan says:

> Everything that counsel submits should put into the reader's mind the information and motivation necessary for a favourable decision. Appeal books, factums and everything else are devoted to that goal and nothing less. You're not writing to entertain, show how smart you are, how many

---

17 Crist, above n 9, 93.

18 Nicholas Cowdery, 'The Power of Persuasion – Some Practical Lessons for the Solicitor Advocate' 5, The College of Law CLE Seminar: A Day of Criminal Law 1 March 2008, available at http://www.odpp.nsw.gov.au/docs/default-source/speeches-by-nicholas-cowdery/the-power-of-persuasion---some-practical-lessons-for-the-solicitor-advocate.pdf?sfvrsn=2.

19 Daniel U Smith, 'Persuasive Legal Writing: Ideas to Strengthen the Lawyer's Connection to the Judge' (2009) *Advocate* np, available at plaintiffsappeals.com/pdf/full-articles/Persuasive_Legal_Writing.pdf.

20 Stephen V Armstrong and Timothy P Terrell 'The Rhetoric of Persuasive Writing' (2007) 15(3) *Perspectives: Teaching Legal Research and Writing* 189.

21 Ibid 189.

> authorities you can cite for one proposition, or even writing to inform. You're writing to *persuade*.[22]

Certain aspects of language have been considered specifically relevant to persuasive writing: an understanding of rhetoric; and the use of **narrative** and **metaphor**.

## *An understanding of rhetoric*

To write persuasively, one must have an understanding of rhetoric. This is because 'law and rhetoric have a common cultural and historical heritage, classical and contemporary rhetorical theory offer conceptual frameworks for understanding and learning legal argumentation'.[23] Or, to put it more pragmatically, in order to catch the attention and convince the reader, the messenger needs rhetorical knowledge.[24]

Classical rhetoric largely derives from the work of the Greek theorists Plato and Aristotle.[25] Aristotle defines rhetoric 'as the faculty of observing in any given case the available means of persuasion'.[26] Rhetoric results from the combination of the speaker's character and the quality of speech (or writing) so that it proves the speaker's case and leads the listener to consider the speaker credible.[27] Aristotle maintained that there were three means of effecting persuasion: logos (logical reasoning); ethos (an understanding of human character and goodness in their various forms);[28] and pathos (an understanding of the emotions).[29] Armstrong and Terrell reinterpret these

---

22 Eugene Meehan, 'Strategic Legal Writing: Preparing Persuasive Documents' (2002) 5, available at http://www.jessupcanada.org/problem_related_materials_and_research_tools/STRATEGIC_LEGAL_WRITING.pdf. Original emphasis.

23 Saunders 566 quoted in DeForrest, above n 12, 112.

24 Bret Rappaport, 'Using the Elements of Rhythm, Flow and Tone to Create a More Effective and Persuasive Acoustic Experience in Legal Writing' (2010) 16 *Journal of the Legal Writing Institute* 65, 66, quoting Amundsen. For articles linking persuasive writing to classical rhetoric, see Kristen K Robbins, 'Paradigm Lost: Recapturing Classical Rhetoric to Validate Legal Reasoning' (2003) 27 *Vermont Law Review* 483; Steven D Jamar, 'Aristotle Teaches Persuasion: The Psychic Connection' (2001–2) 8 *The Scribes Journal of Legal Writing* 61; Michael H Frost, 'Ethos, Pathos and Legal Audience' (1994) 99 *Dickinson Law Review* 85.

25 DeForrest, above n 12, 121.

26 Ibid.

27 Ibid.

28 For ethos in persuasive writing, see Beverly J Blair, 'Ethical Considerations in Advocacy: What First-Year Legal Writing Students Need to Know' (1998) 4 *Legal Writing* 109; Elizabeth Fajans and Mary R Falk, 'Shooting from the Lip: *United States v Dickerson*, Role [Im]morality and the Ethics of Legal Rhetoric' (2000) 23 *University of Hawaii Law Review* 1.

29 DeForrest, above n 12, 122. For use of pathos in persuasive writing, see Laura E Little, 'Negotiating the Tangle of Law and Emotion' (2001) 86 *Cornell Law Review* 974; Lynne N Henderson, 'Legality and Empathy' (1987) 85 *Michigan Law Review* 1574; Peter H Huang and Christopher J Anderson, 'A Psychology of Emotional Legal Decision Making: Revulsion and Saving Face in Legal Theory and Practice' (2006) 90 *Minnesota Law Review* 1045.

aspects of rhetoric specifically for persuasion in the context of litigation. Of logos they observe:

> The argument must reflect, and be based carefully within, the systemic reasoning of the law. It must accept the constraints of internal consistency and logical coherence that judges impose on themselves (we hope), even if that means abandoning an attractive line of pseudo-reasoning or an easy **hyperbole**. In effect, judges look for lawyers who can think 'with' them as a professional equal, not an over-the-top advocate for a position. And a worthy argument will be one that produces 'principled' results – results that 'do justice', and can therefore be the basis of judicial pride.[30]

They write of ethos:

> [judges] respond positively to a writer whom they can look 'at' as a professional equal, someone on whom they can rely to argue truthfully, rationally, and calmly. This requires a credible persona, one that has the qualities of veracity and integrity and professionalism – and that does not try to have the judge look down on opposing counsel: Sneering at the other side, although remarkably common, is off-putting to any sensible judge.[31]

And in relation to pathos, good persuasive writing should:

> *evoke* emotion: to lay out calmly a story or an argument that eventually arouses an emotional response in the readers – but a response that seems their own spontaneous reaction rather than one forced on them. The facts are presented in such a way that the reader begins to think, 'Wait a minute. I bet that witness was lying'.

Persuasive writing has also been influenced by the contemporary discipline of argumentation – 'a relatively new branch of philosophy that seeks to study and identify the process and substance of argumentation, particularly logic and rhetoric' – [32] and by communication psychology and advertising.[33]

---

30 Ibid 190.

31 Armstrong and Terrell, above n 20, 190.

32 Stanchi, above n 11, 80. See for example, Kurt M Saunders, 'Law as Rhetoric, Rhetoric as Argument' (2006) 3 *Journal of the Association of Legal Writing Directors* 166; Linda Levine and Kurt M Saunders, 'Thinking Like a Rhetor' (1993) 43 *Journal of Legal Education* 108; Austin Sarat and Thomas R Kearns (eds) *The Rhetoric of Law* (University of Michigan Press 1994).

33 See for example, James Stratman, 'Investigating Persuasive Processes in Legal Discourse' (1994) 17 Discourse Processes 1; Kathryn M Stanchi, 'The Science of Persuasion: An Initial Exploration' (2006) *Michigan State Law Review* 411.

### *Invisibility*

Many commentators emphasise the importance of invisibility to persuasive legal writing. What is meant by invisibility is that the audience appears to come to the writer's conclusion of their own accord:[34] '[t]he best argument is that which seems merely an explanation'.[35] Invisibility is placed in opposition to 'strident advocacy' which, it is argued, is ineffective for a number of reasons: the audience will recognise and unconsciously resist a strategy that is too obvious; strident advocacy may detract from the writer's credibility; and it may offend the audience.[36] At the same time, it is equally unpersuasive to adopt the neutral tone of objective documents.[37]

### *Narrative and metaphor*

Narrative and metaphor are said to be at the core of good persuasive writing:[38]

> Engage the judge by telling a compelling story … Your story needs a logical narrative that leads directly to your desired outcome. The narrative need not be chronological, although a chronological narrative often works best. The events, the characters, and the theory must come together in a credible plot. Maintain the [reader's] focus by starting, developing, and ending your narrative on a high note.[39]

Sheppard also claims that 'narrative is a powerful tool for persuasion',[40] appealing to all three aspects of rhetoric. She suggests that lawyers can become more persuasive by paying more attention to what stories they tell, and to the elements of narrative.[41] Meehan provides some practical ways this can be done:

---

34 Armstrong and Terrell, above n 20, 191.

35 Meehan, above n 22, 2. See also Meehan, above n 22, 18: 'The Harder you Argue the Less Persuasive you are'.

36 Robin Wellford Slocum, *Legal Reasoning, Writing and Other Lawyering Skills* (Lexis Nexis 2006) 363, 363.

37 Ibid 363.

38 See, for example, Jennifer Sheppard, 'Once Upon a Time, Happily Ever After, and in a Galaxy Far, Far Away: Using Narrative to Fill the Cognitive Gap Left by Overreliance on Pure Logic in Appellate Briefs and Motion Memoranda' (2009–10) 46 *Willamette Law Review* 255; Ruth Anne Robbins, 'Harry Potter, Ruby Slippers, and Merlin: Telling the Client's Story Using the Characters and Paradigm of the Archetypal Hero's Journey' (2006) 29 *Seattle University Law Review* 767; J Christopher Rideout, 'Storytelling, Narrative Rationality, and Legal Persuasion' (2008) 14 *Legal Writing* 53; Kenneth D Chestek, 'The Plot Thickens: Appellate Brief as Story' (2008) 14 *Legal Writing* 127.

39 Lucero Hidalgo and Gerald Lebovits, 'Persuasive Writing for Lawyers' (1 November 2009) 3. Practicing Law Institute, available at http://ssrn.com/abstract=1514002.

40 Sheppard, above n 38, 257.

41 Ibid 258.

> 'Figure out what your story is, map out the main components, write it down and then build the necessary legal elements around that framework. Include a couple of simple elements:
>
> - setting your story in a particular time and place;
> - including a human element;
> - some familiar details;
> - simple, ordinary and disarming language;
> - visual words;
> - an event of personal importance that everyone can relate to;
> - an absence of argument (the reader doesn't want to feel like you are manipulating them down a garden path).'[42]

Smith urges attention to the use of metaphor, arguing that metaphor pervades persuasive legal writing, being present on four levels: '(1) the legal principles governing an issue; (2) the tools of analysis applied to the governing principles; (3) the writing style of an advocate who is presenting the legal argument; and (4) the inherent nature of language itself, which serves as the foundation of any written legal argument'.[43] Acknowledging and utilising the ubiquity of metaphor can make us more persuasive writers and advocates: '[m]ake your audience see, experience, and become a part of what you are talking about'.[44] Meehan recommends the use of charts and diagrams to help persuade the reader.[45]

### *Flow*

Flow is an important component of persuasive writing. Rappaport argues that rhythm, flow, and tone are essential to persuasive writing. He claims that 'humans are instinctively attuned to music. So we need to get into the "habit of listening to the words we write"'.[46] Similarly, Dubose advises persuasive writing should flow, 'analytically and lyrically'.[47] Meehan recommends that one way to achieve flow is to:

> Consciously incorporate connectives in your writing. Forget topic sentences – bridge your sentences by creating 'echo' links. This connective technique allows you to cause a figurative echo in your reader's mind by repeating an

---

42 Meehan, above n 22, 12.
43 Michael R Smith, 'Levels of Metaphor in Persuasive Legal Writing' (2006) 58 *Mercer L Rev* 919, 920.
44 Meehan, above n 42, 3.
45 Ibid 11.
46 Rappaport, above n 24, 114 quoting Peck.
47 Kevin Dubose, 'Writing a Persuasive Supreme Court Brief' (nd), available at www.adjtlaw.com/assets/kd_persuasive_brief.pdf.

earlier used word. A subtler technique may be to use a derivative of an earlier word.[48]

Two aspects of flow are language and the logic of distance. In relation to language, the recommendation is to use plain language. Flammer undertook empirical work with judges and found that two-thirds of judges preferred arguments written in plain language, rather than 'legalese'.[49] While acknowledging that pleadings should not be 'too informal' he advises that, 'when making a writing-style decision, it is probably better to err on the side of informality and clarity than formal Legalese'.[50] In relation to distance, it has been suggested that persuasion is a matter of distance and resistance, ie persuasive force = distance x resistance:

> The amount of persuasive force you will need to 'move' a judge's mind from one location to another is a function of the 'distance' you want that judge's mind to go, legally speaking, and the 'resistance' or 'friction' that hinders that movement. Your goal is to reduce the force with which you need to argue by reducing both the distance and the resistance. You point out that your argument requires the judge to go only a very short distance ('You've already taken much the same approach in a very similar case, your honor.'), and your opponent's argument requires a long journey ('Your honor, they are asking you to stretch the law inappropriately.'). And, through clear and concise writing, you reduce the reader's resistance by making it as easy as possible to assimilate your argument.[51]

## Ethics

### Honesty

Certain ethical obligations have been highlighted for persuasive writing. The first is honesty, enshrined in the professional rules: ASCR r 4.1.2. Although, as a lawyer, your task in persuasive writing is to persuade and convince, you must be vigilant that persuasion is not marred by manipulation or deceit.[52] Persuasive writing should always rigorously adhere to the facts and the applicable law, even if these do not support the argument.[53] A particular aspect of honesty in persuasive writing is to acknowledge – and seek to counter – opposing arguments[54] rather than to avoid material that goes against your case. ASCR r 19 requires that a solicitor must not 'knowingly or recklessly mislead the court'; ASCR r 19.6 demands that a solicitor

48 Meehan, above n 22, 7.
49 Flammer, above n 15, 211.
50 Ibid.
51 Armstrong and Terrell above n 20, 190.
52 Stanchi above n 11, 85.
53 Dubose, above n 47, 6.
54 Smith, above n 19.

must inform the court of any binding authority and ASCR r 19.6.1 says the same in relation to any applicable legislation. ASCR r 19.6.3 maintains this is the case even if this goes against the client's case. You may find this challenging, but such acknowledgment can actually enhance your persuasiveness:

> Nothing instills trust more than facing up to your weaknesses. Better it come from you than from your opponent. The right concession not only enhances your credibility, it is itself a persuasive technique and, I may say, an underused technique. A well-timed concession does not merely narrow the focus of the appeal, which judges like, but also makes your strong arguments seem even stronger.[55]

Attempted distortions will be discovered, and so will not only be unsuccessful but will damage your credibility. The legal writer must be 'meticulously accurate and scrupulously honest':[56]

> [h]onesty is both a legal and a rhetorical requirement because your credibility is at stake. If you are not honest at every point, you will lose the credibility battle, and even your valid points may be rejected. Lapses in honesty occur in many ways: exaggeration, misstatement, omission or disregard for the standard of review.[57]

Hidalgo and Lebovits counsel:

> State the facts accurately, clearly, and completely. Do not misrepresent facts, either affirmatively or by omission. Misstatements signal a lack of knowledge of the case or, worse, a desire to avoid unfavorable aspects of your case. Prove your integrity – and make it easy for the court to find your facts – by giving record citations.[58]

In a similar vein, Dubose counsels that legal writing is much more persuasive when the 'writer writes with wisdom rather than with cleverness. Cleverness is shallow, insubstantial, and trivializing ... A wise argument is not only substantively sound, but it also explains why it is the right thing to do'.[59]

The professional rules also highlight honesty in relation to third persons. For instance, a solicitor must not make any statement which grossly exceeds the legitimate assertion of the rights or entitlements of the solicitor's client, and which misleads or intimidates the other person ASCR r 34.1.1. ASCR r 34.1.3 can be interpreted to mean a ban on sneering on opponents, that is, the use of tactics that

---

55 Meehan, above n 22, 17 quoting Justice Laskin.
56 Dubose, above n 47. Meehan, above n 22, 18 makes the same point.
57 Smith, above n 19.
58 Hidalgo and Lebovits, above n 39, 6.
59 Dubose, above n 47, 8–9.

go beyond legitimate advocacy and which are primarily designed to embarrass or frustrate another person.

In addition, solicitors often provide undertakings to others. This can be a personal undertaking from the solicitor, or one given on behalf of a client. Rule 6 of the professional rules specifically deals with these, requiring solicitors to scrupulously observe what they have promised.

### *Courtesy*

Courtesy is an ethic of persuasive writing and, again, this finds expression in ASCR r 4.1.2. In the context of appellate briefs, courtesy is often overlooked, but improper tone or casting aspersions on opposing counsel detract from your arguments and taints your credibility.[60] This issue, again, finds specific expression in the professional rules in ASCR r 21.1. ASCR r 21.1.3 provides that 'A solicitor must take care to ensure that decisions by the solicitor to make allegations or suggestions under privilege against any person must not invoke the coercive powers of the court to harass or embarrass a person'; while ASCR r 21.2 prohibits a lawyer from making allegations or suggestions under privilege against any person that are not reasonably justifiable; and ASCR r 21.5 prohibits lawyers from making suggestions in cross-examination that would diminish the credibility of the evidence of a witness unless she has reasonable grounds to do so. In general terms, ASCR r 4.1.4 requires lawyers to avoid any compromise to their integrity and professional independence. ASCR r 5.1.1 prohibits them from engaging in conduct that would be considered to be prejudicial to or diminish the public confidence in, the administration of justice; or (under ASCR r 5.1.2) bring the profession into disrepute.

Lastly, **gender-neutral** language is considered an ethical obligation of persuasive writing:

> Eliminate sexist language. Sexist language is insulting. And sexist language affects credibility because it makes the judge focus on your style instead of on your content. Sexist language represents the male or female as the norm, gratuitously identifies the referent's gender, and demeans and trivializes.[61]

---

60 William Eich 'Writing the Persuasive Brief' (2003) 76(2) *Wisconsin Lawyer*, available at http://www.wisbar.org/newspublications/wisconsinlawyer/pages/article.aspx?Volume=76&Issue=2&ArticleID=614.

61 Hidalgo and Lebovits, above n 39, 7.

# III OUTLINING AND DRAFTING

## A *keep it simple and clear*

The drafting of persuasive documentation should aim to simplify the law. ASCR r 7.1 states that a solicitor must provide clear and timely advice to assist a client to understand relevant legal issues and to make informed choices about action to be taken during the course of a matter, consistent with the terms of the engagement.

Persuasive writing should thus utilise '[s]imple, direct assertions' as these 'are powerful and command attention'.[62] Persuasive writing should be without superfluous words or distractions;[63] simple, clear and brief and structured for understanding.[64] Smith observes that, in law: '[o]ur subject is complex – applying complex law to complex facts. The cure for this complexity is simplicity in our writing (to the extent the subject allows)'.[65] Similarly, Meehan calls for legal writing that is simple: '[i]deas still need to be big, but to be effective they must be clear and focused. Try to be simple enough that a stranger, preferably even a non-lawyer, can read and understand'.[66] Smith maintains that brevity is at the core of good persuasive writing: brevity is achieved in by eliminating what is unnecessary or redundant, and writing as concisely as possible.[67]

To achieve clarity and brevity, Younger urges careful attention to the first draft:

> Rewriting doesn't always cure the defects of a rushed draft. Whether scrawled on a legal pad or displayed on a monitor, words that are visible take on a permanence that is dangerous. Resisting revision, balking at erasure, first words have a subversive tendency to persist into the final version. Let those first words be less than your best words and your final version will suffer. The remedy is hard work, the hard work that precedes all persuasive writing.[68]

Meehan, relying on work by a Canadian, Judge John Laskin, advises that the persuasive writer should 'Begin Well' (the initial, overview paragraph should tell the reader in a nutshell what the argument is about) and to 'Point First' (always start with the point you are trying to make rather than the details of your argument.

---

62 James W McElhaney, 'A Matter of Style: What It Takes to Make Legal Writing Look Persuasive' (1996) 82 *American Bar Association Journal* 84, 84.
63 Flammer, above n 15, 184.
64 Dubose, above n 47, 7.
65 Smith, above n 19.
66 Meehan, above n 22, 2.
67 Smith, above n 19.
68 Younger, above n 16, 122.

Readers understand information better when they first know why it matters and how it is relevant).

Most commentators recommend careful attention to sentences (keep them to one idea and keep them short); and to paragraphs: '[a] good rule of thumb is that a paragraph should not be so long that it cannot be read aloud in one breath (generally 2–3 sentences). If you have more to say, then break the ideas into separate paragraphs'.[69]

Headings are important to persuasive documentation. Olson advises the writer to draft headings to encapsulate everything discussed underneath them. As he notes, the arguments made under the heading should directly support and relate to the heading; if an argument does not fall directly under the heading but is important, you need to either revise the heading or create a new one, and the heading should not be broader than the ensuing discussion under it. 'Used this way, headings create the discipline necessary to make sure that the argument truly does proceed simply and logically from one idea to the next'.[70] At the same time, headings should not be overused. There should be only 3–5 major headings in a document,[71] and you should not have more than three levels of headings (eg 1.1.2).[72]

Lastly, good persuasive writing utilises authority. Various commentators have explored the meaning of authority in persuasive writing.[73]

## IV REVISING AND EDITING

### *Revising*

It is important to ensure you leave sufficient time to edit and rewrite your documentation – 'clear thinking is the product of a lot of tinkering'.[74] Hidalgo and Lebovits[75] provide an editing process for persuasive writing:

1. Review to improve macro-organisation:
   - Does each paragraph develop a single point?
   - Is discussion of each concept grouped in one place?
   - Is the position of each concept within the whole document appropriate?

---

69 Meehan, above n 22, 7.
70 Robert Olson, 'A Few of my Favourite Things: Tips for Persuasive Writing' (2004) *Verdict* 38, 40.
71 Ibid 39.
72 Meehan, above n 22, 6.
73 Ellie Margolis, '*Closing the Floodgates: Making Persuasive Policy Arguments In Appellate Briefs*' (2001) 62 *Montana Law Review* 59; Robert C Berring, 'Legal Information and the Search for Cognitive Authority' (2000) 88 *California Law Review* 1673; Dan Hunter, '*Teaching and Using Analogy in Law*' (2004) 2 *Journal of the Association of Legal Writing Directors* 151.
74 Meehan, above n 22, 4–5.
75 Hidalgo and Lebovits, above 39, 124.

- Does the first paragraph of each section set a roadmap for the details that follow?
- Do transitions between paragraphs serve to connect the concepts?
- Does the last paragraph in each section reach the conclusion set out in the first paragraph?

2. Review to improve small-scale organisation:
   - Is the first sentence of each paragraph a topic sentence or a transitional sentence that connects one paragraph to the next?
   - Does each sentence express one idea only?
   - Do transitions between sentences connect them to convey the point?
   - Do sentences move from short to long, from simple to complex, and from old to new?
   - Does the last sentence answer that paragraph's thesis?
3. Review the narrative:
   - Have you used stylistic and grammatical devices to persuade?
   - Have you made the best use of rhetorical devices and metaphors?[76]

## *Presentation*

Particular attention should be paid to the presentation of legal documents: typeface, font, whitespace and so on.[77] Meehan observes that lawyers spend much time thinking about what to say and how to say it, but relatively little time organising material on a page. This, he maintains, is a mistake. He argues that an attractive document helps the reader get the point faster and retain it longer: '[a]well-organized easily accessible reader-friendly document is simply more persuasive. Cornflakes in grey boxes don't sell well'.[78] Similarly, Dubose advises to:

> [c]reate a product that is easy on the eyes. Make sure there is ample white space on the page. Make liberal use of spacing. Choose fonts that are comfortable to look at and large enough to be read by readers with declining vision. Make sure the document filed with the Court is clean and free of distracting errors.[79]

Importantly, Meehan urges respect for any page limits imposed by the Court and reminds us that page limits are not an invitation to cram information onto the page: '[t]his tactic defeats the spirit of the page limit, aggravating the judge and ruining the visual impact of your submissions, and maybe ruining your case'.[80]

---

76 Hidalgo and Lebovits, above n 39, 10.
77 McElhaney, above n 62, 85.
78 Meehan, above n 22, 6.
79 Dubose, above n 47, 8.
80 Meehan, above n 22, 20.

# V CONCLUSION

Persuasive writing is an art that is essential to good lawyering. The keys to effective persuasive writing are considering the audience, staying true to purpose, synthesising and simplifying information, and being discriminating in both content and presentation.[81] Persuasive writing is 'accurate, credible, simple, short, and strong arguments supported by good storytelling and citations to authority, all written in clear, concise, precise, and plain English'.[82]

81 Olson, above n 70, 38.
82 Hidalgo and Lebovits, above n 39, 1.

# REVIEW MATERIALS

## SUMMARY

This chapter focused on the writing of persuasive documents, such as appellate briefs, which seek to argue, convince, and induce action. It covered the elements of rhetoric, narrative, and the concepts of flow and invisibility, as well as the ethics of persuasive writing, and set out the process, from reflection to outlining, drafting, revising, editing, and presenting.

## KEY POINTS

1. The aims of persuasive writing are to argue, convince and (sometimes) induce action. These documents must therefore be compelling.
2. Persuasive writing utilises narrative and metaphor and is based in the fundamentals of rhetoric.
3. While seeking to persuade, the legal writer has to ensure that they retain the professional conduct expectations of integrity and civility.
4. Good persuasive writing is simple, clear and well-constructed.
5. In good persuasive writing, the advocacy is said to be 'invisible' rather than strident.

## QUESTIONS FOR REFLECTION

1. In everyday life, when you want to persuade someone to your point of view, what strategies do you use?
2. Why has metaphor been considered a powerful tool of persuasion?
3. Reflect on a piece of writing that you have read (this may be fiction or non-fiction) that has 'flow'. What is it about the writing that induces the sense of 'flow'? Are there aspects of this writing that you could use in your own writing to facilitate 'flow'?
4. What would you consider the elements of 'strident advocacy'? How can those elements be ameliorated to provide 'invisible' persuasion?
5. What are the key elements of narrative? Why are narratives compelling?

## EXERCISES

1. Select a decided case. How is the narrative constructed? What metaphors are used?
2. Reflect on three or four advertisements you have read or watched. Are they persuasive? Why (or why not)?

## FURTHER MATERIALS

Example of persuasive writing for lawyers (persuading the Court):

Evan Schaeffer, 'Five Steps Towards Persuasive Writing', available at http://www.evanschaeffer.com/five-steps-towards-persuasive-writing.html

Justice Davies, 'Effective and Persuasive Written Advocacy' (2013), available at http://www.fedcourt.gov.au/publications/judges-speeches/justice-davies/davies-j-20130807

Troy Simpson, 'Persuading Judges in Writing: Tips for Lawyers and How Technology Can Help' (2007), available at http://www.llrx.com/features/persuadingjudegesinwriting.htm

# CHAPTER 9

# FORM WRITING: STANDARD FORMS AND USE OF PRECEDENTS

## I INTRODUCTION

This chapter continues our consideration of the most common genre structures of professional legal writing and specifically focuses on what we have termed 'form writing'. The word 'form' can have a number of meanings. It can refer to:

- legal documents that are forms – 'a printed document with spaces in which to write';[1]
- a genre, that is, writing that has 'a particular form, content, technique'[2] or has a particular style[3] associated with legal writing; or the elements required when writing the specified documents ('the overall arrangement or breakdown of the unit of writing');[4] and
- a form of reference. This relates to footnoting. Footnotes take the form of providing a source for the text it relates to or may include notes that elaborate on the point made in the text. In both instances, the assumption is that what is in the text should be self-contained, and that anything included in the footnotes only plays a supporting role for the text.[5]

---

1 The Free Dictionary, 'form', available at http://www.thefreedictionary.com/form.
2 Dictionary.com, 'genre', available at http://dictionary.reference.com/browse/genre.
3 The Free Dictionary, 'writing style', available at http://www.thefreedictionary.com/writing+style.
4 Jaro Mayda, 'On Style and Form in Legal Writing' (1962) 31 *Revista Juridica De La Universidad De Puerto Rico* 9, 19.
5 Ibid 20–1.

The first two definitions will inform the initial discussion in this chapter. More specifically, we will be discussing what are commonly called **standardised forms**, with a particular emphasis on standard form contracts and wills. It seems these developments may 'come with a price'[6] both for clients who use the standard forms and for lawyers whose income can be affected by loss of custom.

In the second part of this chapter, we discuss a different use of the word 'form'. This is the practice of using forms and templates – precedents – to draft contracts and pleadings.

## II STANDARDISED FORMS

In recent years, lawyers have moved beyond the use of websites for the purposes of promotion and advertising.[7] In the US, companies such as Docracy, DocStore, LegalZoom and RocketLawyer are making basic legal services like wills or company incorporations available online at a relatively low cost for consumers and small and medium-sized businesses.[8] Similar services are provided in Australia by LawPath. Effectively, these sites offer consumers inexpensive alternatives to paying for the experience, expertise, or assistance of a lawyer in certain circumstances.[9] Such sites allow the public to generate their own legal documents by filling out a standardised form online, resulting in efficiencies and, arguably, increasing access to justice. These forms include powers of attorney, business name registration, and wills. Standardised forms only require those who use them to 'fill in the blanks'.[10]

### *Access to justice or consumer traps?*

Some see these developments as positive, particularly from the perspective of access to justice. Cooper, for instance, notes the significant problem of access to justice in the US and ways in which that problem is being addressed, including standardised forms developed by courts for pro se litigants; adoption of technology to improve the experience of self-representation; and the provision of a variety of legal documents to consumers by LegalZoom and others at a relatively low price. He writes:

> Indeed, in some cases involving routine work – obtaining an uncontested divorce, drafting a simple will, filing a tax return – good forms and/or

6 William A Scott, 'Filling in the Blanks: How Computerized Forms are Affecting the Legal Profession', (2002–2003) 13 *Albany Law Journal of Science & Technology* 835, 836.

7 Lindzey Schindler 'Skirting the Ethical Line: the Quandary of Online Legal Forms' (2012) 16 *Chapman Law Review* 185, 185.

8 Nick Abrahams, 'The Legal Frog is Comfortably Numb' *Lawyers Weekly* 2 July 2014.

9 Schindler, above n 7, 186.

10 Scott, above n 6, 835.

> assistance from a nonlawyer professional might serve consumers just as well as a lawyer and at a lower price.[11]

Increasing numbers of people are now relying on computer-generated wills or do-it-yourself handbooks and websites, bypassing lawyers altogether.[12] It has also been argued that these developments may also stimulate the creation and supply of contractual innovation.[13]

But these developments have been controversial. In the US, LegalZoom was subject to class actions brought on the basis that its website provides services amounting to the unauthorised practice of law.[14] It has been suggested that, on the one hand, such legal actions are based on a desire to protect the public from potentially damaging legal products. There are obviously questions about the suitability of such standardised and generalised materials. As Greene et al recount, a client who sought legal advice after trying some legal software remarked – 'I don't know what I don't know'.[15] This is in keeping with the observation by a US judge, that '[f]orms without knowledge are just useless pieces of paper'.[16] Two types of standardised products, in particular, have given rise to concern.

### *Standard-form contracts*

It is now well known that most commercial transactions rely upon the use of standard-form contracts. Businesses particularly favour them, as they are predominantly contracts that have been 'prepared by providers and presented to consumers on a "take it or leave it basis"'.[17] The terms are not negotiated as between the parties.[18] Indeed, in many cases, the consumer may not even realise what these terms are, as it is believed they simply accept the contracts without reading them (believing that even if they read the terms, they would not understand them).[19] One author suggests

---

11 Benjamin P Cooper, 'Access to Justice Without Lawyers' (2014) 47(1) *Akron Law Review* 205, 209.

12 Edith Greene, Kethera Fogler and Sheri C Gibson, 'Do People Comprehend Legal Language in Wills?' (2012) 26 *Applied Cognitive Psychology* 500, 500.

13 Kevin E Davis, 'Contracts as Technology' (2013) New York University Law and Economics Working Papers, Paper 341, http://lsr.nellco.org/nyu_lewp/341.

14 Schindler, above n 7, 186.

15 Greene et al, above n 12, 500.

16 Cooper, above n 11, 214, quoting Judge Denise S Owens.

17 *George Mitchell* [1983] QB 284, 297 (Lord Denning MR) cited in Jeannie Patterson, 'The Australian Unfair Contract Terms Law: The Rise of Substantive Unfairness as a Ground for Review of Standard Form Consumer Contracts' (2009) 33 *The Melbourne University Law Review* 934, 940.

18 Shmuel I Becher, 'Behavioral Science and Consumer Standard Form Contracts' (2007–2008) 68 *Louisiana Law Review* 117, 119.

19 Wayne Barnes, 'Consumer Assent to Standard Form Contracts and the Voting Analogy' (2009–2010) 112 *West Virginia Law Review* 839, 839.

that this creates a situation of 'forced passivity, power inequalities and commercial privilege'.[20] Ultimately this may result in poor deals for consumers.[21] This is not to suggest that there are no remedies for consumers, but such remedies would also come at a cost in terms of legal fees. For instance, a claim of unfair contractual terms under s 23 of the *Australian Consumer Law*[22] might be made, but in order to prove this, s 24(c) of the same legislation requires the consumer to show 'detriment (whether financial or otherwise) to a party if it were to be applied or relied on'. It is also possible to claim unconscionability, defined by the Full Court of the Federal Court in the case of *Australian Competition and Consumer Commission v Lux Distributors Pty Ltd* [2013] FCAFC 90 at [41], as 'conduct against conscience by reference to the norms of society', but that, too, must be proved.

## *Do-it-yourself wills or will kits*

There are now a number of sites that allow individuals to use published forms to make a will.[23] While this may create a perception that creating a will is easy,[24] this may in fact be far from the truth, and the legislation regulating wills and estates can differ dramatically depending on the jurisdiction. For instance, if a person is divorced in most Australian jurisdictions then any disposition that provides for that person's former spouse will be revoked, but in Western Australia, a divorce revokes the entire will.[25] It is also the case that where a person has superannuation and leaves company assets or has trusts, then these matters are quite complicated. But even simple mistakes made by testators in writing their wills can result in costly litigation to their families.[26]

There are also questions about testamentary capacity, particularly in light of the increasing incidence of Alzheimer's Disease and the fact that, in general, many people sign legal documentation that they have not read or properly understood.[27] At the very least, as Cooper observes, whether these products are effective in allowing consumers to accomplish their legal goals 'is an empirical question that requires continued monitoring'.[28]

---

20 Katherine Hall, 'Power and Privilege: Objectivity, Commercial Interests and Standard Form Contracts' (1997) 6 *Griffith Law Review* 30, 31.

21 Becher, above n 18, 119.

22 *Competition and Consumer Act 2010* Schedule 2.

23 For instance, Online Will Centre: https://www.onlinewillcentre.com.au/?gclid=Cj0KEQiA1NWnBRDchObfnYrbo78BEiQA-2jqBRmZk7aPCB_acD81ktWT-26EiACjj9BCnpxB-J6DDOMaAijM8P8HAQ; and The Australian Will kit - http://www.legalkits.com.au/willkits/.

24 Rod Genders, 'DIY Wills Create Potential for Family Disaster' (2011) 125 (2) *InFinance* 21, 21.

25 Ibid.

26 Ibid.

27 Greene et al, above n 12, 500.

28 Cooper, above n 11, 213.

## *Consumer protection or protection of lawyer monopolies on legal services?*

While consumer protection is a concern, opposition to standardised forms might be attributable to the desire by lawyers with specialised practices, such as estate planning, to protect their businesses against more affordable competitors.[29] Standardised forms may potentially increase competition; commoditise legal services, facilitating consumers to make easier price comparisons; and bring in new entrants, as suppliers of legal services and low cost providers of inputs to lawyers.[30] Indeed, some observers have described the developments in technology that allow the creation and dissemination of these forms, as well as other changes to legal practice, as the 'great disruption' to the role of lawyers in the delivery of legal services:

> And when machine intelligence becomes as good as lawyers in developing some service or some factor of production that contributes to a service, it does not stop improving. Intelligent machines will become better and better, both in terms of performance and cost. And unlike humans, they can work ceaselessly around the clock, without sleep or caffeine. Such continuous technological acceleration in computational power is the difference between previous technological improvements in legal services and those driven by machine intelligence. This difference makes it the single most important phenomenon with which the legal profession will need to grapple in the coming decades.[31]

The opposition to pre-prepared forms might thus be viewed as a means by which lawyers protect their professional monopoly. The argument that lawyers commonly mount is based in the prohibition against the unauthorised practice of law.

Notably, the standardised forms we have discussed predominantly take place without the assistance of a lawyer even though we have noted that this often results in consumers, in the case of contracts, and families, in relation to do-it-yourself wills, paying a high cost when difficulties arise. Individual lawyers have no recourse against those who prepare, sell or provide standardised forms for the public, but an action alleging unauthorised practice may be made, and this is usually pursued by professional bodies or regulators.

---

29 Schindler, above n 7.

30 John O McGinnis and Russell G Pearce, 'The Great Disruption: How Machine Intelligence Will Transform the Role of Lawyers in the Delivery of Legal Services' (2014) 82 *Fordham Law Review* 3041, 3042.

31 Ibid 3041-3042.

### United States

The American Bar Association includes a rule against the unauthorised practice of law in its *Model Rules of Professional Conduct*. Rule 5.5, and Comment [2] explain that:

> [2] The definition of the practice of law is established by law and varies from one jurisdiction to another. Whatever the definition, limiting the practice of law to members of the bar protects the public against rendition of legal services by unqualified persons.

The question to be answered is, of course, 'What constitutes the practice of law?' The variation in meaning across the American states can produce different answers. This accounts for the different results in class action lawsuits claiming that LegalZoom.com, as a national firm which provides consumers in all fifty states with the opportunity to formulate their own legal documents, is guilty of unauthorised practice of law.[32] In Texas, for instance, legislation was passed in 2011 which states that there is no unauthorised practice of law where a company states clearly on its website that the information it provides does not take the place of a lawyer's advice.[33] The South Carolina Supreme Court in 2014 held that LegalZoom was simply acting as a **scrivener** – merely recording 'the customer's original information verbatim', not using any professional judgment or discretion[34] and, therefore, not engaging in the unauthorised practice of law.

While other states have not adopted this principle and still entertain legal complaints against the company, there appears to be some acceptance of companies like LegalZoom by legal ethicists in the US. For instance, Deborah Rhode, who is the director of the Center on the Legal Profession at Stanford Law School, asserts that 'it is time for the legal profession to drop efforts to shut down such companies for UPL and instead focus on how best to regulate them to protect their customers'.[35] Andrew Perlman, director of the Institute on Law Practice Technology and Innovation at Suffolk University Law School, also argues that new regulation is needed to encourage innovative legal services.[36] This acceptance is not universal, however. Milan Markovic, a law academic, maintains that there is no empirical evidence to suggest that companies like LegalZoom are needed as these services are already provided by lawyers. He does concede, however, that if there are legitimate

---

32 Schindler, above n 7, 186.

33 Ibid 186.

34 Karen Rubin, 'LegalZoom: Unauthorized Practice? Or New Legal Services Model?' (2014), available at http://www.thelawforlawyerstoday.com/2014/08/LegalZoom-Unauthorized-Practice-or-new-legal-services-model.

35 Robert Ambrogi, 'Latest legal victory has LegalZoom poised for growth' (2014) *ABA Journal*, available at http://www.abajournal.com/magazine/article/latest_legal_victory_has_legalzoom_poised_for_growth.

36 Ibid.

gaps in legal services, then he would support the introduction of new 'regulatory or licensing schemes that would allow for alternatives'.[37]

### Australia

Currently, lawyer regulation in Australia is still firmly focused on penalising those who are not qualified to provide legal services. All of the Australian jurisdictions regulate legal practice, and the *Legal Profession Uniform Law*, which has been adopted by New South Wales and Victoria, provides in Part 2.1 that non-lawyers are not to provide legal services. These restrictions are sometimes criticised as mechanisms that aim to protect legal work for lawyers, but s 9 of the *Legal Profession Uniform Law* states the objectives of the regulation very clearly:

> 9 Objectives
>
> The objectives of this Part are:
>
> a. to ensure, in the interests of the administration of justice, that legal work is carried out only by those who are properly qualified to do so; and
> b. to protect clients of law practices by ensuring that persons carrying out legal work are entitled to do so.

However – and as is also the case for regulation of lawyers in the United States – determining whether or not there has been unauthorised practice of law depends on the interpretation of 'legal practice'. Guidelines provided by the Law Institute of Victoria are useful, as they refer to:

> 2 (a) drawing documents of a legal nature; and (b) giving advice as examples of legal services, and alternatively that 3 (b) selling of legal documents do not fall into that category.[38]

Further, in *ACCC v Murray* (2002) 121 FCR 428, 448, the Court held:

> This is the essence of legal practice, the advising of a particular person in a particular situation and the production of a document which affects legal rights and which is tailored to the particular needs of that person.

The Court decided in that case that if a provider of legal forms who is not a legal practitioner helps to select the appropriate form, explains terminology, or assists in the completion of the form, that would constitute legal advice. Alternatively, when standardised forms are just supplied without any assistance or advice being given, then this would not be held to be legal practice. This would then seem to suggest

---

37 Ibid.

38 Law Institute of Victoria, 'Unqualified Practice Guidelines', available at http://www.liv.asn.au/PDF/Practising/Ethics/2004GuideUnqualifiedPractice.aspx.

that any software run by non-lawyers, that provides some 'interactive help',[39] may fall into the category of providing legal services, and therefore be illegal as providing unqualified legal advice.

A further recent example of where the provision of a standard form may result in unqualified legal practice is the Advance Care Directive DIY Kit created by the Department of Health and Ageing of South Australia. The Law Society of South Australia's submission to the Minister for Health and Ageing warned:

> In our opinion, the requirement that the witness has 'explained the effects of giving an Advance Care Directive to the person giving this Advance Care Directive' may constitute a breach of s 21 of the *Legal Practitioners Act 1981* leading to a penalty of up to $10,000 (and we highlight that amendments to the *Legal Practitioners Act 1981* will increase the maximum penalty to $50,000).[40]

Obviously the Department was making these proposals in order to assist its consumers. It was not intentionally trying to offend the legal regulation against providing unauthorised legal practice. In this situation it is difficult to be fully convinced of the value of only allowing legal practitioners to carry out tasks that may be defined as practising law. Surely there is also value in allowing certain non-practitioner specialists to encourage consumers to think about completing health directives, delegating their care to those they trust. In fact, in these circumstances it may actually be preferable to allow paralegals to provide advice to consumers, particularly when it is a real possibility that this directive would not happen at all if it could only be created with the assistance of legal practitioners.

### *Lawyers' obligations in completing contracts and wills*

However, while the current system continues to hold legal practitioners wholly responsible for providing legal services, it is important to consider their obligations when they assist consumers with contracts and wills. As highlighted in the definition of 'form' in our introduction, along with standardisation of documents, 'form' can also mean genre, that is, writing that has 'a particular form, content, technique'[41] or has a particular style[42] associated with legal writing or the elements required when writing the specified documents 'the overall arrangement or breakdown of the unit of writing'.[43] Contracts and wills created specifically for clients would fall within this

39 Scott, above n 6, 846.

40 Law Society of South Australia, 'Advance Care Directive', available at https://www.lawsocietysa.asn.au/submissions/140328_Draft_Advance_Care_Directive_DIY_Kit.pdf.

41 Dictionary.com, above n 2.

42 The Free Dictionary, above n 3.

43 Mayda, above n 4, 19.

definition of 'form', as they need to include particular elements and comply with statutory requirements (for example, statutes dictate that some contracts and all wills must be in writing).

While this chapter will not focus on the legal elements to be included in contracts and wills, as any competent lawyer should be aware of these (ASCR r 4.1.3), it will consider a lawyer's duty, in terms of how they should act for the client, as set out in the legal professional rules.

As might be expected, lawyers are required to 'follow a client's lawful, proper and competent instructions' (ASCR r 8.1) and to act in the best interests of the client (ASCR r 4.1.1). However, in doing so they need to recognise that their paramount duty is to the court and the administration of justice (ASCR r 3.1). In practical terms this includes guarding their independence, ensuring that they 'not act as the mere mouthpiece of the client' (ASCR r 17.1) and more generally ensuring that they 'avoid any compromise to their integrity and professional independence' (ASCR r 4.1.4) or avoid engaging in conduct that will 'diminish the confidence of the public in the administration of justice' (ASCR r 5.1.1) or 'bring the profession into disrepute' (ASCR r 5.1.2).

Taken together, the rules provide that lawyers 'have a broader function than solely delivering focused legal advice for clients'.[44] This function extends to encouraging their clients to consider the consequences of their decisions on their family, peers, and ultimately on the community as a whole,[45] when they are formulating contractual terms. This implies that lawyers should encourage clients to reflect on adjusting contractual terms that may very well be legal, and may not go so far as to be unfair, but may potentially be burdensome on the other parties involved. Taking this approach may avoid the matter being litigated and thus reduce the demand for public resources being expended or alternatively free up the court system to deal with more contentious issues.

A similar example can apply to lawyers advising clients who are making their wills. Lawyers in that situation, have the opportunity to advise the will-maker to think more carefully about those who have an expectation that they will be beneficiaries under the will. The inclusion of explanatory clauses may very well avoid emotional distress, family provision claims, and consequently avoid the use of estate funds for legal costs.[46]

---

44 Ronit Dinovitzer, Hugh P Gunz and Sally P Gunz, 'Reconsidering Lawyer Autonomy: The Nexus Between Firm, Lawyer, and Client in Large Commercial Practice' American Business Law Journal (2014) 51 (3) *American Business Law Journal* 661, 718.

45 Mark Tushnet, 'Citizen as Lawyer, Lawyer as Citizen' (2008–9) 50 *William and Mary Law Review* 1379, 1387 n 39.

46 Lillian Corbin, 'Australian Lawyers as Public Citizens' (2013) 16 (1) *Legal Ethics* 58, 70.

It should also be noted that there are some very specific rules regarding possible conflict situations between lawyers advising clients about their wills. For instance ASCR r 12.4.1 warns that a lawyer who is to be appointed as an executor under the client's will must advise the client that she would be entitled to claim executor's commission and legal costs in relation to the administration of the estate. In addition, the lawyer is obliged to advise the client that if another person is appointed, then no executor's commission may be claimed.

While considering a lawyer's duties regarding acting for clients, it should also be noted that s 47(6) of the *Legal Profession Uniform Law* allows Australian legal practitioners to be charged with supervising others such as non-lawyer employees, or those whose practising certificate is conditional upon them being supervised. This obliges supervising lawyers to be responsible for the work completed by those they are supervising for clients. (Supervising lawyers cannot themselves have a practising certificate subject to a condition requiring them to engage in supervised legal practice: s 49.)

## III PRECEDENTS: USE OF FORMS AND TEMPLATES

There is another use of the word 'form'. This is not a form in the 'fill in the blanks' sense, but an actual document the lawyer or someone she works with has used previously.[47] Although law school stresses the importance of originality and the need to produce independent, non-plagiarised work, much writing in legal practice is rather different. First, legal writing is often collaborative: practitioners frequently employ associates and junior lawyers to draft documents under supervision. Second, copying is the norm rather than the exception. Lawyers often borrow from the writings of others, particularly in the preparation of transactional documents but also for letters, court documents and other types of non-transactional documents.[48]

Use of precedents saves time and money: '[t]he time and expense that would result from writing everything from scratch would be enormous'.[49] Use of forms and templates may influence consistency in interpretation. Indeed, it has been argued that one reason legal language is often archaic is that lawyers repeat wording verbatim, repeatedly, so as to avoid inconsistency or variation in interpretations.[50] Even in litigation, lawyers may 'borrow' language from a document that was successful in

---

47 Claire A Hill, 'Why Contracts Are Written in Legalese' (2001) 77 *Chi-Kent Law Review* 59, 59. Available at: http://scholarship.kentlaw.iit.edu/cklawreview/vol77/iss1/5Hill, 59.

48 Wayne Schiess 'Legal Writing Is Not What It Should Be' (2009) 37 *Southern University Law Review* 1, 10.

49 Ibid.

50 KK DuVivier, *Nothing New Under the Sun-Plagiarism in Practice* (2003) 32 *Colorado Lawyer* 53, 53.

another case.[51] As DuVivier points out, '[o]ur precedent-based system emphasizes consistency over originality and bases ideas on those of others in the past'.[52]

Use of forms and precedents may be efficient, but it can also be dangerous. Over time, forms evolve, often for the better, with improvements and correction of mistakes. But the evolution of forms can lead to their unnecessary length and complexity and a failure to address ambiguities.[53] Schiess identifies four problems with the use of forms: first, forms can lead to rushed and lazy writing because they are easy to use; second, forms are often outdated in style and language; third, forms usually have text and terms originally written by several different writers. They are thus often a 'hodgepodge' of inconsistent styles and ambiguities and can lead to confusion; fourth, lawyers generally add to, but do not delete from, forms. The resulting document can thus contain unnecessary language, irrelevant text, and 'extra stuff that isn't needed'.[54] Schiess recommends that lawyers should be more systematic about forms and their use; and that the legal office should prepare and maintain a database of up to date forms.[55] In addition, lawyers need to be careful to customise a form or previously drafted document for a new client's purpose:[56] '[e]ven though work environments are becoming more rationalised and mechanised, the essence of professional work is still the largely intangible application of individual creativity, experience and judgment'.[57]

There is, of course, an ethical issue here about the unacknowledged use of earlier work. But because of the customary use of forms and reuse of client materials is the norm, it is unusual for plagiarism allegations to be brought against lawyers, although it has happened. And in 2002, a New York law firm threatened action for copyright infringement against other lawyers, sending cease and desist letters to a number of law firms, demanding that they stop copying and using the firm's pleadings.[58] Bast and Samuels argue that standards should be enforced in legal practice against plagiarism:

> a [practising] attorney should not be excused if he or she borrows from a copyrighted work. Additionally, even with transactional documents and

---

51 Carol M Bast and Linda B Samuels, 'Plagiarism and Legal Scholarship in the Age of Information Sharing: The Need for Intellectual Honesty' (2008) 57 *Catholic University Law Review* 777, 804.
52 DuVivier, above n 50, 53.
53 Hill, above n 47, 60.
54 Schiess, above n 48, 11–12.
55 Ibid 12.
56 DuVivier, above n 52, 54.
57 Marion Brivot, 'Controls of Knowledge Production, Sharing and Use in Bureaucratised Professional Service Firms' 24, available at http://spectrum.library.concordia.ca/7742/1/Brivot_M__2010.pdf.
58 Janet L Conley, 'Firm Claims Its Words are Stolen' (2002) *National Law Journal* A21, in Bast and Samuels, above n 51, 805.

> pleadings, an argument can be made that the clients have the right to know the source of the attorney's work. Therefore, in the future, the plagiarism standard for practitioners should move closer to that for original scholarship.[59]

The use of forms and templates in law is not new: McGinnes and Pearce trace the practice back to the Middle Ages. But what is new is the use of computer intelligence to generate legal documents and further efficiencies. McGinnes and Pearce recount the story of one law firm in Silicon Valley that developed a program for automatically developing documents for the incorporation of startups:

> their technology officer, said: 'It reduced the average time we were spending from about 20 to 40 hours of billable time down to a handful of hours … In cases with even extensive documents, we can cut the time of document creation from days and weeks to hours.

McGinnes and Pearce predict that advances in technology will enable the automatic creation of forms, tailoring them to specific facts and legal arguments, and tracking the effects of the form in future litigation so that, in 10 to 15 years, the first draft of most transactional documents will be computer-generated.[60]

Of course, ethical issues can attach to this reproduction of documents. Is it ethical to charge the original client for the amount of time taken to create the document when it is recognised that the document will be used repeatedly over many years? Similarly, is it ethical to charge repeat clients the same fee as the original client when the time taken to create their documents is minimal compared with that taken for the original document?[61]

## IV CONCLUSION

In this chapter, we have considered the issues relating to the provision of forms – standard form contracts and wills. We noted the tensions between access to justice, protection of consumers and protection of the lawyers' monopoly over legal services. We also considered forms in the sense of the use of precedents and noted issues relating to repeated use of documents, such as length, wordiness, repetition of errors and ambiguities.

What is common to both these discussions, however, is the disruptive impact of new technologies on lawyering. McGinnes and Pearce observe that, as the exponential impact of machine intelligence on lawyering increases, it will alter at

59 Bast and Samuels, above n 51, 810.

60 McGinnis and Pearce, above n 30, 3051.

61 C Parker and A Evans, *Inside Lawyers' Ethics* (Cambridge University Press, 2007) 207.

least five areas of legal practice significantly: discovery, legal search, generation of documents, creation of briefs and memoranda, and predictive analytics. Eventually, they argue, much lawyering will be overtaken by machine intelligence as it is faster and more efficient than many lawyers in providing those services. Their prediction is that this will mean a major, and irreversible upheaval in the legal services market:

> Lawyers will continue to provide services that cannot be commoditized if they are superstars, practice in highly specialized areas of law subject to rapid change, appear in court, or provide services where human relationships are central to their quality. Otherwise, no effective barriers to the advance of machine lawyering in legal practices exist – not even in the law and ethics of lawyering. Lawyers will continue to embrace machine intelligence as an input and fail to prevent nonlawyers from using it to deliver legal services. Ultimately, therefore, the disruptive effect of machine intelligence will trigger the end of lawyers' monopoly and provide a benefit to society and clients as legal services become more transparent and affordable to consumers, and access to justice thereby becomes more widely available.[62]

62 McGinnis and Pearce, above n 30, 3065–6.

# REVIEW MATERIALS

## SUMMARY

This chapter considered genres of professional writing that rely on standard forms and precedents, focusing on issues arising from their use rather than process. It considered ethical issues including access to justice and consumer protection in regard to situations where online templates are available and computerisation makes reproduction of forms and precedents easy.

## KEY POINTS

1. Technological advances are rapidly changing the practice of law.
2. Standardised legal documents offer savings to the consumer, but are not always appropriate.
3. Although there is increasing use of the internet to provide legal forms and precedents, there are some concerns that such practices may constitute unauthorised practice of law.
4. Much legal work relies on the use of pre-existing forms and precedents, but these should always be used carefully and thoughtfully and tailored to the matter at hand.
5. Although the customary use of forms and reuse of client materials is the norm, the practice does raise ethical issues.

## QUESTIONS FOR REFLECTION

1. What is meant by the unauthorised practice of law? Is the prohibition against unauthorised practice justified, or monopolistic? Justify your answer.
2. Do you consider that technological advances in the provision of legal services are of benefit to the profession? Why?
3. What does it mean to act as 'the mere mouthpiece of the client'? Why do the professional rules express concern about this practice?
4. Ethically, is it wrong to use a precedent from another legal firm without the firm's permission? Why?
5. What are the advantages and disadvantages of using pre-existing forms and precedents?

## EXERCISES

1. Non-lawyers and unqualified legal practice

   There are now a number of organisations owned by non-lawyers, such as *LegalZoom*, *SmartLegalForms*, and *WhichDraft*, which take information fed into their systems over the internet and use specialised document assembly software to generate documents for clients, who can then submit those to courts.[63]

   In your opinion:

   - Should the non-lawyer owners of these websites be found guilty of unqualified practise of law?
   - If you think there is value in clients accessing online legal information, should this be a priority over the goal of protecting the public?

2. Plagiarism

   Which of the following are examples of plagiarism?[64] Justify your answer.

   a. A lawyer uses large portions of an article posted on a law firm's website in a brief filed with the court without referring to the law firm as the author.
   b. A lawyer uses language from a set of pleadings drafted by a fellow lawyer in your firm.
   c. A lawyer uses language from a set of pleadings drafted by a lawyer from another firm, or from a judicial opinion.
   d. A lawyer incorporates language into a contract they are drafting taken from a contract drafted by lawyers in another firm.
   e. A lawyer is asked to sign a set of pleadings drafted by other lawyers in their firm.

3. Completing a power of attorney

   Put yourself in the place of a lay person and complete an Enduring Power of Attorney. You will find a form at http://www.lpi.nsw.gov.au/__data/assets/pdf_file/0010/187282/Enduring_PoA.pdf.

   You may want to read the fact sheet that the government provides for this purpose: http://www.lpi.nsw.gov.au/__data/assets/pdf_file/0009/25947/PoA_Fact_Sheet.pdf.

   In your opinion, would a lay person be likely to feel confident completing this form?

---

63 Marc Lauritsen, 'Liberty, Justice and Legal Automata' (2013) 88(3) *Chicago-Kent Law Review* 945, 947.

64 This exercise has adapted examples referred to in Diane B Kraft, 'When is Copying OK in Legal Writing?' (2013) *Law Faculty Popular Media* Paper 5, available at http://uknowledge.uky.edu/law_facpub_pop/5.

## FURTHER RESOURCES

1. Report of the Summit on the Use of Technology to Expand Access to Justice (2013): http://www.lsc.gov/media-center/publications/report-summit-use-technology-expand-access-justice.
2. Law Institute of Victoria, 'Warning on Unqualified Legal Advice': http://www.liv.asn.au/Practice-Resources/News-Centre/Media-Releases/Media-Release-Archive/Warning-on-Unqualified-Legal-Advice.
3. Jason Harrop, 'Document Product Strategy: Optimizing Precedent Investment for Higher Profits and Better Service', Law and Technology Resources for Legal Professionals: http://www.llrx.com/features/precedent.htm.

# CHAPTER 10

# TECHNICAL WRITING

## I INTRODUCTION

'Technical writing', sometimes called 'technical communication', refers to communications that provide information to users who need to accomplish a defined goal or task.[1] It focuses upon direction, instruction or explanation. The key to technical writing is the creation of clear and organised content.[2] Technical writing, in fact, encompasses a range of products, including reports, instruction manuals, policy manuals, white papers, proposals, training materials and so on. It has been observed that, 'students who are expected to write in technical and professional settings need to develop multiple literacies'.[3]

In this chapter we consider very specific forms of technical writing relevant to law: report writing and legislative drafting. Although students and those with legal training may commonly be expected to write reports, relatively few will experience legislative drafting. However, it may be that, during your time as a student, you are asked to draft a legislative provision as an assignment. We have thus provided the basics of drafting. This is a highly specialised skill and we cannot pretend to offer more than the basics.

The key principles behind technical writing are the same as the principles we have highlighted throughout this book: know your purpose and audience, write clearly and in a non-personal style; and ensure your research is thorough and accurate. As we will see, however, there are some specific ethical issues involved in both reports and legislative drafting.

---

1 Susan Bodnick, 'What is Technical Writing?', available at http://online-learning.com/technical-writing/.

2 Ibid.

3 Florence Elizabeth Bacabac, 'Creating Professional ePortfolios in Technical Writing' (2013) 27(1) *Journal of Business and Technical Communication* 91, 93 citing Jablonski and Nagelhout.

## II REPORTS

A report is a systematic, well-structured document that defines, analyses and presents information succinctly and clearly. Generally, the purpose of a report is to either account for actions; to provide 'accurate, timely, objective and concise information to make effective decisions';[4] to record progress, to present the findings of an investigation or project; or to make proposals or recommendations for change.

Effective reports have been described as a combination of science and art, particularly where the report is seeking to persuade the reader to take action.[5] Interestingly, research suggests that many professionals believe that they write clear and accessible reports. This belief may not be well founded – a rather different assessment is given when the report is rated objectively, or by typical readers of reports.[6]

### *Reports and their conventions*

Reports are written in sections, separated by numbered headings and subheadings. In common with most formal writing, the report will have an introduction, a main body, which will detail findings where these are appropriate, and a conclusion. Often, however, reports use other, specific sections.

### *Executive summary*

Executive summaries are generally included in longer reports, and provide the reader with a succinct general statement of the aims, scope and methodology of the project, key findings and main conclusions (including recommendations where appropriate). An executive summary is generally no more than 10 per cent of the overall length of the report.

### *Terms of reference*

The terms of reference of a report define the task, its scope and limitations, who the report is for, and the timescale for the report.

### *Recommendations*

Most reports include recommendations for action. Recommendations should be specific, measurable, realistic and achievable.[7] They should generally be numbered.

---

4 JP Bowman and BP Branchaw, *Business Report Writing* (Chicago: The Dryden Press, 2nd ed) 12.

5 Sarah M Mastoras, Emma A Climie, Adam W McCrimmon and Vicki L Schwean, 'A C.L.E.A.R. Approach to Report Writing: A Framework for Improving the Efficacy of Psychoeducational Reports' (2011) 26(2) *Canadian Journal of School Psychology* 127 at 129, citing Applebaum 1970.

6 Ibid 132.

7 Judith Wiener and Laurie Costaris, 'Teaching Psychological Report Writing: Content and Process' (2012) *Canadian Journal of School Psychology* 119, 122.

### *Tables and graphics*

Reports often use tables and other illustrative figures, such as graphs, diagrams and charts, to present data. These should assist the reader's understanding of the ideas, not just repeat written information.

### *Appendices*

The appendix contains detailed information that the author does not want to include in the main body of the text, often because that information is long or complicated and would break the coherence of the text. Such documentation might include, for example, questionnaires used, organisations or individuals who contributed to the report, tables and charts or technical information. Anything used in the appendix should be referred to in the main body of the report.

### *Glossary*

Some reports will include a glossary to detail acronyms or specialised vocabulary. We have included a glossary in this text in the Learning Materials section, so you can turn to that as an example.

## *Researching your report*

Use the key concepts and issues to generate key words for your research. You might wish to review Chapter 3 on researching. Information should be gathered from a variety of sources and documented. These sources should be authoritative, current, reliable and relevant. In particular, if you are doing a report on a particular organisation, don't solely rely on information from that organisation.[8]

Part of the challenge in writing a report is to put the information into an easy to understand format to instruct those who read it. The more unfamiliar your audience is with the material you are presenting, the more information you will need to gather and explain.

## *The process of writing a report*

### *Reflect on the brief*

The first step is to clearly understand your purpose. Analyse your brief to ensure you know and understand the topic, question or case; the purpose of the report; and who the report is for. What is the objective of your report: is it to inform? to argue? to persuade? to evaluate? What does your reader want to see in the report, and what

---

8 University of Melbourne, 'Business Reports', available at http://library.unimelb.edu.au/__data/assets/pdf_file/0004/1226839/Business_Reports.pdf.

will they do with it?[9] One reason your intention is so important is that it focuses the report. Feierman[10] also argues that report writers must be discriminating and ask from the beginning: 'What are the most important things I want to communicate about this topic? What will probably be worth putting in the executive summary?'

In terms of ethical rules, writers of reports should ensure that they write clearly (ASCR r 7.1); write the report in accordance with the client's instructions (ASCR r 8.1); and present findings independently (ASCR r 17.1).

### *Reflect on the audience*

A report may have a number of potential readers, all with different levels of prior knowledge and expertise in the area. Indeed, reports are often written by people with specific expertise, but read by generalist readers. An expert reader will understand certain abbreviations, acronyms and jargon in a particular field. A novice may not understand them, however, so such usages need to be made accessible. In order to ensure your report can be easily understood, consider:

- the prior knowledge of the audience with the subject;
- the experience of likely readers with the background information, technical language, concepts and contexts covered in the report;
- the interest of the audience in the topic;
- the questions or objections they may have with the issues;
- whether the audience is internal to an organisation, or external or both;
- if internal, whether the audience is up, across or down the hierarchy of the organisation;
- what sort of reaction you wish to incite.[11]

Feierman argues that, in fact, the first principle of effective report writing is 'know your reader'.[12] She claims too many report writers imagine their readers going through their reports page by page in a printed form, but many readers read reports on laptops, tablets and smartphones:

> Multitasking, busy readers demand that they receive essential information quickly. Today's readers are impatient – they don't like to scroll down to find the conclusion. They also have short attention spans, so they expect to receive

---

9 Birmingham City University, 'How to Write a Report', available at http://library.bcu.ac.uk/learner/writingguides/1.02%20Reports.htm.

10 Joanne Feierman 'The 7 Deadly Sins of Report Writing' (2012) 61(4) *Journal of Government Financial Management* 50, 51.

11 Drawn from University of Melbourne, above n 8 and Guarav Kapoor and Connie Valencia 'Effective Audit Report Writing' (2013) *The CPA Journal* 36.

12 Feierman, above n 10, 51.

> only essential information. They want to see an executive summary on the first screen. The days of long introductions are gone.[13]

Kapoor and Valencia make a similar point: readers should be able to understand the purpose, value, and results of the report within the first few moments of reading.[14]

## *Drafting the report*

Like all other forms of writing we have covered in this book, writing a report is an ongoing and recursive process of writing and rewriting. With reports, it is generally easier to write parts of the body first, then the conclusions, the introduction and lastly the executive summary (if you are using one).

Effective reports are accurate, clear, succinct and well structured. There is a strong consensus in advice on writing reports that you should:

- always use plain language, that is, clear and concise English, avoiding jargon and colloquial language;[15]
- keep sentences and paragraphs short;[16]
- write in an impersonal and objective style (that is, from a third person perspective);
- balance the need for description and detail with the need to be succinct. You need to be discriminating to only include important and relevant information;[17]
- use the active voice;[18]
- use images where appropriate to assist the reader's understanding;[19]
- ensure you leave enough time to review and edit the draft report.[20]

On the last point, RMIT provides a helpful editing checklist for reports.

> Have you:
>
> - clarified the purpose and audience?
> - selected the most appropriate text type (memo report, long report, etc)?
> - used the correct format?
> - explained the purpose of the report?
> - defined the problem?
> - included all the information needed?

---

13 Ibid.
14 Kapoor and Valencia, above n 11, 36.
15 Feierman, above n 10, 51.
16 Jack Caldwell, 'Technical writing for consultants' reports: Some dos and don'ts' (2013) Australian Mining, available at http://www.miningaustralia.com.au/features/technical-writing-for-consultants-reports-some-dos; Feierman, above n 10, 51; Kapoor and Valencia, above n 11.
17 Kapoor and Valencia, above n 11.
18 Ibid.
19 Ibid.
20 Feierman, above n 10, 52.

- deleted unnecessary information?
- presented factual and objective information?
- organised the information logically and clearly?
- formatted appropriate headings and subheadings?
- written language appropriate to the purpose and audience?
- used 'spell check' and 'grammar check'?
- written paragraphs with clear subjects and purposes?
- summarised the contents and findings?
- made recommendations that offer solutions to any problems mentioned?[21]

## III LEGISLATIVE DRAFTING

### *What is legislative drafting?*

Legislative drafters are lawyers who prepare bills which may later become law. Legislative drafting is the expression of legislative policy as law;[22] the process of constructing a text of legislation.[23] It is the framework by which governments seek to achieve their purposes.[24] Legislative drafting has been described as difficult, extremely onerous, exacting and highly skilled. Crabbe argues that what is conceived in the mind might not be easily expressed with clarity and precision in language; and even where something is relatively easy to express, it may be difficult to do in a way that avoids misunderstanding. Legislative drafting is not a task:

> for children, amateurs and dabblers. It is a highly technical discipline, the most vigorous form of writing outside of mathematics. Few lawyers have the special combination of skills, aptitudes and temperament necessary for a competent draftsman.[25]

He argues that legislative drafters must have capacity in the use of legislative language; experience in legal practice; an interest in drafting; a systematic and orderly mind; the ability to pay meticulous attention to detail; and the ability to work with accuracy under pressure.[26] Stefanou adds to that list the ability to research

---

21 Study and Learning Centre, RMIT University, 'Writing a Report', available at https://www.dlsweb.rmit.edu.au/lsu/content/pdfs/2_assessmenttasks/super_report.pdf.

22 VCRAC Crabbe, 'The Ethics of Legislative Drafting' (2010) 36(1) *Commonwealth Law Bulletin* 11, 16.

23 Helen Xanthaki 'Legislative Drafting: A New Sub-Discipline of Law is Born' (2013) 1(1) *IALS Student Review* 58, 58.

24 Crabbe, above n 22, 15.

25 Ibid 12.

26 Ibid.

background knowledge;[27] while Webster argues that it is not a job suited to those who crave the limelight:

> by all standards, it is a backroom job, without any of the glamour of starring in court appearances which so appeals to young aspiring advocates in developing countries. No press headlines for the successful drafter, as for the successful advocate. Instead, if a Bill is a winner, the credit is the Minister's, whereas if it is a disaster, blame the drafter.[28]

Despite the importance of legislative drafting, it has recently been suggested that there is a lack of training on the legislative process, statutory interpretation and legislative drafting provided at law school,[29] and overall there is a general lack of training.[30] Legislative drafting has traditionally been seen as a practical, rather than an academic, subject.[31] Generally, the presumption has been that legislative drafters will receive 'on-the-job training', though some question whether this is now a reality.[32] Further, Butt and Castle observe that few of those entering law today are familiar with grammar or have been trained in the important analytical skills associated with drafting.[33] Xanthaki notes:

> Until recently legislative drafting was viewed as a mere skill, normally and mostly, served by government lawyers. The idea was that the drafting of legislation was nothing more but know-how learnt via mentoring by brilliant lawyers whose job was to basically switch the table round from the normal lawyer's task of statutory interpretation of existing legislation to the extra-ordinary task of drafting legislation with a vision on how this would be interpreted by the others. But things have changed. Legislation became the focus of regulation, replacing the common law in the preference of regulators.[34]

---

27 Constantin Stefanou, 'Is Legislative Drafting a Form of Communication?' (2011) 37(3) *Commonwealth Law Bulletin* 407, 415.

28 Robin Webster 'Teaching Legislative Drafting: Reflections on the Commonwealth Secretariat Short Course' (2010) 36(1) *Commonwealth Law Bulletin* 41, 41.

29 Tonya Clinton Jaja, 'Teaching Legislative Drafting: The Necessity for Clinical Legal Education' (2012) 14(1) *European Journal of Law Reform* 104, 108.

30 Crabbe, above n 22, 12.

31 Webster above n 28, 44.

32 Jaja, above n 29, 111.

33 In Edwin Tanner, 'Clear, Simple and Precise Legislative Drafting: Australian Guidelines Explicated Using an EC Directive' (2004) 25(3) *Statute Law Review* 223, 224.

34 Xanthaki, above n 23, 57.

## *Reflecting on audience*

The primary audiences for legislative drafting are the Parliament and the courts. Bills as drafted must comply with parliamentary procedure and the expectations that the bill is self-explanatory and that it is arranged so as to facilitate orderly debate.[35] But beyond these primary audiences and their expectations, legislation governs the actions and affairs of the public. Greenberg considers the public to be the 'ultimate' client for legislative drafting.[36] Thus, in the contemporary context, there is considerable effort invested in improving the readability and accessibility of legislation.[37] Legislation is a form of communication and given its importance to citizen activity, it is important that the legislative message is 'loud and clear'.[38]

Because there are different audiences for legislative drafting, however, the task can be difficult, each reader bringing 'to the process of interpretation a unique set of preconceptions, life experiences and understanding of language'.[39] This means that:

> Without the opportunity to sit down individually with each reader and explain the legislation personally, the drafter is bound to fail in the task of conveying the same message to all his or her readers. At best, the drafter can hope to convey a message which is similar enough (for practical purposes) to enough of the readers (ideally, including any judges called on to interpret the legislation).[40]

## *The process*

The process of drafting, like other forms of writing we have discussed, is always iterative[41] but it does require considerable preliminary work: 70 per cent of the effort is in working out what is needed and only 30 per cent involves getting the words down on paper.[42]

Most elements of the drafting process are similar in the Australian states and territories. Some aspects of the management of legislation are rather different; in general, but not always, the state or territory processes are slightly less formal.[43]

---

35 Crabbe, above n 22, 16.

36 Daniel Greenberg, 'The Nature of Legislative Intention and Its Implications for Legislative Drafting' (2006) 27(1) *Statute Law Review* 15, 26.

37 Esther Majambere, 'Clarity, Precision and Unambiguity: Aspects for Effective Legislative Drafting' (2011) 37(3) *Commonwealth Law Bulletin*, 417, 418.

38 Xanthaki, above n 23, 61.

39 Hilary Penfold, 'Legislative Drafting and Statutory Interpretation' (2006) 7 *Judicial Review* 471, 481.

40 Ibid.

41 Ibid.

42 Ibid 478.

43 Ibid 471.

The first stage is that the department or agency with policy responsibility for the proposal gives 'instructions' to parliamentary counsel. These instructions are vital, but it is perhaps particularly important for the drafters to carefully craft the 'objectives' section of a bill as this is heavily relied upon when the bill becomes an Act and the courts are interpreting the law. Penfold notes that the manner and form of these instructions will vary from bill to bill, but generally, initial instructions are in writing and attempt to set out the details of what the proposed bill should achieve. On rare occasions, policy officers may provide a draft bill by way of instructions.[44]

The second stage concerns the drafting of the bill. In some cases, the written instructions provided will be adequate. In others, the drafter may identify a number of issues that need to be discussed and will contact the instructors to arrange that discussion. The discussion may resolve the issues, or there may be a need to seek further advice from other agencies or further policy development may be needed. This stage may result in a preliminary draft bill or production of an 'outline', a document preliminary to drafting which details concepts, the elements of the bill, matters not to be dealt with by the bill and so on.[45] Only after these are resolved will the bill be drafted. In order to achieve a high degree of clarity, Crabbe reminds us that '[i]t may be necessary to revise the draft of a bill many, many times. 'Pride of authorship requires patient consideration and comparison of constructive suggestions for improvement from every source'.[46]

The third stage involves approval for the introduction of the bill. Once the bill is verified within the drafting team, completed to the satisfaction of the instructors and verified by other relevant departments and agencies,[47] it is submitted for introduction.[48] Penfold writes with specific reference to the Commonwealth process, in which case, the bill is submitted to the Department of the Prime Minister and Cabinet for introduction.

Xanthaki outlines a similar process in the UK, though she divides it into five stages:

1. Understanding the proposal.
2. Analysing the proposal.
3. Designing the law.
4. Composing and developing the draft.
5. Verifying the draft.[49]

---

44 Ibid 475.
45 Penfold, above n 39, 477.
46 Crabbe, above n 22, 21.
47 Xanthaki, above n 23, 62.
48 Penfold, above n 39, 478.
49 Xanthaki, above n 23, 57 citing Thornton.

## *Key principles*

There is a general consensus in the literature that the key principles of effective drafting are that the product be clear, succinct and accessible.[50] Crabbe emphasises clarity and places it in opposition to verbosity. He urges drafters to express only one main thought in a sentence;[51] to consider the meaning of words in their context;[52] and to avoid language of 'colour or ornament'.[53] Watson-Brown observes that, despite the exhortations for drafters to use 'plain English' the term is rarely defined, which is problematic.[54] Stefanou refers to the plain language debate, and observes that, in essence, it is:

> about the use of language which is clear and conveys its message without unnecessary complexity. Whether or not it is possible to do so in law, where individual words may carry more than their simple, everyday meaning is a matter of personal belief. However, we certainly do not wish to see twenty-first century drafts in nineteenth-century language. Complex language can certainly produce 'noise' especially if it is caught up in political interpretations.[55]

Xanthaki summarises the principles of drafting in a pyramid with simplicity, plain language and gender neutrality at the base; through efficiency (clarity, precision and ambiguity); to effectiveness and then efficacy at the apex.[56] Similar principles can be found in the recommendations of a New Zealand report produced in 1993, which urged 'that those who are expected to know, obey, apply and advise on the law must be helped, so far as is practicable to understand it'.[57] To this end, the report advocated clearer and more straightforward legislative drafting with shorter sentences, use of the active voice and use of plain language, changes in the formatting of enactments; and commended aids to understanding such as indexes, explanatory notes, examples, flow charts and the use of formulas, maps and diagrams.[58] Butt and Castle's guidelines for effective legislative drafting are:

1. 'Avoid long sense-bites.
2. Use short sense-bites.
3. Use 'must' instead of 'shall' to indicate mandatory force.

---

50 Crabbe, above n 22, Stefanou, above n 27, Majambere, above n 37.

51 Crabbe, above n 22, 21.

52 Ibid 19–20.

53 Ibid 15.

54 See further, Anthony Watson-Brown, 'In Search of Plain English – The Holy Grail or Mythical Excalibur of Legislative Drafting' (2011) 33(1) *Statute Law Review* 7.

55 Stefanou, above n 27, 414–15.

56 Xanthaki, above n 23, 66.

57 Ivor Richardson, 'Simplicity in Legislative Drafting and Rewriting Tax Legislation' (2012) 43(3) *Victoria University of Wellington Law Review* 517, 518.

58 Ibid.

4. Avoid using noun phrases in place of verbs.
5. Avoid overuse of the passive.
6. Avoid wordiness and redundancy.
7. Avoid foreign words and phrases.
8. Avoid legalese and jargon.
9. Avoid peculiar linguistic conventions.
10. Use punctuation to give guidance about meaning.'[59]

## *Reflecting on the ethical obligations of drafting*

Legislative drafting imposes a number of ethical obligations upon the writer. Crabbe delineates these by dividing drafting into the 'amanuensis function', the 'professional function' and the 'composer function'. An amanuensis is a person employed to write what another dictates. In this case, the drafter is putting government's will into words. Crabbe emphasises the primary ethical duty here is for the drafter to understand the dividing line between the drafting function and that of a policy maker:[60]

> Policy decisions are for the policy makers. Parliamentary Counsel should not dictate policy. They should not distort policy. They should not divert policy. Their responsibility in this regard is to comprehend the policy and translate the policy into legislative form.[61]

And he emphasises that, at times, a drafter will need to say no – '[n]ot as a challenge to the will of our political masters, but in response to a higher sense of public duty and a nobility of service'.[62]

Under the professional function, the drafter 'must anticipate the legal difficulties and the pitfalls, the inadequacies in the policy, and the relationship of the policy to the existing body of the law'.[63] Parliamentary Counsel thus has a duty to foresee all possible eventualities that are likely to occur.[64] Crabbe argues that the greatest challenge to this function is that of time: drafters must learn to work under pressure and even under trying conditions.[65] Penfold also takes up this point, observing that workloads for drafters are 'substantial' and the size of the legislative program

59 Tanner, above n 33, 225.
60 Crabbe, above n 22, 17.
61 Ibid 22.
62 Ibid 18.
63 Ibid.
64 Ibid 18.
65 Ibid 23.

means that the only reductions in workloads tend to come during election caretaker periods. She observes:

> in the 2003–2004 financial year, for instance, 27 drafters in OPC (around one-third of them classified as 'trainee' drafters), working in 12 or 13 teams, produced 173 Bills totalling 6,700 pages. As well, consultation drafts totalling over 1,500 pages were prepared. This works out at around 14 introduced Bills, and over 650 pages of draft legislation (including consultation drafts), per team.[66]

The composer function is related to the ability to communicate the law to the audience. Drafters have ethical obligations to maintain the rule of law by ensuring that laws are drafted with clarity, precision and consistency;[67] to ensure that legislation is barrier-free for persons with disabilities,[68] and to use gender-neutral language.[69] Greenberg also argues that the drafter is obliged to determine the nature of their audience, and the facilities available to them in applying and construing the legislation.[70]

In terms of their professional obligations, legislative drafters are encouraged to write with clarity (ASCR r 7.1); but these writers have a particular duty to serve the public, ensuring that they carefully consider any potential legal difficulties with what is being proposed (ASCR r 5.1.1).

## IV CONCLUSION

In this chapter, we have sought to outline the fundamentals of common forms of what we have termed 'technical' writing: report writing and legislative drafting. Both demand a high standard of clarity and organisation. As in other forms of legal writing, the keys to effective technical writing are to begin with a careful consideration of audience and purpose, and to take the time to plan, revise, edit and proofread.

---

66 Penfold, above n 39, 482.

67 Majambere, above n 37, 418.

68 M David Lepofsky and Randal NM Graham. 'Universal Design in Legislative Drafting – How to Ensure Legislation is Barrier-Free for People with Disabilities' (2010) 27 *National Journal of Constitutional Law* 129, 130.

69 Majambere, above n 37.

70 Greenberg, above n 36, 28.

# REVIEW MATERIALS

## SUMMARY

This chapter covered 'technical writing', which focuses upon direction, instruction or explanation. It outlined processes for the two specific forms of technical writing relevant to law: report writing and legislative drafting, emphasising the importance of clarity and good organisation. Finally, it considered the key principles and particular ethical obligations that attach to legislative drafting.

## KEY POINTS

1. Technical writing, particularly report writing, is an important skill for lawyers to master.
2. Successful technical writing relies on excellent organisation and clarity.
3. Successful legislative drafting can be difficult, not least because the writing serves a variety of audiences.
4. Legislative drafting must find the right balance between clarity and complexity.
5. Legislative drafting entails a number of ethical issues.

## QUESTIONS FOR REFLECTION

1. How does report writing differ from writing a legal essay or a hypothetical problem question?
2. How, as a writer, is your work shaped by knowing that your reader is time-poor?
3. Why is legislative drafting considered to be such a specialised role?
4. Can you think of instances when plain language may not be possible in drafting? How can the principles of plain language drafting be utilised in such situations?
5. How, as a writer, is your work shaped by knowing that it must address the needs of multiple audiences?

## EXERCISES

1. Analysing an executive summary
   Access the Final Report 'Connection to Country: Review of the *Native Title Act 1993* (Cth)' at https://www.alrc.gov.au/sites/default/files/pdfs/publications/alrc_126_final_report.pdf.

Does the report answer the following questions,[71] which are often suggested as those that need to be answered in an executive summary?

- What is the report about?
- Why is it important?
- What is included in the report?
- What is included in each section?

2. Consider the report mentioned in Exercise 1 and consider whether its recommendations meet the following criteria:
   - Do they describe a suggested course of action to be taken to solve a particular problem?
   - Are they written in the form of action statements without justification?
   - Are they stated in clear, specific language?
   - Do they express their content in order of importance?
   - Are they based on the case built up in the body of the report, and are written in parallel structure?[72]
3. Choose a recent piece of legislation and evaluate it using Butt and Castle's guidelines for effective legislative drafting.[73] (You will find these in the Legislative Drafting section of this chapter, under the heading Key Principles.)

## FURTHER RESOURCES

1. Massachusetts Legislative Research and Drafting Manual (5th ed, 2010): https://malegislature.gov/Legislation/DraftingManual.
2. Law Society of New South Wales, Sample brief to a Barrister: https://www.lawsociety.com.au/cs/groups/public/documents/internetcontent/026515.pdf.
3. South Australian Community Health Research Unit, 'Evaluation Report Template': http://som.flinders.edu.au/FUSA/SACHRU/PDF/EvalReportTemplate.pdf.

---

71 Processes for Writing an Executive Summary, available at http://writing.colostate.edu/guides/page.cfm?pageid=1508&guideid=76.

72 World Health Organization, 'Writing Effectively for WHO: Module 3, Reports and Proposals', available at http://colelearning.net/who/module3/page43.html.

73 Butt and Castle, in Tanner, above n 33.

# CHAPTER 11

# WRITING WITH CIVILITY

## I INTRODUCTION

We noted earlier in this book that writing is an inherently ethical act in at least three ways: in an awareness of self and other; in an awareness of the discourse community; and in accordance with professional responsibilities. This chapter takes up the issue of professional responsibility and, specifically, the need to write with civility.

But while we are mainly referring to professional responsibility we note that civility also touches on awareness of self and other and the norms of the community of practice. Indeed, civility is said to be fundamental to the legal profession. Justice Griffiths recently observed that '[c]ourtesy and civility are not bourgeois affectations. They are not the mark of the effete or inept litigator. They are part of a practitioner's overriding duty to the court, indeed to the standards of the profession and to the public'.[1] Former Chief Justice of New South Wales, J. J. Spigelman, has said:

> Ours is a profession of words. We must continue to express ourselves in a way that demonstrates respect for others … The tradition of civility in the legal profession goes well beyond the requirements of appearance in court. It is to be found in the full range of discourse between practitioners, both oral and in correspondence. This tradition has been maintained in the law to a greater degree than other areas of social discourse. It is recognised as a fundamental ethical obligation of a professional person.[2]

Although there is widespread agreement that civility is important for the legal profession, there is no unanimity as to the meaning of the term. Most writers consider

---

1 Justice John Griffiths 'Some Ethical Issues: A View From the Bench' [2012] *Federal Judicial Scholarship* 26.

2 Quoted by Rob Reis, 'Fairness and Courtesy in Communications with Third Parties' (2013) March *Ethos* 24, 25.

civility to be wider than, but including, common courtesy[3] and many link it to notions of professionalism.[4] For this chapter, we will use the definition given by Fischer: civility is 'treating others with respect and with consideration for the overall good of clients, the legal profession and society'.[5]

A number of behaviours have been linked to civility. Those involving written communications include: accurate representations, timeliness in communication, restraint from writing 'hostile or aggressive' communications,[6] and refraining from using offensive, provocative or intimidatory language.

Of course, lawyers are only human and sometimes will write in anger in the course of a matter. This is, as we will see, to be avoided. Generally, lawyers will be held to higher standards of civility than the general public in their professional correspondence and, in particular, are expected to maintain an objective and professional demeanour. A more complex situation arises as a result of the fact that lawyers must advocate on behalf of their client and have a duty to speak out when they perceive wrongdoing or abuse of the legal system. Whether such 'robust' communications will attract censure is less clear.[7] In this chapter, we will outline written instances that have attracted the attention of the regulators by way of charges of discourteousness in Australia, but we will also occasionally refer to the discourteous behaviour of lawyers from other jurisdictions. In particular, we will seek to give guidance as to when lawyer advocacy on behalf of the client, or their strongly worded criticisms of an opponent's actions, are likely to become the subject of claims of unethical behaviour and attract professional sanction.

## II INCIVILITY IN WRITING

Civility encompasses a range of behaviours, but here we are particularly concerned with written communications. Justice Griffiths observed that:

> Few things irritate judges more than having to deal with solicitors' letters which are expressed in vitriolic and provocative language. Such language is

3 See for example Steve Mark, 'Civility and Professionalism: Standards of Courtesy' (February 2007) 34 *Without Prejudice* 1.

4 Kara Anne Nagorney, 'A Noble Profession? A Discussion of Civility among Lawyers' (1999) 12 *Georgetown Journal of Legal Ethics* 815; Lillian Corbin, 'Professionalism Redefined: More than Ethics' (2001) 26 *Alternative Law Journal* 139; Judge Helen Wilson Nies, 'Rambo Lawyering: The Need for Civility in Civil Litigation' (1991–1992) 1 *IDEA* 1.

5 Judith D Fischer, 'Incivility in Lawyers' Writing: Judicial Handling of Rambo Run Amok' (2011) 51 *Washburn Law Journal* 365, 366.

6 Josh O'Hara, 'Creating Civility: Using Reference Group Theory to Improve Inter-lawyers Relations' (2006–2007) 31 *Vermont Law Review* 965, 966.

7 Paula Baron and Lillian Corbin (2015) 'Robust Communications or Incivility – Where Do We Draw the Line?' (2015) 18(1) *Legal Ethics* 1.

> intended to be self-serving. It is invariably counterproductive. Extreme cases could well attract adverse cost consequences for practitioners, consistently with s 37N of the *Federal Court Act*.[8]

There are a number of cases in the US of what Fisher[9] terms, 'obnoxious' letter writing. These include *Saldana v Kmart Corp*, 260 F3d 228, 237–38 (3d Cir 2001) where a lawyer wrote referring to an expert witness as a 'Nazi'; and *Revson v Cinque & Cinque*, 221 F3d 71, 79 (2d Cir 2000) where a lawyer threatened to subject opposing counsel to 'the legal equivalent of a proctology exam'. In both cases, the lawyers in question escaped sanction.

In recent years there are cases where discourteous written communications are occurring when the correspondence is by email. As we have noted earlier, email is now widespread among lawyers as a means of communication, but it poses some risks for lawyers: when the majority of correspondence was by mail, there was a 'cooling off' period available between the writing of the letter and the sending of the letter to the recipient. With email, there is no such protection, so lawyers need to think carefully about their correspondence, particularly when they are angry (the issue is, of course exacerbated where texting is used).

In the *In de Braekt* case,[10] there were a number of charges of discourteousness to a magistrate and others against Megan Maree In de Braekt, including racist remarks to a court security officer. However, for the purposes of this discussion, only the discourteous written communications to police officers are of interest. The Court held that emails written by *In de Braekt*, six sent to one detective and one to another, constituted professional misconduct. The emails included the following statements:[11]

> Just because you are a Police officer does not mean you can make up your own laws & impose them on other people.
>
> Police aren't above the law, Detective Broadley.
>
> So do your job in accordance with the law & stop attempting to bully me into doing things I am not legally obliged to do, & will not do.
>
> You do remember the law, don't you?
>
> Do you want me to have to explain your ridiculous approach to the Court?
>
> Am I going to have to make a complaint about you in order to have that DVD sent to me?

---

8 Griffiths, above n 1.
9 Fischer, above n 5, 368.
10 *Legal Profession Complaints Committee v In de Braekt* [2012] WASAT 58 (27 March 2012).
11 Ibid [6].

> It would seem you're not used to a Lawyer standing up against your bullying & unlawful attempts to impose unlawful conditions on the provision of accused's VROI's.
>
> You just don't get it do you[?]
>
> Have you not ever posted anything before Detective Broadley? and
>
> You need to realise Detective Broadley that just because you are a Police Officer does not mean you have limitless powers, nor does it mean that you have the lawful ability to change, alter or add to laws in any way that suits your fancy & enables you to 'get your own way'.

*In de Braekt* sent an email to another detective which included:

> What a load of rubbish.
>
> He *hasn't* made any efforts to serve the materials on me.
>
> It would also appear that you don't understand the law either.
>
> The Police can't require me to adhere to any of their 'policies or practices,' or whims.[12]
>
> I look forward to cross-examining you sometime in the future, in a trial.[13]

In relation to this single email, the Tribunal reasoned that the inclusion of the threat to the detective, a future witness that In de Braekt would have the opportunity to cross-examine, placed her in a position of power which made the matter serious enough to constitute professional misconduct.[14] The Tribunal in this case emphasised the situation of those who were the recipients of the communications:

> In the view of the Tribunal, the practitioner had demonstrated a character and course of conduct that was discourteous, offensive and abusive to other participants in the justice system including police officers and court officials. In the view of the Tribunal, the maintenance of appropriate relationships between legal practitioners and others engaged in the proper functioning of the criminal justice system, such as police officers and court officials was a matter of considerable importance.[15]

The Tribunal also formed the view that the practitioner's conduct seriously undermined the reputation of the legal profession.[16]

---

12 Ibid [7].
13 Ibid [8].
14 Ibid [9].
15 Ibid [17].
16 Ibid.

More recently a Victorian case[17] involved 18 emails and one letter between the solicitor and his client that contained language that was 'hectoring, aggressive, disrespectful and abusive in tone'.[18] The following are examples:

> 9. …
>
> email of 17 October 2011
>
> 3 THINGS:
> 1. THE F…. CONCILIATION IS GOING ON. LISTEN TO ME AT SOME STAGE;
> 2. I WILL MEET YOU AT 2.15 PM IN THE FOYER. I DO9 [sic] NOT NEED MY HEAD FILLED WITH EXTANEOUS [sic] CRAP I KNOW WHAT I AM DOOING [sic] AND
> 3. THE PRICK THAT PUT MY ATTACHMENTS OUT OF ORDER IS GOING TO DIE LIKE A DOG. THINGS GO 11 12 13 NOT 13 11 12.
>
> email of 19 October 2011:
>
> sweetjesus. Don't you buggers ever learn. What in the hell are you writing to the Commissioner for
>
> email of 5 December 2011:
>
> Adam;
>
> YOU HAVE 10 MINUTES TO ANSWER THIS STARTING NOW
>
> On the basis of appropriate lawyering, I send the attached. Based on this, DO YOU WANT TO CHANGE ANYTHING. NOTE if your instructions remain the same, then I shall give it to her with both barrels.
>
> ANSWER BY 4:30 PM TODAY AS AT 4:31 I DO THE ABOVE.
>
> email of 22 April 2012:
>
> Here is the bloody thing. You have until I get back from dinner (in about 3 hours) to advise of any spelling mistakes and or info I need provided. I WILL NOT BE F… AMENDING ANY STUPID SHIT AS IT HAS ALREADY COST U A FORTUNE TO DO WHAT I HAVE DONE NOR WILL IN [sic] BE EXPLAINING AGAIN ANY STUFF 6X IS ENOUGH IF NO CHANGES TONITE IT WILL BE AT YOUR PLACE FOR DELIVERY TOMORROW AND YES YOU DO HAVE TO GIVE THE ATTACHMENTS AGAIN.
>
> ME.

---

17 *Legal Services Commissioner v Lynch* (Legal Practice) [2015] VCAT 772.

18 Ibid [7].

At the hearing the solicitor, Lynch, acknowledged that the communications were discourteous but also suggested 'that the LSC's concerns about language were out of touch with the modern world'.[19] However, the Tribunal rejected this suggestion suggesting that 'practitioners must be careful not to slip down the path towards communication which could be construed as overly aggressive, disrespectful, abusive, imprecise or otherwise unprofessional'.[20] The Tribunal went on to find the solicitor guilty of professional misconduct on this charge alone (even though other charges were involved).

## III ROBUST COMMUNICATIONS OR 'RAMBO TACTICS'?

Could it be argued that such exchanges are commonly 'robust' and therefore justified as being in the interests of the client? Where is the line to be drawn between robust advocacy on the client's behalf and overzealous representation that is discourteous and that will attract professional censure? In the US, there is a term for 'overzealous' lawyer representation: 'Rambo tactics'. Fisher observes that '[t]he varieties of Rambo tactics are limited only by lawyers' imaginations. They include "rudeness, hostility, abrasive conduct, and strident personal attacks on opponents," "overzealous advocacy," "unnecessary combativeness," and "bad manners"'.[21] Fisher[22] observes that civility is fundamental to the practice of law and that, accordingly, there have been calls for courts to actively discourage incivility. Although she acknowledges that there is no way of knowing how often discourteous conduct goes unpunished, a survey of cases decided over the past twenty years shows that numerous US courts have imposed penalties for incivility in lawyers' written documents and disbarment has sometimes followed (although ordinarily other offences are involved as well as the incivility). Discourteous written communications have also resulted in official censure or reprimands.

The fundamental ethical duties required of solicitors as set out in ASCR r 4 include a dictate that solicitors are to 'act in the best interests of a client'. As explained by Lord Reid in *Rondel v Worsley*,[23] 'every counsel has a duty to his client fearlessly to raise every issue, advance every argument, and ask every question, however distasteful, which he thinks will help his client's case'. At the same time, ASCR r 4.1.2 requires solicitors to 'be ... courteous in all dealings in the course of legal practice'. Importantly, this wide wording imposes upon lawyers a duty to be courteous to all parties: clients, other practitioners and third parties.

---

19 Ibid [11].
20 Ibid [14].
21 Fischer, above n 5, 366 (refs omitted).
22 Ibid 394.
23 [1969] 1 AC 191, 227.

The obligation of courtesy may be argued to be inconsistent with acting in the best interests of clients (ASCR r 4.1.1). For instance, it is conceivable that the words or expressions used to assert the rights of clients may be interpreted as discourteous to those to whom the communications are made. As Smithers, the Senior Member of the Victorian Civil and Administrative Tribunal, states in *LSC v Johnson*: 'lawyers will on occasion go close to, or cross the line of breaching these conventions, to advance the case they are putting'.[24] Indeed, sometimes clients will consider that lawyer loyalty and courtesy are at odds. In his study of the civility codes of thirty-two state bar associations in the US, Campbell concluded that lawyers:

> should inform their clients that weakness does not necessarily follow from courtesy and civility, and ensure that clients understand that 'uncivil, rude, abrasive, abusive, vulgar, antagonistic, obstructive, or obnoxious' behavior is not a valid part of effective or zealous representation.[25]

In de Braekt had tried to respond to the charges against her by referring the disciplinary committee to two New Zealand cases.[26] She referred to *N v K*[27] and argued that 'communications between litigants such as defence counsel and Police, are often brusque and aggressive & there is nothing wrong with this'.[28] In this case, the subject of the applicants' complaint was a letter sent by Lawyer K to the applicants, which: asserted that the applicants did not have the right to use the letterhead 'XX Heights' claiming it to be misleading and in breach of intellectual property rights; requested copies of the letters of complaint; and demanded that the applicants cease and desist using the letterhead immediately. The tone of the letter might be described as aggressive.[29] The Legal Complaints Review Officer found the communication 'was not overtly discourteous',[30] and that '[a]lawyer is generally entitled to assert rights on behalf of a client which may or may not ultimately be upheld'.[31]

In de Braekt relied on *S v J*[32] to argue that 'a lawyer not being pleasant to another lawyer, to a Police officer or to another persons [sic], could never justify disciplinary

24 *Legal Services Commissioner v Johnson (Legal Practice)* [2012] VCAT 1426 (24 September 2012) [92].
25 Donald E Campbell, 'Raise Your Right Hand and Swear to Be Civil: Defining Civility as an Obligation of Professional Responsibility' (2011) 47(1) *Gonzaga Law Review* 99, 113. In this summary Campbell quotes the § 2.7 of the Oklahoma Bar Association's 2006 Standards of Professionalism.
26 *N v K* [2009] NZLCRO 1 and *S v J* [2009] NZLCRO 3.
27 Ibid 1.
28 *Legal Profession Complaints Committee v In de Braekt* [2012] WASAT 58 (27 March 2012) [140].
29 *N v K* [2009] NZLCRO 1 [2].
30 Ibid [8].
31 Ibid [9].
32 *S v J* [2009] NZLCRO 3.

proceedings being taken against such Lawyer'.[33] In this case, a complaint that Lawyer J acted discourteously to the applicant when he was suggesting to the applicant's son that he should plead guilty was rejected by the Complaints Review Officer. While the Officer accepted that the lawyer 'acted in a rather forceful manner', he went on to suggest that in order for lawyers to give objective and sometimes unwelcome advice, that 'parties (including lawyers) do not feel that they need to tiptoe around matters' and so '[i]t is not the role of professional discipline to require lawyers to act pleasantly'.[34] These arguments did not dissuade the Tribunal from finding *In de Braekt* guilty of professional misconduct.

## IV REPEATED CONDUCT

As a general rule, repeated questionable behaviour can shift a judge's view of the impugned behaviour from acceptable to unacceptable. In *In de Braekt*[35] the collective conduct of the lawyer was seen to warrant removal from the Roll of Solicitors:

> The Tribunal also concluded that while the other four findings of misconduct would not, if each were viewed in isolation, warrant the removal of the practitioner's name from the Roll, viewed collectively, those matters demonstrated a character and course of conduct on the part of the practitioner which was inconsistent with the privileges of practice as a member of the legal profession.[36]

A similar finding was made in *Byrne v Legal Services Commissioner*.[37] In this case the Victorian Court of Appeal held that the solicitor's 'alleged conduct in repeatedly ignoring … [the] apparently reasonable requests for a copy of the fee agreement, coupled with the appellant's references to idle threats and bullying, were rude and in context sufficiently discourteous, offensive and provocative' to breach the applicable solicitors conduct rules,[38] leading to a possible finding of misconduct.

In *Legal Services Commissioner v Johnson (Legal Practice)*,[39] the matter concerned Johnson's conduct of his own family law proceedings. In these, he filed four **affidavits**

---

33 *Legal Profession Complaints Committee v In de Braekt* [2012] WASAT 58 (27 March 2012) [2012] [140].

34 *S v J* [2009] NZLCRO 3 [46].

35 [2012] WASAT 58 (27 March 2012).

36 *Legal Profession Complaints Committee v In de Braekt* [2012] WASAT 58 (27 March 2012) [17].

37 [2010] VSCA 162 (25 June 2010).

38 *Byrne* [2010] VSCA 162 (25 June 2010) [61]. While the court made this finding by reference to r 21 of the Professional Conduct Rules of Victoria, the Court dismissed the matter due to a failure to follow due process on the part of the Legal Services Commissioner.

39 *Legal Services Commissioner v Johnson (Legal Practice)* [2012] VCAT 1426 (24 September 2012).

which the LSC alleged 'used language which could variously be described as intemperate, discourteous, vulgar, provocative and/or offensive'.[40] In his affidavits, among other things, Johnson referred to his former de facto partner as 'monstrous – a violent, abusive, criminal and insane monster notwithstanding her female gender';[41] referred to his ex-partner's legal counsel as 'unethical, disgraceful and disgusting' with a reputation for being 'slippery'; described other legal practitioners involved in the matter as acting with 'consistent sheer stupidity and incompetence' and 'being grossly misleading and deceptive';[42] referred to the Court-appointed psychologist in the family law proceedings, as 'nightmarishly unprofessional' and 'an egotistical monster, totally unethical and unprofessional'.[43] Senior Member of **VCAT**, Smithers, stated that the affidavit material was 'well beyond statements of fact; contained repeated allegations of unethical, incompetent, fraudulent and corrupt conduct, so as to 'amount to a barrage of abuse'; and the language was 'intemperate, discourteous, vulgar, provocative and offensive'.[44] Johnson was found to have committed professional misconduct and had his practising certificate cancelled.[45] In the course of proceedings, Smithers observed: 'The expression "a lawyer who acts for himself has a fool for a client" was mentioned by Mr Johnson in his correspondence ... This case is clearly an example of the wisdom of that aphorism'.[46]

The principle that repeated questionable behaviour can move impugned behaviour from acceptable to unacceptable is also implied in the legislation governing lawyers. For instance, there are references to 'consistent failure' as shifting a finding that would normally be Unsatisfactory Professional Conduct to Professional Misconduct.[47] As noted above, in *LPC v Johnson*, Smithers expressed concern about the repeated allegations constituting a 'barrage of abuse'.[48]

---

40 Ibid [1].
41 Ibid [13].
42 Ibid [14].
43 Ibid [16].
44 Ibid [92].
45 *Legal Services Commissioner v Johnson (Legal Practice)* [2012] VCAT 1731 (14 November 2012).
46 *Legal Services Commissioner v Johnson (Legal Practice)* [2012] VCAT 1426 (24 September 2012) [102].
47 Note, for example, that a matter can progress from being categorised as unsatisfactory professional conduct to professional misconduct if it is that there is a 'consistent failure to reach or maintain a reasonable standard of competence and diligence' – s 297(1)(a) and 'justify a finding that the lawyer is not a fit and proper person to engage in legal practice' – s 297(1)(b) Legal Profession Uniform Law (NSW) (2014).
48 *Legal Services Commissioner v Johnson* (Legal Practice) [2012] VCAT 1426 (24 September 2012) [92].

## V LANGUAGE AND COMMUNITY STANDARDS

The cases suggest that language generally accepted by the community may be held to be offensive when used by a lawyer in correspondence, effectively holding the lawyer to a higher standard than that accepted in the general public. In the Reports of the Solicitors' Statutory Committee (NSW) in respect of *Constantine Karageorge*, where statements by a solicitor were found to be obscene and racist, it was noted that:

> It may be that the conduct complained of would merely amount to reprehensible rudeness or churlish discourtesy if it were conduct on the part of someone other than a solicitor. There may be some acts which, although they would not be disgraceful in any other person, yet if they are done by a solicitor in relation to his profession may be fairly considered disgraceful and dishonourable conduct: See Lord Esher MR in *Allinson v General Council of Medical Education and Registration* (1894) 1QB 750 at 760. Clearly, such acts may include acts perpetrated towards members of the public. It has long been the view of the profession that only the very highest conduct is consistent with membership of the profession ... Clearly, the use of insulting language or behaving offensively towards members of the public is not conducive to the maintenance of the good name of the profession.[49]

This view is expressed in the jurisdictional rules: practitioners should be courteous to other practitioners. The rules also go on to require lawyers' conduct to be such that it does not bring the administration of justice or the profession into disrepute. The ASCR has a heading, 'Fundamental duties of Solicitors' under which ASCR r 4 requires practitioners to 'act in the best interests of a client' and to 'be honest and courteous in all dealings'. ASCR r 5 requires practitioners to avoid conduct that could be considered 'prejudicial to, or diminish the public confidence in, the administration of justice; or ... bring the profession into disrepute'. This implies that a solicitor's language will be judged from the perspective of its effect on the community.

This approach is illustrated by *Legal Complaints Committee* and *Chin*.[50] When Chin, a Western Australian solicitor, wrote to a client who had decided to dismiss his services, the State Administrative Tribunal of Western Australia found his communications 'intemperate and offensive':[51]

> As a learned person and a professor in your own field, you are now equipped with the 'professional knowledge' that you have improperly and stealthily

---

49 Quoted in *Lander v Council of the Law Society of the Australian Capital Territory* [2009] ACTSC 117 [20].

50 *Legal Complaints Committee* and *Chin* [2012] WASAT 77 (24 April 2012).

51 Ibid [136].

> acquired from us to benefit yourself in a way you think is most fit and most economical to you … In short, you have induced us to provide you with draft copies of our handiwork in order to serve your private purpose to defraud us of our professional fees by refusing to give the necessary details to render the instruments we were preparing for you complete and perfect …[52]

Even comparatively mild language may be seen to be discourteous, offensive or provocative and constituting unsatisfactory professional conduct. In *Legal Services Commissioner v Cooper*[53] there was a family law dispute where Cooper acted for the husband. The following are extracts from the two letters Cooper wrote to the other solicitor:

> We note that according to the documentation that you provided us on the 10th November undercover of the letter of the 7th November, as of 4 November your client had $43,830.01 in her bank account. Presumably she has spent all of that in the period between the 4th November and your letter of the 13th November! Given the manner in which the funds under her control have been depleted, that seems an excessive rate of expenditure even for your client who has already spent over $180,000.00 in joint funds in the last 12 months.
>
> I have advised my client to instruct me not to respond to anymore of your correspondence. It just seems to me that every time you have got no work to do you return to [the wife's] file because there is plenty of money there to pay your legal fees.
>
> …
>
> The children's issues are never going to be resolved at the mediation. The likelihood is that your client and her family have done so much damage to [child] that my client will never have a meaningful relationship with his daughter. Your client will live to regret that in the future, when [child] grows up and becomes as dysfunctional as your client is.

The Tribunal held that 'on any view' the language used by Cooper in these letters was 'intemperate, inappropriate, and discourteous and in some respects offensive'.[54] However, there was little discussion on why that was so, because Cooper accepted that he was guilty. However, the Tribunal, when discussing the penalty to be applied, did rely heavily on the fact that Cooper was a very experienced solicitor. It commented that even though he was acting on the client's instructions, 'he failed to strike an appropriate balance between his professional obligations, and the legitimate

---

52 Ibid [135].

53 *Legal Services Commissioner v Cooper* [2011] QCAT 209 (17 May 2011).

54 Ibid [19].

pursuit of his client's interests'[55] and he 'should have fought harder against allowing the heat in the dispute itself to colour his own language'.[56] The Tribunal also pointed out that this was a novel case and so principles of general deterrence ought to be considered.[57]

The line between incivility and 'robust' communication was differently drawn in *Legal Services Commissioner v Bradshaw*.[58] The correspondence in Cooper took place between two solicitors. In the case of *Bradshaw* the questionable correspondence was between two barristers who were discussing a Queensland District Court judge. A charge of sending correspondence which was scandalous, offensive or likely to bring the profession into disrepute was brought against one of those barristers.[59] The impugned communications included:

> The matter is still up in the air where my next application for Emerson [sic] to disqualify himself, nobody deserves to be threatened and spoken to the way Irene was and that the judgment is clearly a face saving exercise after a week he realised he had acted unjudicially and it was time to protect his own backside. Nothing more ludicrous than adjourning for a week to see whether you were going to adjourn.
>
> …
>
> … knowing Williams and his love of money I could imagine where he will attempt to recoup his losses.
>
> …
>
> Clearly Emerson [sic] is just a person not suited to the bench and for us to continue before him is simply self defeating.

The Queensland Legal Practice Tribunal held that 'the criticism of the Judge is robust. However, it is not scandalous or offensive or likely to bring the profession into disrepute to ask a Judge to disqualify himself'. The Tribunal continued:

> To describe a judgment as a face saving exercise is strong criticism but judges may expect strong criticism from time to time. It might be different if the circumstances of publication were different but this is a letter from one barrister to another. I think judges would be regarded as naive if they thought that barristers do not in contacts between each other sometimes express their criticisms of the judges in strong terms. The system is none the worse for that.

55 Ibid [14].
56 Ibid [15].
57 Ibid [14].
58 [2009] QLPT 21 (8 September 2009).
59 *Legal Services Commissioner v Bradshaw* [2009] QLPT 21 (8 September 2009).

> The Tribunal did suggest, however, that if an 'assertion that the judge is just a person not suited to the bench' were made to the judge then it might be considered offensive, but not when the comment is made by one barrister to another and not made publicly.

The courts have made it clear that if criticisms made by a lawyer are held to be true or, at least, fair comment as understood in defamation law, issues of misconduct or unsatisfactory professional conduct will not arise. In *Lander v Council of the Law Society of the Australian Capital Territory* [2009] ACTSC 117, Lander acted on behalf of an employee of the Department of Education and Training in relation to his potential invalidity retirement. In 2006, Lander wrote a letter to the Chief Executive of the Department of Education and Training about his client's retirement.

In that letter, Lander made a number of general statements about the Department of Education and Training and its staff failing to communicate, being dishonest, rude, unhelpful, obsessive and compulsive, bearing grudges against people who engaged lawyers; and also made general allegations of 'malpractice' and 'maladministration'. He also implied that the Department of Education and Training might engage in recriminations against his wife, who was a teacher employed by the Department, and was not involved in the matter addressed in the letter. The issues raised in the letter were investigated, and a reply sent to Mr Lander, but The Department's Director of Human Relations also referred the letter to the Law Society to ascertain whether it breached required standards of professionalism.

The Legal Practitioner's Disciplinary Tribunal found the letter warranted a finding of unsatisfactory professional conduct; the matter was appealed to Supreme Court of the ACT, which set aside the decision of the Tribunal. The Court pointed out that there is no general obligation on a solicitor: 'to refrain from that which the recipient might find to be discourteous, offensive or provocative statements. That is too broad and a sweeping proposition'.[60] The real issue was:

> If the criticisms the solicitor levelled at the Department were true or, at least, fair comment as understood in defamation law, it could not be misconduct or unsatisfactory conduct to draw them to the attention of the relevant officers of the Department and its Minister. That is not an issue which those considering the statements should have to concern themselves. The fact that it was perceived as discourteous and offensive, even provocative, to parties to whom it is directed, is beside the point.[61]

In some cases, determining whether a comment is truthful will require the decision-maker to determine which party is the most credible. This was the

---

60 *Lander v Council of the Law Society of the Australian Capital Territory* [2009] ACTSC 117 [52].
61 Ibid [53].

situation in *Legal Services Commissioner v McDonald (Legal Practice)* [2013]VCAT 1943 (18 November 2013), where McDonald was accused of two counts of 'failing to ensure that his [sic]communications with other practitioners were courteous and/or by avoiding offensive or provocative language or conduct'.[62] More specifically, in two letters McDonald accused the other practitioner of being 'fundamentally dishonest'.[63] Although the Tribunal could not conclusively decide which account was correct, it favoured the other practitioner's account and found McDonald guilty of two charges of unsatisfactory professional conduct based on its view that just because it was impossible to determine conclusively which account was correct, McDonald should not have persisted with his very serious allegations that the other practitioner was 'fundamentally dishonest', accusations that are offensive and have the 'potential to undermine the integrity and reputation of the profession … [and undermine] cooperation between practitioners which is important to promote the efficient operation of the justice system, and the conduct of legal business'.[64] Interestingly, if Victoria adopts the ASCR, then McDonald might also be found to have breached r 32 ('unfounded allegations').

The discussion of the cases illustrates what the court stated in *In de Braekt* about charges that are solely about discourtesy:

> Discourtesy, in many instances, will be insufficient to warrant a finding of professional misconduct. Even less frequently will that discourtesy result in, or contribute to, a finding that the practitioner should be removed from the Roll. However, the importance of courtesy in the legal system, and in the relationship between the legal profession, the court system, and general public should not be understated. While a practitioner should advocate fearlessly on behalf of the interests of their client, that is not an excuse for discourtesy.[65]

## VI CONCLUSION AND SOME GUIDING PRINCIPLES

In effect, the decision-makers who are tasked with dealing with claims of discourtesy see this as a developing issue, that is, as an area where the principles are not yet defined. However, it is our view that the above analysis can provide some guidance for you, as a legal writer.

As we initially highlighted, if there are repeated or persistent incidents of discourtesy, or if there is other poor behaviour as well as discourtesy, then the lawyer's conduct can move from something excusable to misconduct.

---

62 *Commissioner v McDonald (Legal Practice)* [2013] VCAT 1943 (18 November 2013) [6].
63 Ibid [19].
64 Ibid [72].
65 *Legal Profession Complaints Committee v In de Braekt* [2012] WASAT 58 (27 March 2012) [28].

Lawyers are held to a higher standard of conduct than others. Our discussion of the cases above made this quite evident. The language used by lawyers was held to be discourteous even though that would not be the case for the communications of a member of the public.

While not generally applied, there are instances where courts award a harsher penalty than normal for the purposes of deterring others from similar behaviour, although this may have occurred in the case of *Cooper* because of the seniority and experience of the practitioner.[66]

According to the ASCR, lawyers are not to be discourteous to anyone – clients, other practitioners or third parties. Yet the analysis of the cases reveals that the courts treat much more seriously the discourteous communications of lawyers with other legal actors. This is because it is important to ensure that the legal system functions as it should and that the respect of the community for the administration of justice and the legal profession is maintained.

However, this does not mean that all communications between legal actors must speak courteously of others, even judges. For example, the correspondence between two barristers about a sitting judge was held not to be discourteous. In that situation, however, the court noted that if those communications were made to the judge personally or had been made public, then a different conclusion might have been reached.

Finally, although just as important, we note that the law governing lawyer conduct is developing in accordance with the law more generally. The courts have made it clear that if the criticisms made by a lawyer are held to be 'true or, at least, fair comment as understood in defamation law, it could not be misconduct or unsatisfactory conduct … [not] if the allegations were soundly based, gratuitously insulting or offensive'.[67]

---

66 *Legal Services Commissioner v Cooper* [2011] QCAT 209 (17 May 2011) [1].

67 *Lander v Council of the Law Society of the Australian Capital Territory* [2009] ACTSC 117 [53].

# REVIEW MATERIALS

## SUMMARY

This chapter discussed the relationship of writing to legal professional responsibility and, in particular, the need to write with civility. It covered the broadening obligation of courtesy in the ASCR, applying to clients, other practitioners and third parties, and in advocacy, the duties owed not just to clients but also to administration of justice. The distinction between robust advocacy and incivility was explored, and the chapter set out guiding principles from decided cases.

## KEY POINTS

1. Courtesy is a fundamental expectation of legal professionalism.
2. The ASCR imposes an obligation of courtesy beyond fellow practitioners to clients and third parties.
3. As a lawyer, you must learn where to draw the line between robust advocacy and incivility.
4. Lawyers are held to a higher standard of conduct than members of the public.
5. The courts have considered lawyer communications in context, taking into a number of factors in their determination of whether communications amount to misconduct.

## QUESTIONS FOR REFLECTION

1. Why is civility considered by many to be so fundamental to legal practice?
2. Should senior members of the profession be subject to higher standards of conduct than more junior members, or should the same standard be expected of all practitioners? Justify your answer.
3. A number of empirical reports have expressed concern about the high incidence of bullying and other unethical behaviours in law firms. Is it important for law firms to expect civility within the firm, as well as to clients and parties outside the firm? Justify your answer.
4. What steps can you take to ensure that your own writing furthers the legitimate interests of your client without abandoning civility?
5. What does it mean to 'bring the profession into disrepute'? What behaviour, in addition to incivility, may compromise the profession?

## EXERCISES

1. Rewrite the following communication in terms that would be more professionally acceptable. This exercise draws upon the case of *Legal Services Commissioner v Cooper* [2011] QCAT 209 (17 May 2011), where the solicitor acted for the husband in a family law dispute and wrote the following to the solicitor for the wife:

    > We note that according to the documentation that you provided us … your client had $43,830.01 in her bank account. Presumably she has spent all of that in the period between the 4th November and your letter of the 13th November! Given the manner in which the funds under her control have been depleted, that seems an excessive rate of expenditure even for your client who has already spent over $180,000.00 in joint funds in the last 12 months. [3]
    >
    > I have advised my client to instruct me not to respond to anymore of your correspondence. It just seems to me that every time you have got no work to do you return to [the wife's] file because there is plenty of money there to pay your legal fees. [4]
    >
    > …
    >
    > The children's issues are never going to be resolved at the mediation. The likelihood is that your client and her family have done so much damage to [the child] that my client will never have a meaningful relationship with his daughter. Your client will live to regret that in the future, when [the child] grows up and becomes as dysfunctional as your client is. [5]

2. Remove the unnecessary words from the following statements to achieve more professional communications:[68]
    - Your letter fails to state any legal authority for your absurd claim that my client's fasteners are responsible for the porch collapse.
    - Your request seeks highly unusual documents for a product defect case … Document request no. 13 seeks completely irrelevant documents, and the production of those documents would be unduly burdensome.
3. Writing letters in an adversarial setting[69]

    The following letter might be interpreted by the recipient as overly aggressive or arrogant. Identify mistakes, antiquated phrases, and, in particular, any words and phrases in the following letter that may give rise to this perception:

---

68 This exercise has been adapted from material available at http://www.ericejohnson.com/courses/sales_15/m/Sales_Civility_in_Communication_Special_Module_A_slideshow.pdf.

69 This material, which can be found at International Risk Institute Management (Inc) UK available at https://www.irmi.com/articles/expert-commentary/a-few-tips-on-writing-to-opposing-attorneys, has been modified to reflect an Australian address.

January 5, 2004

BREEN & EVERETT, LLP
PO BOX 456 STAFFORD QLD 4053

RE: Our Claim Number 57638T47R34

Our Policy Number: T-67589
Our Insured: Hart Smyth
Date of Loss: November 30, 2002
Your Client: Sarah Barton

Ms. Breen, I have received our letter of October 30, 2003, along with the demand proposal for your client, Sarah Barton. After review of the medical information provided, I would like to extend an offer of $1,700.00. My offer is based on the following:

Ms. Barton did not seek medical attention until 21 days after the accident. At that time, she was diagnosed with a cervical strain. X-rays were taken and were essentially normal with the exception of some calcification which was present in the past. On April 12, 2003, Dr. Stevens released your client stating that she had full range of motion of the neck and no longer had headaches. He felt that she had healed 100 percent.

In regards to the wage loss, I do not find anything in your client's records that shows a doctor had restricted her from working. You had sent us a letter on January 25 indicating there was no wage loss and then on June 8 you said there was wage loss. It was also stated in the records that on December 29, 2003, the patient had resumed her work which included moving furniture. Therefore, we do not feel we owe any wage loss to your client.

Again, based on the review of the medical information on your client, I wish to offer $1,700.00. We have a lien from Longley Bank in the amount of $913.32 which we will reimburse directly to them. Please review with your client and advise me of your decision.

Respectfully,
ACME Insurance

## FURTHER RESOURCES

1. Wendy Matheson, Torys LLP, 'Civility: Ten Litigators to Watch Out For': http://www.lsuc.on.ca/media/ninth_colloquium_ten_litigators.pdf.
2. Illinois Supreme Court Commission on Professionalism, Jayne Reardon, 'Incivility and Professional Ethics' (2015): http://www.2civility.org/incivility-and-professional- ethics/.

# CHAPTER 12

# REFLECTIVE PRACTICES AND EVERYDAY COMMUNICATION

## I INTRODUCTION

In this chapter we will be suggesting that reflection is an important attribute of professionalism in writing. At its simplest, reflection is an ethical act to ensure that legal writing does not offend those to whom it is written. Many of the examples of poor ethical behaviour that are characterised variously as incompetence or incivility or discourtesy, and can even extend to intimidation, harassment and bullying, have resulted because lawyers failed to think carefully before writing. More importantly, for the novice legal writer, reflection plays a vital role in developing professional identity and in preparing future lawyers for legal practice. As a lawyer, you need to possess the relevant substantive legal knowledge to solve a client's problem (ASCR r 4.1.3 competence), but you also need to recognise the importance of deliberately reflecting on your own performance. This develops the skill of professional judgment. This is the ability to coherently deal with, and choose between, the 'conflicting values within the framework of general rules',[1] and to recognise that your personal choices and society's realities can influence the decisions you make. Further, as Brummer suggests, 'professional' means more than expert or competent; it contains an element of self-restraint',[2] a positive element in professional behaviour.

With these ideas in mind, in this chapter we will consider the meaning of reflection; before turning to a consideration of students' correspondence with their peers, the use of social media and student correspondence with academics and others

1 Katherine R Kruse, 'Professional Role and Professional Judgment: Theory and Practice in Legal Ethics' (2011) 9(2) *University of St Thomas Law Journal* 250, 250.

2 Bennett H Brummer, 'Independent, Professional Judgment: The Essence of Freedom' (1997–1998) 10 *St Thomas Law Review* 607, 608.

(via emails and letters). We outline a schema for reflection, acknowledging Ryan's concern that:

> Despite the common (and often undefined) use of the terms reflection or reflective in assessment tasks ... learners are not often taught *how* to reflect, which different types of reflection are possible, or how best to communicate their disciplinary knowledge through reflection.[3]

Further, we will discuss the importance of reflective practices to the development of your cognition, values and professionalism through the use of reflective practices such as journals and e-portfolios.

## II WHAT IS REFLECTIVE PRACTICE AND WHY DOES IT MATTER?

Although reflection has been variously defined from different perspectives and disciplines, it is generally taken to have two fundamental characteristics: first, 'making sense of experience in relation to self, others and contextual conditions';[4] and second, 'reimagining and/or planning future experience for personal and social benefit'.[5] With specific reference to reflection in the context of professional activities, reflective practice has been defined as follows:

> Reflective practice is the integration of intentional thought and specific action within a professional context. Reflective practice includes consideration of ethical rules and norms in a given field and offers guidance for the skillful application of professional ethics. Reflective practice is not the same as occasional review or reflection about a past professional experience, rather, it is the ingrained habit of constant reflection.[6]

This sort of professional reflection has been distinguished from purely personal reflection, as it involves 'a conscious and stated purpose' and needing 'to show evidence of learning and a growing professional knowledge'.[7]

Characterising lawyers as professionals means that they have a role that requires them to serve the community. But professionalism also implies that the public expects a certain standard of behaviour and consider lawyers to be experts in the law (mandated in the professional rules as competence: ASCR r 4.1.3). As a novice,

3 Mary E Ryan 'The Pedagogical Balancing Act: Teaching Reflection in Higher Education' (2013) 18(2) *Teaching in Higher Education* 144, 144.

4 Ibid 145.

5 Ibid.

6 Timothy Casey, 'Reflective Practice in Legal Education: The Stages of Reflection' (2013–2014) 20 *Clinical Law Review* 317, 322.

7 Ryan, above n 3, 146.

one can study lawyer behaviour and model what one sees. But an inherent aspect of professionalism is the ability to exercise judgment, that is, to use your knowledge to make a decision intuitively. This is what Schön refers to as 'reflection-in-action'.[8] Initially, this is a deliberate, conscious process that can be time consuming. As Ryan points out, 'critical reflection is not an intuitive skill'.[9] But if you have the chance, over time, to apply your knowledge to similar situations effectively, it is likely that you will make the same decisions when dealing with similar factual situations. Psychologists refer to this practice as using judgment heuristics[10] – that is, the use of 'short-cuts, rough judgments' or 'rules of thumb',[11] in order to save time and to conserve cognitive energy.[12]

A note for teachers here: we suggest that students need to be encouraged and, in some instances assessed, on their reflective practices.[13] At a basic level, students should be encouraged to reflect on the performance of practising lawyers. For instance, they may be encouraged to recognise activities that have attracted disciplinary action and reflect on how they might avoid that outcome. Students can also be encouraged to think about their own communications with their peers and with academics and to reflect on the role of the lawyer in society by keeping a reflective journal or e-portfolio. These activities will now be discussed.

## III COMMUNICATING RESPONSIBLY WITH PEERS

Suggesting that you ought to reflect on what you write to your peers may initially seem to be an overly restrictive requirement. However, given some of the consequences of posting comments and photos to Facebook and other social media, such as YouTube and so on, a cautious approach is advisable. A growing literature considers how one should behave in the social media space, a movement known as 'e-professionalism'. E-professionalism has been defined as 'the development of an online persona that is congruent with the values and ethics of the profession and portrays use of self in a way that is respectful and demonstrates professional integrity'.[14]

---

8 Donald A Schön, *The Reflective Practitioner: How Professionals Think in Action* (Basic Books, 1983) 49–69.

9 Ryan, above n 3, 154.

10 Elliot Aronson, *The Social Animal* (Worth Publishers, WH Freeman and Company, 1999), 134.

11 Donald C Langevoort, 'Behavioral Theories of Judgment and Decision Making in Legal Scholarship: A Literature Review' (1998)51 *Vanderbilt Law Review* 1499.

12 SR Fiske and SE Taylor, *Social Cognition* (New York, McGraw Hill, 1991), cited in Aronson, n 10, 120.

13 Casey, above n 6, 319 notes the importance of deliberate reflection as the means to providing 'the new professional with a process to develop professional judgment'.

14 L Chenoweth, and D McAuliffe, *The Road to Social Work and Human Services*, (4th ed, Cengage, 2015) 306.

A person's level of e-professionalism may affect their employability.[15] It is now common for employers to carry out detailed background checks on applicants for positions in firms, using the means available on the internet.[16] In fact, there have been many reports of employment applicants failing to be considered due to the future employer's investigation of the applicant's Facebook page.[17] Much of this information is freely available as the applicant has chosen to post the information publicly, although there are more dubious methods adopted from time to time. For example, some employers have requested or required job applicants to allow them to log in to their social network, or to provide their username and password to the employer so that their social media activities can be viewed. It is reported that some employers have threatened to refuse to hire, discipline or discharge employees if they failed to comply with this request.[18] Generally speaking, the law does not preclude this practice in Australia. There is now legislation in some American states against employers demanding access to the social media sites of future or current employees.[19] Facebook too, as an organisation, has made statements suggesting that employers who demand this information are invading the privacy of future or current employees.[20]

However, there is still quite a lot of interest by government agencies;[21] and financial institutions in accessing this information.[22] Even the Florida Bar's Character

---

15 D McAuliffe, *Interprofessional Ethics: Collaboration in the Social, Health and Human Services* (Cambridge University Press, 2014).

16 Linda B Dwoskin, Melissa Bergman Squire, and Jane Patullo, 'Skeletons in the Closet? Legal Developments in Screening Applicants and Employees' (2014) 39(4) *Employee Relations Law Journal* 24, 24.

17 Alan Finder, *For Some, Online Persona Undermines a Resume, The New York Times*, 11 June 2006, available at http://www.nytimes.com/2006/06/11/us/11recruit.html?pagewanted=all&_r=0 Also see Emma Reynolds, *How Facebook Could Cost You Your Job! One in Five Bosses has Rejected a Job Applicant After Checking Out Their Profile on Social Media Sites*, available at http://www.dailymail.co.uk/news/article-2115927/How-Facebook-cost-job-One-applicants-rejected-bosses-check-profiles-social-media-sites.html#ixzz3MhoBmRvQ.

18 James Delaney, 'Employer Use of Facebook and Online Social Networks to Discriminate Against Applicants for Employment and Employees: An Analysis Balancing the Risks of Having a Facebook Account and the Need for Protective Legislation' (2013) 64(2) *Labour Law Journal*, 86, 87.

19 Aliah D Wright, 'More States Ban Social Media Snooping', Society for Human Resource Management, 8/12/2014, available at http://www.shrm.org/hrdisciplines/technology/articles/pages/social-media-snooping.aspx.

20 *Facebook Warns Employers not to Demand Passwords of Job Applicants, The Australian*, 26 March 2012, available at www.theaustralian.com.au/technology/facebook-warns-employers-not-to-demand-passwords-of-job-applicants/story-e6frgakx-1226309862088?nk=c1e337dc2084b35fff54bae16181ddaa.

21 Kevin Rector, *Maryland Becomes First State to Ban Employers From Asking for Social Media Passwords, Baltimore Sun,* 10 April 2012, available at http://articles.baltimoresun.com/2012-04-10/news/bs-md-privacy-law-20120410_1_facebook-password-social-media-bradley-shear.

22 Trevor Timm, 'If the FBI has a Backdoor to Facebook or Apple Encryption, We Are Less Safe', *The Guardian*, 9 June 2015.

and Fitness Commission recommended that in order for applicants to show their fitness to be admitted to the legal profession they should provide their passwords to their social media sites to the admitting body. This recommendation was rejected by the Supreme Court of Florida but the Court did agree that it was appropriate to investigate social networking websites where the applicants have admitted to a history of lack of candour or substance abuse and are wanting to show that they have been rehabilitated.[23]

It is not only the employment environment that invites reflection when using social media sites. A variety of other circumstances may create issues for future and for current lawyers. For instance, lawyers who provide answers to legal questions on the web, may, in fact, create a lawyer/client retainer.[24] Alternatively, lawyers acting for their clients may be tempted to gain an advantage for their clients by becoming the 'friend' of an unrepresented opposing client on Facebook.[25] If the lawyer fails to provide her true identity, then she may breach the professional rules, specifically ASCR r 4.1.2 (lack of honesty), and possibly ASCR r 33 (dealing with another solicitor's client). The obligation to treat other lawyers with civility applies on social media sites and use of derogatory or course language in reference to other lawyers can be held to be a breach of courtesy under ASCR r 4.1.2.[26] This rule can also be breached in other ways. For instance, if a lawyer asks a judge for an adjournment because of the death of a family member and later the judge discovers photos on social media dated at that time showing that she was actually attending a party, this will also be a breach of honesty.[27] Lawyers who post confidential information about their clients' case on the net, without the informed consent of the clients, will breach ASCR r 9.[28] A breach of confidentiality might also occur, albeit unintentionally, by a lawyer tweeting her location, which ultimately discloses that she is working with an

23 Jan Pudlow, 'On Facebook? FBBE May be Planning a Visit', *The Florida Bar News*, 1 September 2009 available at http://www.floridabar.org/DIVCOM/JN/JNNews01.nsf/cb53c80c8fabd49d85256b5900678f6c/d288355844fc8c728525761900652232!OpenDocument&Highlight=0,social,networking.

24 Marilyn Krawitz, 'May it Tweet the Court: Ethical Considerations Involving Australian Lawyers' Social Media Use' (2013) 2 *Journal of Civil Procedure* 85, 92.

25 David Gottlieb, 'Recent Developments in the Law of Professional Responsibility: Lawyers and Out-of-court Misconduct', 29-30 May 2014, University of Kansas School of Law, available at https://law.ku.edu/sites/law.ku.edu/files/docs/recent-developments/(3)GottliebEthics.pdf.

26 Bar Standards Board Disciplinary Tribunal's findings re: David Harris, 26 January 2012.

27 Helen W Gunnarsson, 'Friending Your Enemies, Tweeting Your Trials: Using Social Media Ethically' (2011) 99 (10) *Illinois Bar Journal* 500.

28 In the Matter of Peshek, Ill AttyReg and Disc Comm, 09 CH 89 (Aug. 25, 2009), Ill S Ct MR 23794 (May 18, 2010) cited in Helen W Gunnarsson, 'Friending Your Enemies, Tweeting Your Trials: Using Social Media Ethically' (2011) 99 (10) *Illinois Bar Journal* 500.

identifiable client.[29] Breaches of ASCR r 4.1.2 (incivility) and r 42 (bullying) might also occur depending on the language used in postings on the web.

We mentioned earlier the desire of the Florida Bar to be able to examine, more carefully, a potential lawyer's private character. In Australia, a student's behaviour prior to admission is similarly important. On applying for admission students are required to disclose anything that might suggest that they are not fit to practice. This includes a consideration of their behaviour as a student. The following section discusses behaviour of a student that may be considered problematic when communicating with academics and other third parties.

## IV COMMUNICATIONS WITH ACADEMIC STAFF AND OTHERS

In recent years in Australia, the relationship between lecturers and students has become less formal and there is a perception that this has resulted in an increase in disruptive classroom behaviour which empirical studies have found results in reduced student learning.[30] It has also been suggested that even students find classroom disruptive behaviour objectionable.[31] For example, Bjorklund and Rehling recently conducted a survey of students to determine their perceptions of behaviour that those authors referred to as 'classroom incivility' and this included a long list of activities which included continuing to talk after being asked to stop; allowing a cell phone to ring; conversing loudly with others; arriving late or leaving early; and text messaging.[32]

### *Email*

Email communications can be used persistently and aggressively; and, on occasion dishonestly. There have thus been instances where a student's inappropriate use of email has seen them banned from university study – for instance where email was used to impersonate a lecturer and gain access to examination answers, or where it was used to harass a university lecturer over an 18-month period (alleging that

---

29 Law Institute of Victoria, 'Guidelines on the Ethical Use of Social Media', 29 November 2012, available at http://www.liv.asn.au/PDF/For-Lawyers/Ethics/2012Guidelines-on-the-Ethical-Use-of-Social-Media.aspx.

30 LJ Feldmann, 'Classroom Civility is Another of Our Instructor Responsibilities' (2001) 49 *College Teaching* 137–40; and AS Hirschy and JM Braxton, 'Effects of Student Classroom Incivilities on Students' (2004) 99 *New Directions for Teaching and Learning* 67.

31 TH Benton, 'Remedial Civility Training' (2007) 53 *Chronicle of Higher Education* 36; and Wendy L Bjorklund and Diana L Rehling, 'Student Perceptions of Classroom Incivility' (2010) 58 *College Teaching* 15.

32 Bjorklund and Rehling, above n 31, 16.

university lecturers were engaged in a 'cover-up' and consequently denying the student access to research facilities).[33]

But emails can also be inappropriate through lack of civility – a consequence of the fact that email is the predominant means by which students communicate with academics and university administrators, and of the informal environment, the instantaneous nature of the medium, and the growing consumerist ethos.

Academics, on the whole, encourage an informal approach, but some concern has been expressed that many academics receive 'a steady stream of e-mail messages … that are too informal or downright inappropriate'.[34] It has been suggested that students, as the consumerist ethos has strengthened, perceive themselves to have a 'right' to be provided with whatever they ask, regardless of their reasons, and that there is an expectation that a response would be forthcoming immediately. Michael J Kessler, an assistant dean and a lecturer in theology at Georgetown University, quoted one student as saying 'I need to know this and you need to tell me right now'. Some of the students' requests reveal their own ethical issues, such as the student who asks for lecture notes, due to their non-attendance, because, by their own admission, they had been drinking all weekend.[35] Or another who wrote 'I couldn't come to class today. Did I miss anything?'[36] It is also relatively common for academics to receive petulant emails from students complaining about their grades. This may often be described as incivility.[37]

Tips for good email etiquette[38] include the following:

- Always address the email with a salutation (ie 'Dear Anna') and sign your email at the end. Include contact information below your signature.
- Never send an email in anger. If you are upset, draft the email without a send address (to avoid inadvertently sending it), then do not look at it overnight or at least for a few hours. Only send it if you then think it is appropriate. Alternatively, ask someone else to look over it before you send it.

---

33 Patrick Lawnham, 'Student Expelled for Email Impersonation' *The Australian,* 22 August 2001, 40; and Gerard Cunningham, '"Obsessed" Student, 42, Waged War by Email' *Daily Mail* 17 April 2010, 8.

34 Jonathan D Glater, 'To: Lecturer@University.edu Subject: Why It's All About Me', *The New York Times*, 21 February 2006, available at http://www.nytimes.com/2006/02/21/education/21professors.html?th.

35 Ibid.

36 'Students E-Mail the Oddest Things' *The New York Times*, 23 February 2006, available at http://www.nytimes.com/2006/02/23/opinion/l23educ.html.

37 See, for example, Marilyn Gilroy, 'Colleges Grappling with Incivility' (2008) 74 (4) *Education Digest* 36.

38 Janice Mac Avoy, Ivan Espinoza-Madrigal and Sherita Walton 'Don't Send an Email Unless You Would be Happy to See It on the Front Page of a Newspaper – or All Over the Internet' (2008) *The Practical Lawyer* 45, 51.

- Avoid unnecessary email – people often receive significant amounts of email daily. Where appropriate, for instance, when you are sending an email for informational purposes, include a notation 'no reply needed' to save your recipient time, and when sending or replying, copy others in only when necessary.
- Ensure you have included any necessary attachments.
- Don't:
  - send jokes unless you are absolutely sure they are appropriate;
  - write anything that you would not be happy to see reproduced on a news site or in a newspaper;
  - use 'all caps' as it is the virtual equivalent of shouting;
  - use emoticons;
  - use slang, jargon or abbreviations.

### *Lawyers and email correspondence*

It is vitally important that law students develop good habits in relation to emails, as there have been some significant issues for practising lawyers in their use of the medium. Emails should be written as carefully as printed communications, for a number of key reasons: first, they are a permanent record. Even if deleted, they remain accessible. Second, email systems may not be secure, so one needs to be careful about sensitive information. Lawyers have a duty of confidentiality in ASCR r 9 and ASCR r 31 sets out very clearly how a practitioner should treat emails sent inadvertently by others. In this context, it is relevant, and of concern, to note that a recent survey of 282 legal professionals, conducted by Lexis-Nexis found that some 89 per cent of law firms collaborated with clients or privileged third parties by email, but only 22 per cent of firms used encrypted email. Seventy-seven per cent relied only on a confidentiality statement in the body of the email.[39]

A related issue is that the sender needs to check the email reply list carefully: a number of difficult situations have arisen because of an accidental 'reply to all'. Fill in the address box only when you're ready to send,[40] and get into the habit of reviewing the 'to', 'cc', 'bcc' and 'from' fields before pressing 'send'.[41] It is easy for an email to be sent to the wrong address, particularly if the autofill function is on. In 2008, in the US for example, a lawyer emailed confidential information about settlement discussions between a corporate client and the federal government – to a *New York Times* reporter. The lawyer thought she was sending the email to her co-counsel,

39 Jeff Goldman, 'Just 22 Percent of Law Firms Use Encrypted Email', *Network World*, 6 June 2014, available at http://www.esecurityplanet.com/network-security/just-22-percent-of-law-firms-use-encrypted-email.html.

40 Gerald Lebovits, 'Email Netiquette for Lawyers' (2009) 64 *NYSBA Journal* 55, 58.

41 George W Kuney, 'Legal Form, Style and Etiquette for Email' (2013) 15 *Transactions: the Tennessee Journal of Business Law* 59, 64.

who happened to have the same family name as the reporter. The newspaper then reported on these negotiations.[42]

A particular problem can be created by lawyers sending their clients 'blind copies'. While it is good practice to ensure your client is kept up to date with what you are communicating on their behalf, the better course of action is to forward copies to them. If clients receive a blind copy they may easily fall into the trap of responding 'to all' and thereby communicate information inadvertently to lawyer representatives of those with whom they are litigating.[43]

Of course, when writing an email you also need to be conscious that the recipient may simply forward it on. In 2006, an American lawyer emailed a prospective employer to say she was declining a position that she had previously accepted. The prospective employer wrote back, noting her lack of professionalism. The lawyer responded that a real lawyer would have put the offer in writing. The prospective employer wrote, counselling against alienating the legal community. The lawyer responded 'bla, bla, bla'. The email chain was forwarded to the media and published in a number of outlets.[44]

Third, email communications are far more likely to be misinterpreted than verbal communications because of the lack of social cues.[45] Indeed, studies have shown that email increases the likelihood of conflict and miscommunication.[46] Care should thus be taken with drafting; and, if the communication does start to degenerate into conflict, try to speak by telephone or in person to the person concerned. Email is not a good means of resolving differences.[47] Similarly, stop emailing when the correspondence turns into a long back and forth discussion (a thread), and try to resolve the issues by telephone or in person.[48] And a reminder of our tip in the etiquette section: do not use all caps or emoticons.

Emails should not contain discriminatory or offensive language, of course, but their tone should also be appropriate. They should be written in keeping with plain language principles and structured carefully. As MacAvoy et al observe, '[c]areless email use can lessen workplace efficiency, damage work relationships, compromise client confidences, and sometimes end promising careers'.[49]

42 Debra Cassens Weiss, 'Did Lawyer's Email Goof Land $1B Settlement on NYT's Front Page?' *American Bar Association Journal*, Feb 6, 2008.

43 Jeffrey M Allen, 'Avoiding Email Hazards' (2014) 24(1) *Experience: The Magazine of the Senior Lawyers Division, American Bar Association* 44, 45.

44 Recounted in Mac Avoy et al, above n 38, 47.

45 Ibid 45.

46 Ibid 46.

47 Lebovits, above n 40, 55.

48 Ibid.

49 Ibid 45.

Lastly, there is another aspect of student email communication that has professional relevance. That is the checking of email accounts. In many universities, email communication is the official form of university communications with students, but students often fail to check their university email account regularly. This often has negative consequences for the student. But there are good reasons why, not only academically but professionally, students should ensure they get into the habit of checking their email accounts regularly.

In the US, as in Australia, electronic filing of court documentation has become the norm. However, in *Blackburn v US Department of Agriculture and Forest Service*[50] a lawyer, Blackburn, filed an action through the Court's electronic filing system, suing the Department of Agriculture. The defendant filed a motion to dismiss. The Court also issued two orders. However, the lawyer failed to respond to either the motion to dismiss or the Court orders. The Court subsequently issued a default judgment dismissing the case. The lawyer argued he had never received copies of the motion to dismiss and the Court orders and that the dismissal should therefore be overturned. However, the Court held that proper notification had taken place through the Court's electronic filing system and that the lawyer had a positive duty to check his email and the status of the case. By using the Court's electronic filing system, the lawyer and his client were bound by its rules, which included an agreement to receive notices via email and to access court information through its electronic system.

The implications of this are that it is good professional training for students to get into the habit of regularly maintaining official email accounts.[51] MacAvoy et al also recommend that you should ensure all substantive email communications are maintained in the client correspondence file and that protocols are in place to maintain this file (particularly if multiple lawyers are involved in the matter); and consider deleting internal emails with drafts of documents that are not forwarded to the client.

## *Texting*

Recognising that the relationship between lecturers and students is now much more informal, many of the examples above could take place in the texting environment. In fact, in one study, students rated text messaging as the discourteous activity most frequently entered into by students,[52] although, in another, texting was only rated as

50 *Blackburn v US Department of Agriculture and Forest Service* No C04-1404RSM (WD Wash, 2005).

51 Practice tips arising from this case can be found in Jessica Belskis, 'Electronic Case Filing: Is Failure to Check Email Related to an Electronically Filed Case Malpractice?' (2005) 2 *Shidler Journal of Law, Commerce & Technology* 13.

52 Bjorklund and Rehling, above n 31, 17.

tenth on a list of twenty-six discourteous activities.[53] The bulk of scholarly literature to date, however, discusses texting primarily as a means of enhancing student learning in classroom activities.[54]

Universities have now introduced strategies to curb inappropriate communications and in some cases to characterise these acts as student misconduct. Most universities have introduced Student Codes of Conduct; Minimum Expectations or similar policy initiatives to make it explicit that certain written communications will not be tolerated. However, more specifically, as a law student you are entering the legal profession's community of practice. You need to recognise that there are specific rules about how a lawyer communicates with other practitioners, the court, their clients and others and, perhaps more importantly, that you must conduct yourself as an officer of the court and ensure that you do not bring the legal profession into disrepute (ASCR r 3.1 and r 5.1.2). In other words, as a trainee lawyer, you need to reflect on what you intend to do and in doing so, exercise professional judgment. In addition, poor conduct on the part of students at academic institutions must now be reported as part of an application for admission (See *Legal Profession Uniform Admission Rules* 2015 r 19).

## V REFLECTIVE PRACTICES

Increasingly, reflective practice is an important component of professionalism, particularly for lawyers.[55] Reflective practice, as we noted earlier, is the integration of thought and action in a professional context. The intention of reflective practice is 'to provide the professional with a self-improvement algorithm, and to increase the capacity of the professional to exercise judgment in the professional context'.[56] The following discussion outlines one reflective model, summarised in Figure 12.1. Initially, the model might seem artificial and somewhat mechanical, but over time, it can become an 'ingrained habit of constant reflection'.[57]

---

53 Ibid 16.

54 Stephen McClean, Paul Hagan and Jason Morgan, 'Text Messaging for Student Communication and Voting', *Bioscience Education e-Journal*, December 2010, 16, available at www.bioscience.heacademy.ac.uk/journal/vol16/beej-16-4.pdf.

55 Mike Robertson, 'Renewing a Focus on Ethics in Legal Education?' (Paper presented at Australian Lawyers and Social Change, Faculty of Law, Australian National University, 24 September 2004), available at https://law.anu.edu.au/sites/all/files/users/u4081600/Conference_docs/mikerobertson.pdf.

56 Casey, above n 6, 321.

57 Ibid 322.

FIGURE 12.1

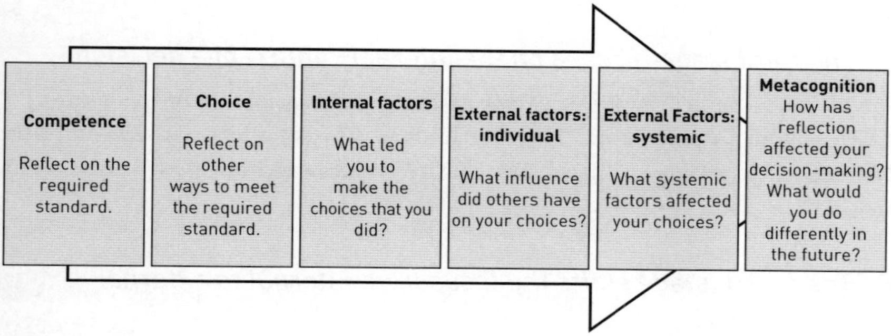


## 1 *The first stage focuses on professional competence*

The key question here is: *Does the writing meet the appropriate standard of competency?* Some prompts for reflection are:

- What would a competent lawyer do in this situation?
- What would be necessary to achieve a basic level of competence in the performance?
- Did you meet the standard of competence?

This methodology starts similarly to the application of IRAC in that it requires you to consider your action in accordance with the professional standard required. It acknowledges the fundamental importance of ASCR r 4.1.3 (to deliver legal services competently, that is, with the level of legal research and knowledge warranted).[58] It also asks you to consider whether the legal standard for performance is adequate. Is it sufficient to perform this minimum standard? Or should you strive to achieve a higher standard?[59] In this way you are encouraged to develop your own professional identity.[60]

## 2 *The second stage focuses on discretion and choice*

The key questions here are: *Are there different, equally successful ways to accomplish the requisite standard of performance? At what point in the performance did you make a choice?*

At this stage, you are invited to reflect on the element of vagueness inherent in professional practice.[61] There are, ordinarily, multiple ways of doing things.

58 Casey, above n 6, 335.
59 Ibid 336.
60 Ibid 338.
61 Ibid 339.

As a decision-maker, you have discretion to determine what is relevant or what is expected of you, and in making decisions, you make choices.[62]

### 3 *The third stage focuses on the internal context of a decision*

The key question here is: *Why have you made the specific choice or decision in the context of your professional performance?* This step leads you to consider your own intrinsic 'preferences, experiences, biases and characteristics' and how they shaped your decision.[63]

### 4 *The fourth stage shifts the focus from internal to external considerations*

The key question here is: *What external factors affected your choice?* This step leads you to reflect upon the preferences, experiences, biases and characteristics of others and how these influenced your choices.

### 5 *The fifth stage continues with the external focus*

The key question here is: *Are there broader considerations (political, economic or social) that affect the decision or choice?* Decisions are made within a context of systemic power dynamics, political and social realities, and economic forces.

### 6 *The sixth stage is one of 'metacognition' (metacognition is knowledge of your own learning processes)*

The key questions here are: *How has reflection affected your decision-making? How do you think differently, or, how has your thinking process changed, as a result of reflection on the lawyering activity in question?*

It is suggested that, with practice, this process will prepare you to be a reflective practitioner – one who has the 'capacity to analyse the context and adapt [your] performance while the decision is still under consideration'.[64] Employing a reflective model will provide you with the tools to track your development towards becoming a lawyer who has professional judgment.

62 Ibid 338–9.
63 Ibid 339.
64 Ibid 350.

## VI REFLECTIVE WRITING

Increasingly, assessment in tertiary education has a reflective component to it. For instance, you may have been asked to complete a journal; an e-portfolio; to 'rework ideas'; or comment on your experience of the assessment. These activities are particularly designed to help you analyse your thoughts and consider how you have developed professionally.[65]

### *Reflective portfolios*

A reflective portfolio is writing that summarises the insights and experiences a student has gained from practical assignments. It can take many forms, including an e-portfolio, an extended written piece, or a collection of short writings and documentary evidence.[66] Despite the difference in forms, the common characteristics of portfolios are collection, selection, reflection,[67] connection and reconstruction. The purpose is for you to explore and reflect upon your own learning processes[68] and to develop a critical awareness of your own skill development.[69] Portfolios can provide a developmental view of professional growth and achievements.[70]

Portfolios are thus not a mere collection of writings and assignments. Ideally, they are the product of discrimination and choice: rather than 'undifferentiated pieces of paper seasoned with a sprinkling of commentary', a reflective portfolio is 'carefully shaped'.[71] In a reflective portfolio, you not only keep a record of your work but reflect on what you learned, how this fits into the 'bigger picture' of your personal and professional goals, and how you might use your experiences in the future. In this way, reflective portfolios move you to a professional level of personal responsibility[72] and actively engage you in your own learning.[73]

Generally, if used as an assessment item in a subject, you will be given instructions for constructing a portfolio. But you may wish to construct a portfolio yourself to

---

65 Andrea McArdle, 'Writing Across the Curriculum: Professional Communication and the Writing that Support It' (2009) 15 *Journal of the Legal Writing Institute* 241, 246.

66 Ivory Research.com, 'Reflective Portfolio – How to Write 1st Class Reflective Portfolio', available at http://www.ivoryresearch.com/reflective-portfolio-how-to-write-1st-class-reflective-portfolio/.

67 Yves Labissiere 'Using Reflective Electronic Portfolios to Enhance Student Learning: Theory and Practice', nd, (citing Yancey, 2001), available at http://www.frinq-workshop.michael flower.com/resources/Wednesday-the-17th/ReflectiveEP.pdf.

68 Ivory Research.com above n 66.

69 Ibid.

70 San Diego State University, 'The Reflective Student Learning Portfolio', available at http://interwork.sdsu.edu/main/system/files/Student%20Learning%20Portfolio%20Handbook%20%5BUPDATED%20FALL%202011%5D_0.pdf.

71 Barbara J Millis, 'Shaping the Reflective Portfolio: A Philosophical Look at the Mentoring Role' (1995) 6(1) *Journal on Excellence in College Teaching* 65, 66.

72 San Diego State University above n 70.

73 Labissiere above n 67, 3.

document your progress towards becoming a professional. Portfolios are increasingly useful, too, in the job application process. Used in this way, they can become an evolving collection of documents and materials which change over time. In general, the process of developing a reflective portfolio is as follows:

- Step 1: *Reflect on the goals of the portfolio process.*
- Step 2: *Collect samples of your learning*: In particular, use samples or experiences that you found to be exciting, challenging, confusing, surprising or to which you had some other significant response.
- Step 3: *From your collection, select an example or examples that are particularly significant to you:* You may find the sample referred to an 'artefact' in some of the literature about portfolios. Start by using the prompts:
  - What is the artefact?
  - Why did I select it?
- Step 4: *Reflect on your learning:* Here you should take a critical approach. This is a process of self-assessment and you should acknowledge strengths and weaknesses. The key attributes of your reflective commentary should be integrity and lucidity.[74] You can use the reflective process we outlined above, or you can use the following prompts:
  - What happened?
  - Why did it happen?
  - What do I think about it happening?
- Step 5: *Reconstruction:* Consider how this experience, and the reflection upon it, affects the future. Some prompts you mind find useful include:
  - What do I want to happen in the future?
  - What did I learn that I did not know before?
  - What are the implications of this experience for my personal and/or professional goals?
- Step 6: *Add your sample and your reflection to the portfolio:* As in all writing, you should ensure the portfolio is professional and well-presented.[75]

### Reflective essays and other writing

In addition to portfolios, other forms of reflective writing are increasingly used in universities. These may take a variety of forms, including formal reflective essays or reports (which have a clear structure of introduction, body and conclusion) and more informal reflective writing tasks, such as blogs, discussion entries or journals.

---

74 Millis, above n 71, 70.
75 Ivory Research.com above n 66.

Regardless of the form, reflective writing generally has certain key features, as shown in Figure 12.2.[76]

FIGURE 12.2

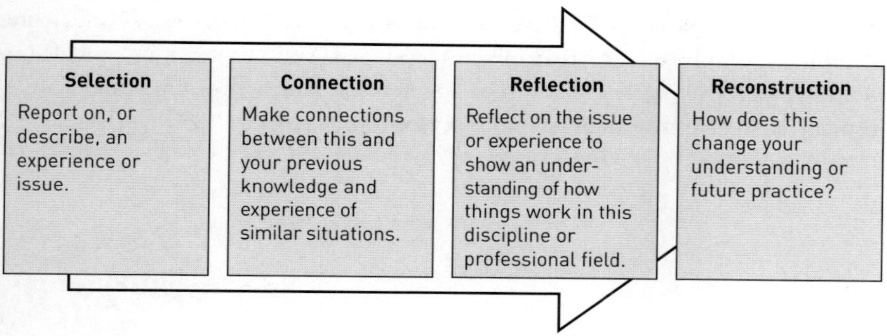


- *Selection:* Report on, or describe, an experience or issue. This corresponds to the 'sample' in the e-portfolio. Explain what happened and in what context.
- *Connection:* Relate the issue or experience to your own skills, professional experience or development or discipline knowledge. Have you had similar or related experiences? What is your subjective response? Make connections between this and your previous knowledge and experience of similar situations. The examination of your beliefs, values, attitudes and assumptions is foundational to this sort of writing. At the same time, this is a form of academic writing, so although you are writing about your own experiences and responses, you need to be objective and rigorous.
- *Reflection:* Reflect on the issue/incident to show an understanding of how things work in this discipline or professional field. What factors in the experience are important for a new understanding? Relate these back to the academic literature. Discuss different perspectives involved (these may be ethical, social, legal, organisational or professional).
- *Reconstruction:* How does this change your understanding or future practice? Outline the changes in your understanding and/or your behaviour as a result of the experience and your reflection upon it. What are the implications for your future professional practice? What actions will you take and why?

76 Adapted from http://www.citewrite.qut.edu.au/write/reflectivewriting.jsp.

## VII CONCLUSION

In this chapter, we have considered the relationship between writing and reflection. Reflecting on our writing; and writing to enhance reflection are both important aspects of professional identity. We have thus outlined the need for reflection in everyday communications. We have argued that reflective practice is a key attribute of professionalism, and one that can be developed. The chapter thus provided a model of reflective practice that can be adopted and which, over time can become instinctive. And we have outlined processes for formal reflective writing tasks.

# REVIEW MATERIALS

## SUMMARY

This chapter focused on reflection in writing, including its role in maintaining civility within and beyond the profession, and as an aspect professional identity. Reflection was defined and its place in student correspondence with peers and in social media was examined. The chapter included a schema for reflective practice and suggestions for using reflective journals and portfolios.

## KEY POINTS

1. Reflective practice is the integration of thought and action in a professional context.
2. Reflective practice is an important aspect of professionalism and can foster the development of a professional identity.
3. As a student, reflective and careful use of social media and electronic communications can enhance your professional identity, in the short term and the long term.
4. Always maintain a professional and objective tone in electronic communications (never send an email or text in anger!).
5. The use of a schema for reflective practice can develop your capacity for reflection so that reflective practice then becomes second nature.

## QUESTIONS FOR REFLECTION

1. In what circumstances might communicating in writing be more appropriate than a conversation? When is a conversation more helpful than communicating in writing?
2. There has been much discussion about the importance of mindfulness for lawyers, particularly in the lawyer well-being discourse. What is the relationship between reflection and mindfulness?
3. Do you use good email etiquette? How could you improve your use of email and other forms of instantaneous communication?
4. Do you use a reflective journal or portfolio in relation to your learning or practice of law? If not, could such a reflective practice be of benefit? What steps could you take to introduce reflective practice into your work?
5. In what ways can you protect your individual professional 'brand' on social media?

## EXERCISES

1. Rewrite the following in a more professional voice:
   a. If you don't respond to me by COB today, I will report you to the managing director TOMORROW and there goes your brilliant career. Ha Ha. I am fed up with your stupidity and incompetence;
   b. I checked out your file, and I don't think your case has a chance☹ but your previous lawyer was AWESOME;
   c. You promised me that case file would be on my desk YESTERDAY. I still don't have it. Are you incompetent or what? No wonder everyone says you're an idiot.
2. Are the following emails acceptable? Justify your answers.
   Student to teacher
   a. Can you please read my attached draft assignment and provide me with feedback within 24 hours?
   b. I have read the feedback you have provided but I am a little confused about some of your remarks. May I please have an appointment to see you?
   c. I was unable to attend your class last Monday. Can you please answer the attached questions?
   d. General question – is it appropriate to email a teacher before the results are published praising them for their teaching methods?
   Student to student
   a. Can I please have your assignment answer so that I can get an idea how to answer the question?

## FURTHER RESOURCES

1. Ten Rules of Effective Peer-to-Peer Communications[77]

   'Much of the work we do every day depends on having a positive working relationship with our colleagues. Yes, having a good rapport with the boss is important, but some of us can go days without speaking to our boss. Ah but co-workers? We talk to them every single day.

   Being able to communicate effectively with our peers helps us get our jobs done by answering questions, sharing information, and offering feedback. Not to mention that effective communication can bring fun and energy to the workplace.

77 These rules appeared in a post by Sharlyn Lauby '10 Rules of Effective Peer-to-Peer Communications', available at http://www.halogensoftware.com/blog/10-rules-of-effective-peer-to-peer-communications, dated 4 February 2014.

To make the most of your peer-to-peer (P2P) communications, there are 10 rules you should follow:

1. Understand your communication style. The first rule of communication is to become self-aware and realize how you like to communicate.

   Are you a direct, "just the facts ma'am" communicator? Are you a story teller? Are you more systematic and logical? Is your relationship with the other person a critical aspect of the communication?

   Knowing your preferred style of communication will be incredibly valuable when dealing with others. And essential when the message you need to deliver isn't a positive one.
2. Reflect on how others react to your communications. Think about the last five conversations you had that didn't go well, and ask yourself the reason. Then think about the last five communications you had that went really well and the reason. Identify the common elements or trends.
3. Share the best way for others to communicate with you. Years ago I had a boss who, every time he took a personality assessment, would share a copy of the results with his team. At first, I thought it was goofy. But then I realized he was trying to tell me how to communicate with him. And that was priceless….
4. Communicate on the other person's channel. Once you know how another person wants to receive communication, it's your responsibility to communicate that way.

   If you don't know how someone wants to hear the message, ask them. "I'd like to talk with you about the ABC proposal. Would tomorrow morning be a good time?" or "I need some answers from you regarding the ABC proposal. Would you like me to setup a meeting to discuss it or should I send an email?"
5. Learn how stress impacts communications. When people are under stress, they react differently. I've seen employees totally botch up conversations because they so desperately needed to get their message out, they couldn't wait for the recipient to be ready to receive it. That's what stress will do.
6. Deliver messages at the right moments. Ever work with an employee who came in early, never said hello, and immediately started working? I felt sorry for the co-worker who would saunter over with their coffee to talk about last night's game. Obviously, they didn't read the signs that the employee was trying to get something done, and it was the wrong time for conversation.
7. Use the proper tools. …time for all of us to realize there are some messages you can send on Twitter, others that should be sent via email, and then those that need a voice-to-voice conversation. Using the right medium to send a

message can make all the difference in the world when it comes to how your message will be received.

8. Recognize others in a way that makes them feel good. Recognizing others isn't just a task for management. You should recognize your co-workers for a job well done and when they help you do your job better.

   And, this is where tip #1 is so necessary. The way you want to be recognized isn't always the way others want to be recognized. For recognition to be effective, it has to be given in a way that makes the other person feel important.

9. Be empathetic. This applies to many of the rules above. If you take a moment to put yourself in your co-workers shoes, it can positively impact your communications with them. Whether they're happy or stressed, you can either share in their enthusiasm or not contribute to their frustration.

10. And if, after all of this, the communication gets messed up, don't let it fester. **Fix it**. Yes, there will be times when, no matter how hard you try, the communication will not go as planned. Instead of ignoring the situation and potentially having it get worse, have a conversation with your co-worker. Let them know that having a positive working relationship is important, and you'd like to talk it out.

    The working relationships we have with our peers can make us or break us. Developing good communications with them benefits everyone and makes coming to work a whole lot easier.'

CHAPTER 13

# CONCLUSION

In concluding this book, we come full circle. We began with reflection: reflection upon audience, purpose, genre and ethical obligations. We end, again, with reflection: reflection upon lawyering, ethics and the importance of written communication to the professional identity of the lawyer.

We have claimed in this book that good legal writing is inherently ethical in at least three ways. It shows: awareness of self and other; engagement with the community of practice; and awareness of, and respect for, the writer's professional obligations.

On the first point, awareness of self and other, we have suggested that good legal writing starts from reflection upon the self: your purpose in writing; your biases; your knowledge; and the message you want to convey. It is these reflections that shape your pre-writing, that is, your research and your planning. Your reflection on the other entails consideration of your audience. Who is your audience? What do they know? What do they want from your writing? What are their expectations? These considerations of audience shape, in particular, you drafting, revising, editing and proofreading.

On the second point, engagement with the community of practice, we have suggested that good legal writing evidences an awareness of the norms and conventions of the discourse community, that is, the academic and legal writing communities. As a writer, you will, over time, become familiar with, and develop mastery in, the genres, vocabulary, construction and styles of academic and legal writing.

On the third point, awareness of, and respect for, your professional obligation, we have sought to make the links between professional conduct, particularly the provisions of the ASCR, and your legal writing. We have sought to show that legal writing should adhere to professional expectations, including competency, honesty, duty to law, duty to the client, and courtesy.

We noted that, although in a sense this is a 'how to' book, it is modelled on the fundamentals of academic writing, particularly respect for sources, and it has stressed that there are no 'quick fixes' – legal writing is messy and recursive, and learning legal writing can be difficult and frustrating. We have tried to emphasise that writing is not a merely mechanical task. Yes, grammar, spelling and plain language are inherently important and form an important aspect of the norms and conventions of legal writing. Ultimately, however, developing mastery in academic and legal writing is profoundly rewarding and an integral part of your own professional identity. To learn to be a good legal writer is to learn how to be a good lawyer. We thus leave you with a challenge: who are you as a legal writer? What is your professional 'voice'? What does your legal writing convey about you as a legal professional?

We have also urged caution in relation to changes in the way we write. The increased use of technological forms of writing – such as emails, SMS and social networking – offer opportunities and advantages to legal writers, but they can also be dangerous to the creation and maintenance of your professional identity. Reflecting on the ethical dimensions of writing and keeping in mind the links between writing and professional identity can protect you from falling into some of the traps of instantaneous communications.

This chapter concludes the substantive content of this book. In Part 3, the section following this chapter, we provide a section of learning materials. This section includes an account of different theories of writing, tables outlining professional rules, a grammar primer, and a glossary of terms. We hope these materials prove useful to you and we wish you well in your development as a legal writer.

# PART 3

# LEARNING MATERIALS

# THEORIES OF WRITING

You will recall our diagrammatic summary of the theories of writing outlined in Chapter 2 (Figure 2.3).

This appendix provides further information on each of these theories of writing and their implications for audience and purpose and for legal writing more generally.

## THE RHETORICAL THEORY

The rhetorical theory of writing is based on the concept of 'a rhetor as a purposeful agent in a rhetorical context who seeks through persuasion or identification to affect the minds of others'.[1] The rhetorical perspective assumes writing is analogous to oratory, that is, a speaker addressing an audience she wishes to persuade. On this view, the writer must understand the audience's beliefs, traits and audiences, in order to persuade.[2] But the rhetorical theory is said to have limitations: one drawback of the rhetorical approach is that when we teach students that all writing involves argument, we convey the mistaken view that their writing should always be assertive and argumentative. The audience is perceived to be an adversary, much like the opponent in a debate. A second drawback is that the author is expected to know a lot about her audience. But sometimes the audience is so broad that only very general assumptions about its characteristics can be made.[3] A third drawback is that the theory assumes a relatively passive reader.[4] Thus, Park argues that in the rhetorical tradition, the term audience 'might almost be said to mean too much, to block thought by making us think we know what we are talking about when we often do not'.[5] Audience, from the rhetorical perspective, means 'something like people-as-they-are-involved-in-a-rhetorical-situation'. This concept has to do with 'final

1 Linda Flower, 'The Construction of Purpose in Writing and Reading' (1988) 50(5) *College English* 528, 529.
2 Barry M Kroll, 'Writing for Readers: three Perspectives on Audience' (1984) 35(2) *College Composition and Communication* 172, 172.
3 Ibid 174.
4 Ibid 175.
5 Douglas B Park, 'The Meanings of "Audience"' (1982) 44(3) *College English* 247, 248.

and formal cause-what a piece of discourse sets out to do and how it is shaped to accomplish that end'.[6]

## THE INSTRUMENTAL OR FORMALIST THEORY

This is the theory that underlies the traditional view of legal writing and its instruction[7] (although, as Pollman[8] observes, instruction in legal writing is a relatively recent development in law schools, emerging as a distinct discipline in the US in the 1980s). This theory holds that the purpose of writing is to convey information; that is, the writer seeks to transmit a message to the reader as effectively as she can.[9] Writing is simply a tool for expressing, rather than forming, thought.[10] The emphasis is upon the 'product' of legal writing and the assumption is that language is a transparent medium for meaning, that is, it does not contribute to the construction of meaning.[11] Thus, the primary formal concern in the writing of the text is with clarity of organisation, style and word choice, and with accuracy.[12] Traditional instruction in legal writing has focused on the application of 'rigid rules and formulae that [emphasise] the formal properties of model legal texts'.[13]

This theory of legal writing has been criticised by some members of the academy and the profession as failing to produce good legal writers.[14] As a basis for writing instruction, it has been argued that it encourages students to imitate various writing styles, often generating 'documents replete with run-on sentences, multisyllabic words, obscure Latin phrases, and jargon that they may not even understand'. In addition, this approach tends to separate writing from thinking and analysing law.[15] It has also been argued that the theory is based on a false assumption that readers are 'empty vessels'. It fails to appreciate the extent to which readers 'construct' the text.[16] Readers decode and 'process' writing, integrating new information with information already in memory. Writers thus need to understand this process.[17]

---

6 Ibid 249.

7 J Christopher Rideout and Jill J Ramsfield, 'Legal Writing: A Revised View' (1994) 69 (35) *Washington Law Review* 35, 49.

8 Terrill Pollman, 'Building a Tower of Babel or Building a Discipline? Talking about Legal Writing (2002) 85(4) *Marquette Law Review* 887, 894.

9 Kroll, above n 2, 176.

10 Pollman, above n 8, 897.

11 Rideout and Ramsfield, above n 7, 49.

12 Ibid 49.

13 Pollman, above n 8, 893.

14 Jo Anne Durako et al, 'From Product to Process: Evolution of a Legal Writing Program' (1996–97) 58 *University of Pittsburgh Law Review* 719, 720.

15 Durako et al, above n 14, 721.

16 Kroll, above n 2, 178, quoting Dillon.

17 Ibid 176.

## THE COGNITIVE THEORY (OR PROCESS THEORY)

This theory of writing derives from research into psychology and artificial intelligence and seeks to construct accurate models of the behaviour of writers in the writing process.[18] This model is particularly notable for shifting the emphasis in writing from the product to the process of writing:[19] it seeks to change the goal of writing instruction from 'perfecting the product to teaching life-long skills adaptable to new writing situations'.[20] This theory explicitly acknowledges that students start their studies with varying degrees of experience and competence. Learning to write is a process of developing mastery.[21] This theory of writing is linked to the epistemic view – that is, writing is not only about communication, but also about the generation of knowledge.[22] This is important for legal writing:

> Because a critical function of law school is to teach legal analysis and argument, a function in which legal writing instruction plays an important role. Especially for law students, but no less in law practice, the act of writing is intimately involved with the act of "constructing" the law-describing and synthesizing the applicable law, applying legal rules, drawing analogies and distinguishing facts, and developing legal arguments.[23]

Commentators adopting this view of legal writing, such as Kissam,[24] advocate more critical writing in the law school curriculum.

The cognitive theory holds that 'writing is a recursive process that overlaps and intertwines prewriting, writing and revision activities'.[25] Within this process, the writer will move through '*generating* (using long-term memory to gather ideas in order to write on a specific topic), *organising* (selecting the useful memories and placing them into a logical structure), *translating* (transforming that logical structure into written sentences), and *reviewing* (rereading, evaluation, and perhaps editing the sentences to better conform to the writer's goals)'.[26] In turn, because reading is also a complex constructive cognitive process, the reader's own goals, assumptions and context affect meaning making.[27] From the cognitive perspective, the

---

18 Rideout and Ramsfield, above n 7, 51.
19 Ibid 52.
20 Durako et al, above n 14, 722.
21 Rideout and Ramsfield, above n 7, 53.
22 Ibid 55.
23 Ibid 55.
24 Philip C Kissam, 'Thinking (By Writing) about Legal Writing' (1987) 40(135) *Vanderbilt Law Review* 135.
25 Durako et al, above n 14, 722.
26 Alecia Marie Magnifico, 'Writing for Whom? Cognition, Motivation and a Writer's Audience' (2010) 45(3) *Educational Psychologist* 167, 171.
27 Flower, above n 1, 540.

audience serves primarily as a tool for thought and memory – a trigger for prior knowledge'.[28]

## THE SOCIAL OR SOCIO-CULTURAL THEORY

Under the **socio-cultural theory**, writing is viewed as an essentially social act. Magnifico observes that where cognitive scholars focus on the *writer's position* in the world (that is, the processes by which the writer makes individual meaning from experience, remembers it, and records it), sociocultural theorists focus on the writer's position *in the world*, how she creates meaning from the social factors that make up experiences.[29] On this theory, the process of writing for readers inevitably involves social thinking, or 'social cognition'.[30] On the socio-cultural theory of writing, the audience is not an external consideration, but rather internal and embedded within the writing. Writers write *to* someone and *for* some purpose.[31] Writing, from this perspective, is not a matter of remembering or of internal processing according to complex genre schemata, as the cognitive view would hold. It is, rather, both interpretive and inextricable from 'the writer's language community, social position, values, and actions in the world'.[32]

The intertwining of the individual, the cultural and the social, Gee[33] called 'Discourse'. 'Discourses' are ways of being in the world, by which individuals learn, interact with others, and become members of communities of practice. He thus distinguishes 'Discourse' from 'discourse', the latter referring to any spoken or written stream of language in the world. A 'Discourse' is particular to a community of practice.[34] Legal writers, on this view, become expert not only by learning the genres and writing conventions of the law, but by interacting with the legal community and adopting its Discourse of 'situated practices and specific ways of thinking, talking, writing, acting, believing, and being'.[35] It is not just a matter of learning a series of increasingly complex schemata and thinking processes but of becoming an active member of the Discourse community, adopting common practices and values and, in turn, being seen by an audience of other members as a knowledgeable participant and, eventually, as an expert.[36] On this view, it is essential to gain feedback from the Discourse community: the novice writer gains

28 Magnifico, above n 26, 175.
29 Ibid 173.
30 Kroll, above n 2, 182–3.
31 Magnifico, above n 26, 173.
32 Ibid.
33 Gee 1996, cited by Magnifico, above n 26.
34 Magnifico, above n 26, 173.
35 Ibid 173.
36 Ibid 174.

'a clearer metacognitive understanding of themselves as writers and participants through their audience members' feedback … what the other members will accept as a valid contribution, and why it is important to take those readers into account'. Thus, a key role that the audience plays is to offer feedback and reactions to the writing.[37]

Three features will determine how language is structured in a discourse. These are: the field of discourse (what the text is about); the tenor of discourse (who is taking part, and what are their roles and relationships in the text and context?); and the mode of discourse (what part is language playing in the text? Is the function of the text to persuade? To describe? To explain?).[38] Commentators such as Rideout and Ramsfield consider the social perspective highly significant for legal writing:

> This broader perspective is especially important for a field like legal writing, which takes place within a discourse that is complex and highly conventionalized and which is also closely constrained by the institutional characteristics of law-the roles of lawyers, the organization of law practice, the purposes of law as a social and economic institution, and the underlying ideology of the law.[39]

This view explicitly acknowledges that acculturation to legal discourse continues beyond law school into professional practice. The process is gradual, as novices move closer to expert status and more sophisticated writing techniques.[40]

But difficulties for law students are implicit in this view. First, as Rideout and Ramsfield[41] observe, the student is caught in something of a paradox: the student must master the conventions of a discourse in order to be a member of the discourse community and thus an accomplished legal writer. But those conventions are, by definition, only known to the discourse community, so learning to write as a lawyer writes means becoming a lawyer. For students, mistakes and confusion are inevitable – they mean that they are finding their way into the discourse community.

Second, Kroll observes that too often students have far too few opportunities to experience the social dimensions of writing. Because the process of writing is typically done alone, 'because writing tasks can often be perceived as mere exercises, and because written products are often seen only by a teacher/judge', students often fail to perceive the social nature of writing and writing may then be

37 Ibid 175.
38 Mary Ryan, 'Improving Reflective Writing in Higher Education: a Social Semiotic Perspective' (2011) 16(1) *Teaching in Higher Education* 102, citing Halliday and Hasan, 1985.
39 Rideout and Ramsfield, above n 7, 57.
40 Ibid 93.
41 Ibid 58.

viewed as a mechanical task 'with no more social implications than completing a set of arithmetic problems'.[42] Similarly, Magnifico observes that the external goal of getting reasonable grades remains the key motivation for many students, and they are still writing primarily to be evaluated by their teachers. Thus, little attention is paid to questions such as: What is the purpose of the writing? What form should it take? Who is the audience?'[43] Park, too, specifically refers to situations where the contemplated 'audience' is the teacher. Often students take the attitude, 'You asked me the question, and here's the answer'. But at tertiary level, Park notes, teachers 'expect situations in which the student writes within some kind of rhetorical context and in which the teacher serves not as audience but as editor and judge of success'.[44]

Third, students must accept an inevitable loss of originality:

> To learn legal writing is to learn how to write within the conventions and practices of a particular professional group more than it is to write original ideas that the law might then claim as its own, as being 'legal'. This seeming loss of the ability to 'be original' is something every law student encounters.[45]

The sociocultural perspective need not replace the other perspectives on legal writing, rather it can enhance them.[46] Indeed, Rideout and Ramsfield, in their revised view of legal writing, take into account the various theories of legal writing:

> The revised view suggests that writers start projects by systematically recording purpose, audience, scope, and context. The institutional constraints of writing in a particular practice indicate that writing is more than the final product, that the social context can influence and change the writing process and writing habits, and that new approaches to writing can be put to advantage by the new lawyer. Systematic and continued writing in the new environment can help acculturate the new lawyer to the analytical, linguistic, and stylistic expectations of all audiences.[47]

## Implications for law students

So, what are the implications of these various theories for learning legal writing? First, 'planning activities, analysis, and writing are inextricably linked'.[48] Rideout and Ramsfield advocate that 'writers start projects by systematically recording purpose,

42 Kroll, above n 2, 180.
43 Magnifico, above n 26, 174.
44 Park, above n 5, 255.
45 Rideout and Ramsfield, above n 7, 59.
46 Ibid 60.
47 Ibid 94.
48 Ibid 96.

audience, scope, and context'.[49] But from here, the student of legal writing needs to understand the importance of the discourse community and the way in which it determines the choices available to the writer: '[t]he better the understanding of those rhetorical, analytical, and practical choices, the better able the writer will be to meet the reader's needs and to generate techniques that will mature and adapt to new writing situations'.[50] New legal writers need to be aware of a variety of approaches to process that are practised by experts, and consider carefully the structuring, drafting, and revising of their legal writing.[51] But in addition to incorporating such new techniques, new writers should also build in a reviewing stage to examine the document and consider whether or not it fits its purpose and is directed appropriately to its audience.[52]

49 Ibid 94.
50 Ibid 96.
51 Ibid.
52 Ibid 97.

# COMPARATIVE TABLES

## INTRODUCTION

In this book the authors have chosen to refer specifically to the Australian Solicitors Conduct Rules (ASCR). However, as noted in Chapter 1, these have so far only been adopted by New South Wales, Victoria, Queensland, and South Australia. Therefore, the following tables are provided to outline the equivalent solicitors rules for the other states of Australia, and the equivalent Australian Bar Association Barristers' Conduct Rules (Bar Rules, which are now adopted by New South Wales, Victoria, Queensland, South Australia and Western Australia, and also the equivalent rules governing barristers in the other States that have not adopted the Bar Rules.

The book mentions the *Legal Profession Uniform Law*, which has only been adopted by New South Wales and Victoria, only a few times, but the table below sets out the equivalent legislation in the other states for those sections.

## PROFESSIONAL RULES FOR SOLICITORS

All of the ASCR rules are included here, although particular rules are referred to in the book only where they relate specifically to the topic being discussed.

The following jurisdictional rules apply:

- New South Wales, Victoria, South Australia and Queensland: *Legal Profession Uniform Law Australian Solicitors' Conduct Rules 2015* (ASCR).
- Australian Capital Territory: *Legal Profession (Solicitors) Rules 2007.*
- Northern Territory: *Rules of Professional Conduct and Practice 2005.*
- Tasmania: *Rules of Practice 1994.*
- Western Australia: Legal Professional Conduct Rules 2010.

| | ASCR | ACT | NT | TAS | WA |
|---|---|---|---|---|---|
| NATURE AND PURPOSE OF THE RULES | | | | | |
| Application and Interpretation | 1 | Intro and 4 | Intro and 4 | 3 | 4 |
| Purpose and effect of the rules | 2 | | | | |

(Continued)

| | ASCR | ACT | NT | TAS | WA |
|---|---|---|---|---|---|
| FUNDAMENTAL DUTIES OF SOLICITORS | | | | | |
| Paramount duty to the court and admin of justice | 3/3.1 | | | | 5 |
| Other fundamental ethical duties | 4 | | | | 6 |
| Client's best interests | 4.1.1 | 16.1 | 17.1 | | 6(1)(a) |
| Honest and courteous | 4.1.2 | 24 | 1; 18 | | 6(1)(b) |
| Competently, diligently and promptly | 4.1.3 | 1.2; 1.3(a)(i) | 1.1 | 10 | 6(1)(c); 7(e) and (g) |
| Integrity and independence | 4.1.4 | | | | 6(1)(d) |
| Compliance with rule and law | 4.1.5 | | | | 6(1)(e) |
| Dishonest & disreputable conduct | 5.1 | | | | 6(2) |
| Undertakings | 6.1 | 25.1; and 30 | 19 and 25 | | 22(2) and (3) |
| | 6.2 | 25.2 and 25.3 | 19A, 20 | | |
| RELATIONS WITH CLIENTS | | | | | |
| Communication of advice – understand legal issues | 7.1 | 16.2 | 17.2 | | 8; 10(1) |
| Advise alternative dispute resolution | 7.2 | | 10A.3; 10A.7 | | |
| Client instructions | 8.1 | | | | 7(a) |
| Confidentiality | 9.1 | 2.1 | 2.1 | 11(1) | 9(1);(2) |
| | 9.2.1 | 2.1(a) | 2.1.1 | 11(1) | 9(3)(a) |
| | 9.2.2 | 2.1(b) | 2.1.2 | | 9(3)(b) |
| | 9.2.3 | | | | 9(3)(c) |
| | 9.2.4 | | | | 9(3)(d) |
| | 9.2.5 | | | | 9(3)(e) |
| | 9.2.6 | | | | 9(3)(f) |

| | ASCR | ACT | NT | TAS | WA |
|---|---|---|---|---|---|
| Conflicts – former clients | 10.1 | 3 | 3 | | 13 |
| | 10.2 | 3 | 3 | | 13(2) |
| | 10.2.1 | | | | 13(3)(a) |
| | 10.2.2 | | | | 13(3)(b) |
| Conflicts – current clients | 11 | 7.2 | 7.2 | 12(2) | 14 |
| | 11.1 | | | | 14(1) |
| | 11.2 | | | | |
| | 11.3 | | | | |
| | 11.4 | | | | |
| | 11.4.2 | | | | 14(3) |
| | 11.5 | | | | |
| Conflicts – solicitors own interests | 12.1 | 8.1(a) and 8.2 | 8.1.1 and 8.2 | | 12 and 15(2) |
| | 12.2 | 8.1(b) | 8.1.2 | | |
| Borrow money from clients | 12.3 | 10.1 | 10.1 | | 15(6) |
| Benefit under a Will | 12.4.1 | 9.2 | 9.1 | | 15(5)(a)(iii) |
| | 12.4.2 | 9.3 | 9.3 | | 15(5)(b) |
| Referral fees | 12.4.3 | 34.2 | 29.2 | | 18(5) |
| | 12.4.4 | 34(1)(a) | 29.1.1 | | 18(5)(a) |
| Completion or termination of engagement | 13.1 | 5.1 | 5.1 | | 27(1) |
| | 13.2 | 5.2 | 5.2 | | 27(3) |
| | 13.3 | 5.3 | 5.3 | | 27(4) |
| Client documents | 14.1 | 6.2; 26.2 | 6.3; 21.3 | | 28(2) |
| | 14.2 | 6.1 | 6.2 | | 28(3) |
| Lien over essential documents | 15.1 | 6.3 | 6.4 | | 29 |
| Charging for document storage | 16.1 | | | | 30 |

(*Continued*)

| | ASCR | ACT | NT | TAS | WA |
|---|---|---|---|---|---|
| ADVOCACY AND LITIGATION | | | | | |
| Independence – not act as mere mouthpiece | 17.1 | 17.1 | 17.3 | | 32(1) |
| | 17.2 | 17.2 | 17.4 | | 32(2) |
| | 17.3 | 17.3 | 17.5 | | 32(3) |
| Not act as surety for client's bail | 17.4 | 15 | 16 | | |
| Formality before court | 18.1 | 22.6 | 17.40 | | 37(6) |
| Frankness in court | 19.1 | 18.1 | 17.6 | | 34(1) |
| | 19.2 | 18.2 | 17.7 | | 34(2) |
| | 19.3 | 18.3 | 17.8 | | 34(3) |
| | 19.4 | 18.4 | 17.9 | | 34(4) |
| | 19.5 | 18.5 | 17.10 | | 34(5) |
| | 19.6 | | | | 34(6) |
| | 19.7 | 18.7 | 17.12 | | 34(7) |
| | 19.8 | 18.8 | 17.13 | | 34(8); 34(9) |
| | 19.9 | 18.9 and 28 | 17.14 | | 34(10) |
| | 19.10 | 18.11 | 17.16 | | 34(12) |
| | 19.11 | 18.12 | 17.17 | | 34(13) |
| | 19.12 | | | | |
| Delinquent or guilty clients | 20.1 | 11.1(a); 14; and 19.1 | 11.1; 15; and 17.18 | | 35(1) |
| Client admission of guilt | 20.2 | 19.2 | 17.19 | | 35(2) |
| | 20.2.2 | 13 and 19.2(b) | 14; 17.19(b) | | 35(3) |
| Client intends to disobey court order | 20.3 | 19.3 | 17.20 | | 35(4) |

| | ASCR | ACT | NT | TAS | WA |
|---|---|---|---|---|---|
| Responsible use of court process and privilege | 21.1 and 21.2 | 11.2; 20.1 | 11.2; 12; and 17.21 | | 36(2);(3) |
| | 21.3 | 20.3 | 17.22 | | 36(4) |
| | 21.4 | 11.2; 20.2; and 20.7 | 11.2; 12; and 17.26 | | 36(3); (8) |
| | 21.5 | 20.4 | 17.23 | | 36(5) |
| | 21.6 | 20.5 | 17.24 | | 36(7) |
| | 21.7 | 20.8 | 17.27 | | 36(9) |
| | 21.8 | | | | 36(10) |
| Communication with opponents | 22.1 and 21.2 | 22,1 and 22.2 | 17.35 | | 37(1) |
| | 22.2 | 22.2 | 17.36 | | 37(2) |
| | 22.3 | 22.3 | 17.37 | | 37(3) |
| | 22.4 | 22.5(a) | 17.39(a) | | 37(5) |
| | 22.5 | 22.6 | 17.40 | | 37(6) |
| | 22.6 | 22.7 | 17.41 | | 37(7) |
| | 22.7 | 22.8 | 17.42 | | 37(7) |
| | 22.8 | | | | |
| Opposition access to witnesses | 23.1 | 21.6 | 17.33 | | 38(1) |
| | 23.2 | 21.7 | 17.34 | | 38(2) |
| Integrity of evidence – influencing evidence | 24.1.1 | | | | 39(1) |
| | 24.1.2 | 21.1 | 17.28 | | 39(2) |
| | 24.2 | 21.2 | 17.29 | | 39(3) |
| Integrity of evidence – two witnesses together | 25.1 | 21.3 | 17.30 | | 40(1) |
| | 25.2 | 21.4 | 17.31 | | 40(2) |
| Communicating with witnesses under cross-examination | 26.1 | 21.5 | 17.32 | | 41 |

(*Continued*)

| | ASCR | ACT | NT | TAS | WA |
|---|---|---|---|---|---|
| Solicitor as material witness in client's case | 27 | 12 | 13 | 95(1) | 42 |
| Public comment during current proceedings | 28.1 | | 17.43–17.45 | | 43(2) |
| Prosecutor's duties | 29.1 | 23.1 | 17.46 | | 44(2) |
| | 29.2 | 23.2 | 17.47 | | 44(4) |
| | 29.3 | 23.3 | 17.48 | | 44(5) |
| | 29.4 | 23.4 | 17.49 | | 44(6) |
| | 29.5 | 23.5 | 17.50 | | 44(3) |
| | 29.6 | 23.6 | 17.51 | | |
| | 29.7 | 23.7 | 17.52 | | |
| | 29.8 | 23.8 | 17.53 | | 44(7) |
| | 29.9 | 23.9 | 17.54 | | 44(8) |
| | 29.10 | 23.10 | 17.55 | | 44(9) |
| | 29.11 | 23.11 | 17.56 | | 44(10) |
| | 29.12 | 23.12 | 17.57 | | 44(11) |
| RELATIONS WITH OTHER SOLICITORS | | | | | |
| Another solicitor or other person's error | 30.1 | | | 8 | 23 |
| Inadvertent disclosure | 31.1 | | | | 24 |
| Unfounded allegations | 32.1 | 31 | | | |
| Communication with another solicitor's client | 33.1.1 | 22.4(a) | 17.38(a) | | 37(4)(a) |
| | 33.1.2 | 22.4(b) | 17.38(b) | | 37(4)(b) |
| | 33.1.3 | 22.4(c) | 17.38(c) | | 37(4)(c) |
| | 33.1.4 | 28.1 | 23.1 | | 37(4)(d) |
| Dealing with other persons | 34.1.1 | 31.1(b) | 26.2 | | |
| | 34.1.2 | 31.1(c) | 26.3 | | |
| | 34.2 | | | | |

| | ASCR | ACT | NT | TAS | WA |
|---|---|---|---|---|---|
| Contracting with third parties | 35.1 | 29 | 24 | | 25 |
| LAW PRACTICE MANAGEMENT | | | | | |
| Advertising | 36.1 | 38.2(a) | | 7-8 | 45(1) |
| | 36.2 | | | | 45(2) |
| Supervision of legal services | 37.1 | 35 | | | 16(4)<br>17(2)–(4) |
| Returning judicial officers | 38.1 | 41 | | | |
| Sharing premises | 39.1 | 33 | | 5 | 46 |
| Sharing receipts | 40.1 | | | | |
| Mortgage financing and managed investments | 41 | | | | |
| Anti-discrimination and harassment | 42.1 | 40 | | | 17(5) |
| Dealing with the regulatory authority | 43 | 39 | 32 | | 50 |

## ASCR EQUIVALENT RULES FOR BARRISTERS

Only the specific ASCR rules mentioned in the book and their equivalent other jurisdictional rules are included in the table below.

The following jurisdictional rules apply:

- New South Wales, Queensland, South Australia, Victoria and Western Australia: Legal Profession Uniform Conduct (Barristers) Rules 2015 (Bar Rules).
- Tasmania: *Rules of Practice 1994.*
- The Australian Capital Territory: *The Australian Capital Territory Barristers' Rules 2008.*
- The Northern Territory: Northern Territory Bar Association Barristers' Conduct Rules (Schedule to the Constitution).

| ASCR | HEADINGS USED IN THE BAR RULES | BAR RULES | ACT | NT | TAS |
|---|---|---|---|---|---|
| 3 | 4. These Rules are made in the belief that:<br>barristers owe their paramount duty to the administration of justice;<br>23 A barrister has an overriding duty to the court to act with independence in the interests of the administration of justice. | 4(a)<br>23 | 1 | 1 | |
| 4.1.1 | A barrister must promote and protect fearlessly and by all proper and lawful means the client's best interests to the best of the barrister's skill and diligence, and do so without regard to his or her own interest or to any consequences to the barrister or to any other person. | 35 | 30 | 30 | 51 |
| 4.1.2. But not courteous<br>4.1.3 | Barristers as specialist advocates in the administration of justice, must act honestly, fairly, skilfully, bravely and with competence and diligence; | 4(c) | 3 | 3 | |
| 4.1.4 | Negotiating for a client with an opponent to compromise a case. | 11(c) | | | |
| 7/7.1 | A barrister must seek to assist the client to understand the issues in the case and the client's possible rights and obligations, sufficiently to permit the client to give proper instructions, including instructions in connection with any compromise of the case. | 37 | 17 | 17 | |
| | Independent advice to clients – admin of justice | 5(e) | | | |

| ASCR | HEADINGS USED IN THE BAR RULES | BAR RULES | ACT | NT | TAS |
|---|---|---|---|---|---|
| 7.2 | A barrister must inform the client or the instructing solicitor about the alternatives to fully contested adjudication of the case which are reasonably available to the client, unless the barrister believes on reasonable grounds that the client already has such an understanding of those alternatives as to permit the client to make decisions about the client's best interests in relation to the litigation. | 36 | 17A | | |
| 8/8.1<br>Follow a client's instructions | | | | | |
| 9/9.1 | A barrister must not disclose (except as compelled by law) or use in any way confidential information obtained by the barrister in the course of practice concerning any person to whom the barrister owes some duty or obligation to keep the information confidential unless or until: | 114 | 103 | 103 | |
| 5/5.1 | 6(a) A barrister whose practising certificate is issued in a participating jurisdiction, except to the extent that the conduct of the barrister in relation to practice in a non-participating jurisdiction is regulated by Barristers' Rules for that jurisdiction;<br>7 These Rules are not intended to be a complete or detailed code of conduct for barristers. Other standards for, requirements of and sanctions on the conduct of barristers are found in the inherent disciplinary jurisdiction of the Supreme Court, the legislation regulating the legal profession and in the general law (including the law relating to contempt of court). | 6(a); 7 | 9 | 9 | |

*(Continued)*

| ASCR | HEADINGS USED IN THE BAR RULES | BAR RULES | ACT | NT | TAS |
|---|---|---|---|---|---|
| | Conduct also governed by legislation and common law. | 10 | 9 | 9 | |
| | WAIVER OF RULES | | | | |
| | Bar counsel may waive compliance | 11 | | | |
| | ADVOCACY RULES | | | | |
| | A barrister must not engage in conduct which is:<br>(a) dishonest or otherwise discreditable to a barrister;<br>(b) prejudicial to the administration of justice; or<br>(c) likely to diminish public confidence in the legal profession or the administration of justice or otherwise bring the legal profession into disrepute | 8 | | | |
| 12.4.1<br>No conflict drawing a Will | | | | | |
| 17.1 | A barrister must not act as the mere mouthpiece of the client or of the instructing solicitor and must exercise the forensic judgments called for during the case independently, after the appropriate consideration of the client's and the instructing solicitor's wishes where practicable. | 42 | 18–20 | 18–20 | |
| 19/19.1 | A barrister must not deceive or knowingly or recklessly mislead the court. | 24 | 21 | 21 | |
| 19.2 | A barrister must take all necessary steps to correct any misleading statement made by the barrister to a court as soon as possible after the barrister becomes aware that the statement was misleading. | 25 | 22 | 22 | |

| ASCR | HEADINGS USED IN THE BAR RULES | BAR RULES | ACT | NT | TAS |
|---|---|---|---|---|---|
| 19.6<br>19.6.1<br>19.6.3 | 29. A barrister must, at the appropriate time in the hearing of the case if the court has not yet been informed of that matter, inform the court of:<br>(a) any binding authority;<br>(b) where there is no binding authority any authority decided by an Australian appellate court; and<br>(c) any applicable legislation;<br>known to the barrister and which the barrister has reasonable grounds to believe to be directly in point, against the client's case. | 29 | 25 | 25 | |
| 21/21.1/21.3 | 60. A barrister must take care to ensure that the barrister's advice to invoke the coercive powers of a court:<br>(a) is reasonably justified by the material then available to the barrister;<br>(b) is appropriate for the robust advancement of the client's case on its merits;<br>(c) is not given principally in order to harass or embarrass a person; and<br>(d) is not given principally in order to gain some collateral advantage for the client or the barrister or the instructing solicitor or a third party out of court. | 60 | 35 | 35 | |
| 21.2 | 61. A barrister must take care to ensure that decisions by the barrister to make allegations or suggestions under privilege against any person:<br>(a) are reasonably justified by the material then available to the barrister;<br>(b) are appropriate for the robust advancement of the client's case on its merits; and<br>(c) are not made principally in order to harass or embarrass a person. | 61 | 36 | 36 | |

(*Continued*)

| ASCR | HEADINGS USED IN THE BAR RULES | BAR RULES | ACT | NT | TAS |
|---|---|---|---|---|---|
| 21.5 | 65. A barrister must not allege any matter of fact amounting to criminality, fraud or other serious misconduct against any person unless the barrister believes on reasonable grounds that:<br>(a) available material by which the allegation could be supported provides a proper basis for it; and<br>(b) the client wishes the allegation to be made, after having been advised of the seriousness of the allegation and of the possible consequences for the client and the case if it is not made out. | | 38 | 38 | |
| 22 | 49. A barrister must not knowingly make a false or misleading statement to an opponent in relation to the case (including its compromise). | 49 | 51; 52 | 51; 52 | |
| 26 | 73. A barrister must not confer with any witness including a party or client called by the barrister on any matter related to the proceedings while that witness remains under cross-examination, unless | 73 | 48 | 48 | |
| 31 – Inadvertent disclosure | | | | | |
| 33 | 52. A barrister must not deal directly with a party other than his or her client who is legally represented unless: | 52 | 55(a) | 55(a) | |
| 34 –Not make any statements beyond legitimate claims.<br>34.1.1<br>34.1.2<br>34.1.3 | | | | | |

| ASCR | HEADINGS USED IN THE BAR RULES | BAR RULES | ACT | NT | TAS |
|---|---|---|---|---|---|
| 42 | 123. A barrister must not in the course of practice, engage in conduct which constitutes:<br>(a) discrimination;<br>(b) sexual harassment; or<br>(c) workplace bullying | 123 | | | |

## LAWYER LEGISLATION

The following table identifies the few select sections of the National Law that have been referred to and which have only been adopted by New South Wales and Victoria and provides the equivalent Parts or sections in the legislation governing lawyers in the other Australian states and territories.

The following jurisdictional legislation applies:

- *Legal Profession Uniform Law (2014)* adopted by New South Wales and Victoria.
- *Legal Profession Act 2006* (NT).
- *Legal Profession Act 2007* (QLD).
- *Legal Practitioners Act 1981* (SA).
- *Legal Profession Act 2007* (TAS).
- *Legal Profession Act 2008* (WA).

| | UNIFORM LAW | ACT | NT | QLD | SA | TAS | WA |
|---|---|---|---|---|---|---|---|
| CHAPTER 2 THRESHOLD REQUIREMENTS FOR LEGAL PRACTICE | | | | | | | |
| Part 2.1 UNQUALIFIED LEGAL PRACTICE | | Part 2.2 | Part 2.1 | Part 2.2 | Part 3 Div 3 | Part 2.1 | Part 3 |
| Objectives | 2.1.1/9 | 15 | 17 | 22 | | 12 | 11 |
| Prohibition on engaging in legal practice by unqualified entities | 2.1.2 | 16 | 18 | 24 | 21;23 | 13 | 12 |
| Prohibition on advertisements or representations by or about unqualified entities | 2.1.3 | 17 | 19 | 25 | 23 | 14 | 13 |
| Part 4.3 LEGAL COSTS | | | | | | | |
| DISCLOSE COSTS | 4.3.6/274 | 269 | 303 | 308 | | 291 | 260 |

# A GRAMMAR PRIMER

## I COMMONLY MISUSED OR CONFUSED WORDS

***A priori*** means based on hypothesis or theory rather than experiment. It does not mean 'in advance'.

**Abdicate/abrogate:** *abdicate* means to resign from the throne, or more generally to cast off responsibility; *abrogate* means to repeal a law or terminate an arrangement.

**Adverse/averse:** *adverse* means something unfavourable, contrary or hostile; to be *averse* to something is to have a strong feeling of opposition towards it.

**Advice/advise:** *advice* is a noun, and it refers to a recommendation about what to do; *advise* is the verb, meaning to recommend something.

**Affect/effect:** *effect* is the noun (the result of something); and *affect* is its verb (to influence the result). Sometimes 'affect' is used as a noun, but its meaning is different. As a noun, affect refers to someone's emotional state.

**Alternately/alternatively:** *alternately* means in turn, one after the other; *alternatively* means on the other hand, one or the other.

**Aggravate/mitigate:** *aggravate* means to make worse; *mitigate* means to alleviate something, to make it less bad.

**Amount/number:** *amount* refers to something that cannot be counted; *number* refers to individual items that can be counted (compare less/fewer)

**Between/among:** *between* should be used to refer to individual items that are clearly separated; *among* should be used to refer to things that are not clearly separated (that is, they form part of a group or mass of objects).

**Censure/censor:** *censure* means to criticise strongly; *to censor* is to ban parts of a communication; *a censor* is someone who does this.

**Complement/compliment:** *complement* means something that completes the whole; a *compliment* is an expression of admiration.

**Contingent/contingency:** *contingent* refers to a representative group; a *contingency* is a possible event.

**Criteria/criterion:** *criterion* is the singular; *criteria* is the plural. Hence, one criterion, three criteria.

**Disburse/disperse:** *disburse* means to give out or distribute, especially money; *disperse* means to scatter.

**Discreet/discrete:** *discreet* means careful, cautious or showing good judgment; *discrete* means individual, separate, or distinct.

**Disinterested/uninterested:** *disinterested* means that a person is independent, lacking in bias; *uninterested* means they are indifferent, they have no interest.

**Emigration/immigration:** *to emigrate* is to leave a country indefinitely; to *immigrate* is to arrive in a new country to live.

**Elicit/illicit:** to *elicit* is to draw out, to extract; *illicit* is illegal or unlawful.

**Farther/further:** *farther* refers to distance; to *further* means to advance or progress.

**Flaunt/flout:** *flaunt* means to show off; *flout* is to communicate contempt for something or someone.

**Forego/forgo:** forego means to go before; *forgo* means to give up or do without.

**Hung/hanged:** *hung* is something dangled above the ground; to be *hanged* is to be executed by by hanging.

**ie/eg:** ie is an abbreviation of *id est* and means 'that is' or 'in other words'; eg is an abbreviation of *exempli gratia* and means an example.

**Illusion/allusion:** illusion is a mistaken belief; allusion means a reference.

**Imply/infer:** something is *implied* if it is a suggestion intended by the person speaking or writing; a conclusion is *inferred* if it is reached by the person listening or reading.

**Insure/ensure:** *insure* means to take out insurance; *ensure* means to make sure.

**Irregardless:** is *not* acceptable as a word in professional use; it is only ever a joke or a mistake.

**Lay/lie:** *lay* should be used to refer to placing an object in a location; *lie* means to rest on something.

**Less/fewer:** use *less* should be used when comparing quantities that can't be counted ('I would like less noise, please'); use *fewer* if you are comparing things that can be counted ('I would like fewer cupcakes'). Compare amount/number.

**Lose/loose:** to *lose* is to fail to win, or to misplace or to cease to be in possession; *loose* means the opposite of tight, or tighten.

**Me/I/myself:** 'I' is a *subject* pronoun, that is, it is used when a person is the subject of the sentence ('I read the book'). 'I' is also used in comparison statements with 'than' ('She is faster than I am').

'Me' is an *object* pronoun, which is used when a person is the object of an action, or the object of a preposition: 'She followed me'; 'He gave me the book'.

'Myself' is a *reflexive pronoun*, which is used when the subject and object of the sentence are the same (that is, where the subject of the sentence is performing the action of the sentence onto himself or herself): 'I tricked myself into believing I was invincible'. It can also be used for emphasis: 'I myself believe in the power of reading'.

**Mitigate/militate:** to *mitigate* is to make something milder, typically something undesirable. A 'mitigating factor' is something that affects someone's case by lessening the degree of blame. To *militate* is to fight or exert pressure for something to happen or not to happen.

**Past/passed:** *past* should be used to refer to events that have previously occurred ('I knew him in the past'); *passed* is the past tense of 'to pass' ('I passed him in the street'; 'Parliament passed the bill').

**Peek/peak/pique:** to *peek* means to take a quick look at something; a *peak* is a summit or sharp point; and *pique* means to provoke or instigate.

**Peruse:** means to review a text in depth, not to skim over quickly.

**Practice/practise:** *practice* is the noun and *practise* is the verb. Thus, we practise law, but maintain a legal practice. (American English uses practice for both noun and verb.)

**Prescribe/proscribe:** to *prescribe* means to command or recommend something; to *proscribe* means to outlaw something.

**Precede/proceed:** *precede* means to come before; *proceed* means to begin or continue.

**Principle/principal:** *principle* is a noun meaning a rule or belief ('she had high principles'); *principal* is an adjective meaning main or key, or a noun meaning the head of an organisation ('she was the principal of the firm').

**Redundant:** is often used to mean 'useless' or 'unable to perform its function', but in correct usage it refers to a surplus, so something redundant is no longer needed.

**Remuneration/enumeration:** *remuneration* is payment for goods or services; *enumeration* is a listing of items or numbers.

**Slander/libel:** *slander* is a false statement that is spoken and is harmful to an individual's reputation; *libel* refers to a written statement that is harmful to an individual's reputation. Both are old common law categories of the wider class of defamation, now covered by legislation.

**They're/their:** *They're* is the contraction for *they are* ('they're playing today'). *Their* is the possessive ('they took their positions').

**Who/whom and who/that:** *who* refers to the subject of the sentence, while *whom* refers to the object. They are often confused. An easy way to test whether to use who or whom is to realise that they work in the same way as she and her; or he and him. Thus you can ask:

'Who did this? She did'. You would not reply 'her did this'. Thus 'who' is correct.

'Whom should I tell? I should tell him'. You would not reply, 'I should tell he'. Thus 'whom' is correct.

Who is always used in reference to a person; 'that' should only be used in relation to an object. For instance, 'This is the pen that has ink'; 'Who can say?'

**Who's/whose:** *Who's* is the contraction of 'who is'. *Whose* is the possessive. Thus, 'Who's interested in dessert?' and 'Whose wine glass is this?'

**Your/you're:** *your* is the possessive ('She likes your car'); *you're* is a contraction of you are ('You're lucky to have such a beautiful car').

# II COMMON PROBLEMS

## Active and passive voice

Verbs are either *active* or *passive* in voice. The active voice would read: 'the judge decided the case', while the passive would read 'the case was decided by the judge'.

You can see in this example that, in the active voice, the relationship between the subject and the verb is straightforward. The subject is doing the action. In the passive voice, things are turned around so that the subject of the sentence becomes the target of the action. The subject is *acted upon* by some other agent.

The passive voice is not wrong, as such, but it can be problematic. Lawyers are notorious for writing in the passive voice. Interestingly, there is an ethical dimension to this: the passive voice tends to conceal, or deflect, responsibility. Thus, there is a difference between 'the company distributed asbestos products' and 'asbestos products were distributed by the company' or, worse, 'asbestos products were distributed'. The passive voice can be used intentionally to obscure the agent responsible for the action.

In addition, over-use of the passive voice can make your writing dull, wordy and vague. Your grammar check on the computer can easily identify passive voice which you can then revise to the active voice.

## American spellings

The use of American English (eg 'organize' instead of 'organise'; 'criticize' instead of 'criticise') can rub Australian assessors up the wrong way.

## Archaic and unnecessary words

Many lawyers are particularly fond of archaic words. Try to avoid the use of:

- heretofor
- henceforth
- herein
- hereafter
- hereinafter
- aforesaid
- thereby
- thereto
- hereinbefore
- thereunto

Try to avoid unnecessary words: said, same, such when you mean 'the'; one (before a person's name).

## Basic sentence structure

Often poor student work is characterised by incomplete sentences. Sentences have, at a minimum, certain components:

- *a subject*: the subject is a represented by a noun (common or proper or a pronoun);
- a *verb;*
- *expression of a complete thought:* represented by a principal clause;
- *fundamental punctuation:* beginning with a capital letter and ending with a full stop (or question mark or exclamation mark if a question or common respectively). Thus: *The student is a good writer. She writes well. He wrote a client letter.*

## Commas

One of the most frequent errors made by novice writers is the over-use of commas. There are some basic rules for comma usage:

- *Use commas to separate items in a series*: eg 'I need a pen, a pencil, a ruler and a notebook'.
- *Use commas to separate introductory words or phrases*: eg 'Finally, I wish to thank my legal writing teacher'.
- *Use commas to separate independent clauses*: an independent clause is one that could stand alone as a sentence, but is joined with a conjunction (such as and or but). Thus, 'My legal writing teacher is most particular, and she has been critical of my work'.

## Dangling modifiers

These are ambiguous clauses at the beginning or end of sentences, which modify something that is not clearly stated in the sentence. Compare:

- Making her way along the top of the fence, my sister called to the cat.
- My sister called to the cat, making her way along the top of the fence.

Ensure that your sentence clearly identifies the person or thing undertaking the action in the modifier.

## Ending sentences with prepositions

A preposition at the end of the sentence can make for a very awkward sentence. A preposition is a word that gives the context (eg time or place) of a noun (eg a possum ran up …).

Thus in formal English a sentence such as 'This is the building I work at' is more correctly stated as 'This is the building at which I work'.

This is not a hard-and-fast rule, however, and in a very few cases it will be inappropriate. 'This is something I will not put up with' sounds very odd when expressed as 'This is something up with which I will not put.'

## Failure to use parallel structure

Each sentence or sentence fragment in a list should have the same grammatical structure. Consider this confusing list of steps to take in research:

- *Consider* the research problem.
- *Generating* key words can be helpful.
- *You should* make sure that you note your bibliographic details.
- *A summary* of each of your sources is helpful.
- A parallel structure is easier to read:
- *Consider* the research problem;
- *Generate* key words;
- *Note* your bibliographic details;
- *Summarise* each of your sources.

## Gender-neutral language

Consistent use of masculine pronouns is to be avoided. To this end:

- Avoid gender-specific titles (eg use 'Chair' rather than 'Chairman').
- Use the appropriate noun in place of a pronoun (eg 'the student loves legal writing' rather than 'he' loves legal writing.
- Utilise the feminine pronoun when writing in generalities (eg 'When speaking to the judge, address her directly' (not strictly gender neutral, of course, but it overcomes the assumption of the masculine as the norm).

There are differing opinions on the use of 'their' or 'them' to ensure gender neutrality (eg 'the student often has difficulty with legal writing, and it is helpful to work with them'). Grammatically it is incorrect ('the student' is singular but 'them' is plural) but, in fact, as writers we have been asked by editors to work in this way.

## Incomplete comparisons

When you compare a thing to something else, make sure you always clarify what that something else is. Otherwise, the comparison is meaningless.

For example, 'Her writing is clearer and more concise' does not tell you what the comparison refers to. Her writing may be clearer and more concise than that of her colleague. Or her writing may be clearer and more concise than it was before she read this book.

## Misplaced apostrophes

The misplaced apostrophe is the most common error made in student texts. Avoid errors by following a few simple rules:

- Apostrophes are *never* used to make a word plural.
- Apostrophes are used to:
  - indicate possession – something belonging to something or someone else; OR
  - to indicate a contracted word (eg don't is a contraction of do not).
- If you are indicating possession,
  - if something belongs to one person or thing, the apostrophe goes before the 's';
  - if something belongs to more than one person or thing, the apostrophe goes after the 's'; *but*
- 'it's' is only ever used when short for 'it is'. The possessive is always 'its', without the apostrophe.

## Nominalisations

Nominalisation is the creation of a noun from a verb or adjective. Verbs are often converted into nouns ending in *-ion, -ment, -tion, -ence, -ancy, -ant*, and changing them back to verbs can improve your writing. Some examples include:

- conversion to convert;
- commencement to commence;
- determination to determine;
- resolution to resolve.

Watch, too, for nouns that follow verbs that add little value. For instance,

- 'take into consideration' can be reworded to the much more economical 'consider';
- 'undertake an analysis of' can be replaced with 'analyse'.

Examples of nominalisation of adjectives include:

- enforceable to enforceability;
- distinguishable to distinguishability;
- applicable to applicability;
- specific to specificity;
- important to importance.

Some nominalisations are useful, but, like the passive voice, their overuse can make sentences difficult to understand, less persuasive, wordy and awkward.

Compare: 'The album's significance is in the fact that it evidences society's recognition of the value of traditional music'; to: 'The album is significant because it demonstrates that society recognises the value of traditional music'.

## Noun strings

A noun string is a series of nouns or other words, all of which modify the final noun. For example: 'Underground Mine Worker Safety Protection Procedures'; 'University written assessment mechanisms'.

The longer the string, the more difficult for a reader who is unfamiliar with the term to understand it.

The problem is fixed by identifying the final noun and inserting appropriate prepositions: For example, 'Procedures for protecting the safety of mine workers'; 'Mechanisms used by the University for assessment of written work'.

## Plain language

It has been said that 'no one technique defines plain language. Rather, plain language is defined by results – it is easy to read, understand, and use'.[53] Although there is no single technique, certain principles can guide your use of language:

- Consider the reader, the context and the purpose of your writing.
- Use specialist legal terms only when they are the most appropriate and effective words to use. Otherwise use simple and straightforward language.
- Eliminate:
  - archaic or unnecessary words (see separate section above);
  - redundant words ('each and every'; 'any and all'; 'authorised and empowered'; 'final and conclusive'; 'null and void');
  - unnecessary sentence introductions (eg 'It is possible that you may not be able to apply to the court' can be rephrased to 'You may not be able to apply to the court'; 'There are four people who have refused to testify' can be rephrased to 'Four people have refused to testify');
  - noun strings (see separate section).
- Replace difficult words or legal jargon with words your reader is likely to understand. Writers are often encouraged to use short, rather than long words, but unfamiliar words are more likely to be the issue.
- Define or explain unfamiliar words.
- Use the active voice.
- Use gender-neutral language.

---

53 Plain Language.gov, 'What is Plain Language?', available at http://www.plainlanguage.gov/whatisPL/.

- Keep sentences short.
- Use the positive unless you want to accentuate the negative (negative statements are more difficult to process. Words that signal the negative include unless, failure, absent, except, until, deny.)
- Adhere to accepted grammar, punctuation and usage.
- Consider the readability of your text and think about organisation, layout and presentation that will help to engage the reader.

## Run-on sentences

A run-on sentence is a sentence that joins two independent clauses without any punctuation or a conjunction. The run-on sentence 'Legal writing is difficult I have to practise to improve my expression' can be changed in a number of ways, for example:

- It can be split into two sentences: 'Legal writing is difficult. I have to practise to improve my expression'.
- A conjunction can be used: 'Legal writing is difficult and I have to practise to improve my expression' OR 'I have to practise to improve my expression, as legal writing is difficult'.
- A semicolon and transitional word can be used: 'Legal writing is difficult; therefore, I have to practise to improve my expression'.

## Semicolons

You can use a semicolon to connect two independent clauses that are closely related. For example, you could use a semicolon in the sentence: 'The writing is much improved on your last attempt; I appreciate the renewed effort'.

You can also use semicolons to separate items in a list when those items contain commas themselves.

## Split infinitives

To split an infinitive is to insert an adverb between the two words of an infinitive form of the verb. The classic example is 'To boldly go where no one has gone before'. Some readers take exception to split infinitives, but you can find many examples of its use by careful writers, so avoiding it is not a universal rule.

## Subject and verb agreement

Most plural subjects take verbs without an 's': 'he writes' but 'they write'. It is quite common, particularly in long sentences, to overlook this rule.

# GLOSSARY: WORDS AND ABBREVIATIONS

***ASCR:*** Australian Solicitors Conduct Rules. Developed by the Law Council of Australia as a step towards creating a national legal profession, the Rules are intended to provide solicitors with a first point of reference for dealing with ethical dilemmas, the management of risk and the management of practice.

***Affidavit:*** a written declaration made upon oath before a person authorised to administer oaths, especially for use as evidence in court.

***Analysis:*** the separation of something into its constituent elements.

***Analytical writing:*** a form of writing that is based in comparison, contrast, assessment or evaluation. It does not present an argument, so is a form of balanced, rather than persuasive writing.

***Analogise:*** to reason in a way that points to similarities between two cases. If two cases are so similar that the reasoning of the first should also apply to the second, they are ***analogous***.

***Antonym:*** a word opposite in meaning to another (for instance, light and dark are antonyms).

***Argument:*** a series of statements used to persuade an audience of something or to present reasons for accepting a conclusion or adopting a course of action.

***Audience:*** the intended or imagined readership for a piece of writing.

***Authentic voice/authentic writing:*** generally, a writer's 'voice' is said to refer to an individual writing style, that derives from a combination of the writer's common use of grammar, diction, punctuation and so on. With specific regard to legal writing, we suggest an authentic voice is one that conveys the lawyer's professional authority, competence and courtesy, written to the needs of the audience, which also conveys a sense of the writer's genuine and individual writing style.

***Authorial:*** coming from, or typical of the writer.

***Balanced writing:*** genres of legal writing are often divided into balanced and persuasive. Balanced writing provides a balanced analysis of a legal issue. Letters to clients and inter-office memoranda are often placed in the category of balanced writing.

***Bibliography:*** a list of sources, such as books, scholarly articles, reports, web sites and so on, consulted in the preparation of an essay or research paper. The bibliography should appear at the end of your paper and conform to the appropriate style guide that you have used.

***Bracketing:*** placing elements into groups, classifications or classes.

***Cognitive theory of writing:*** a theory of writing that holds that both reading and writing are complex cognitive processes and that meaning is affected by the reader's goals, assumptions and context.

***Community of practice:*** in relation to law, this term refers to that group of people who share the profession and learn how to improve their professional practice through interaction.

***Descriptive writing:*** a form of writing that describes or outlines the way things are, or how events occurred. It does not establish relationships between the pieces of information, as in analytical writing, and does not present a position to be argued. Student work is often criticised as being 'too descriptive', meaning that the work is insufficiently analytical or persuasive.

***Distinguish:*** you distinguish a case from a precedent when you show that there are fundamental differences between the case and the precedent that lead to the conclusion that the case should be decided differently.

***Doctrine:*** a particular principle, position, or policy taught or advocated.

***Doctrinal:*** relating to, or concerned with doctrine.

***Drafting:*** the act of preparing preliminary versions of a document or other piece of writing.

***Diction:*** word choice in writing. Legal writing demands an appropriate vocabulary that is at once fairly formal but concise and clear.

***Discourse:*** communication of thought by words. The term can also refer to a formal discussion of a subject in speech or writing (as in a dissertation or thesis).

***Discourse community:*** a group of people involved in and communicating about a particular topic, issue, or in a particular field. They share certain language-using practices, basic values and assumptions, and ways of communication.

***Dissertation:*** A lengthy essay, often termed a thesis, about a specific topic. This is usually the term given to an essay written for a doctoral degree at a university.

***Empirical:*** based on observation or experience. Thus, empirical evidence is information acquired by observation or experimentation.

***Formalist/formalistic:*** adhering strictly to a prescribed form; emphasis of organisation and style over content.

***Formalist theory of writing:*** the theory that holds that the primary purpose of writing is the transmission of information. Writing is a tool for expressing, rather than constructing, thought.

***Free writing:*** a compositional strategy of writing for a set time, without looking back, crossing out or worrying about spelling or grammar. The technique is very simple: set a timer and write. It is a good strategy if you are procrastinating about writing or are otherwise blocked in a writing task.

***Gender-neutral language:*** using words, where appropriate, that are free of reference to gender. Our Grammar Primer has guidance on using gender-neutral language.

***Genre:*** a specific type or form of writing. In this text, we have proposed that client letters, memoranda and so on are specific genres of legal writing. But more generally, a genre is an appropriate response to the rhetorical situation in which the writer is operating.[54]

***Hermeneutic:*** concerned with interpretation, rather than explanation.

***Heuristic:*** an approach to problem solving that employs a practical method that may not be perfect, but provides a 'short-cut' for analysis. IRAC is a heuristic.

***Hyperbole:*** an obvious and intentional exaggeration not intended to be taken literally (pronounced *hy-PER-bol-ee).*

***Hypothesis*:** a proposed explanation that is made as a starting point for further investigation, which can then be tested by evidence.

***Hypothetical:*** a problem question that poses an imagined fact scenario based on an actual case or cases. It requires the student to formulate an answer by applying their knowledge of legal rules to a new fact situation.

***Ineluctable:*** unable to be resisted or avoided.

***Instrumental:*** serving or acting as an instrument or means to an end.

***Interdisciplinary:*** combining or involving two or more academic disciplines or fields of knowledge.

***IRAC:*** IRAC stands for Issue, Rule, Analysis, Conclusion. It is a tool used to structure an answer to a law hypothetical question. It is useful, but not the only tool available to structure your answer and it is not universally required in law school. Some lectures will advocate – in some cases mandate – its use. Others do not like it. But as is the case with any such structuring tool, it can be helpful, particularly if you are novice writer, to guide your writing.

***Iteration:*** the repetition of a stage or a process in order to better achieve a desired goal or result. (Adjective: ***iterative***.)

***Legalese:*** communication that contains language containing an excessive amount of legal terminology or jargon.

***Literature review:*** an evaluative report of information found in the literature related to your topic. The review should describe, summarise, evaluate and clarify the relevant literature.

54 Mary Kay Mulvaney and David A Joliffe, *Academic Writing: Genres, Samples and Resources* (Pearson Longman, 2005) 2.

***Mastery:*** comprehensive knowledge or skill in a regard to a particular subject or activity.
***Metaphor:*** a word or phrase that ordinarily refers to one thing, but is used in reference to another. The meaning is carried over, thus making an implicit comparison.
***Methodology:*** a system of methods used in a particular area of study or activity.
***Narrative:*** *a* story or account of events or experiences.
***Nominalisation:*** conversion of some other part of speech into a noun. Nominalisations are discussed in our Grammar Primer.
***Normative:*** considered to be the normal or correct way of doing something. An ideal standard.
***Paraphrase:*** to take some else's idea or theory and put it into your own words.
***Passive and active voice:*** the two forms or modes of verbs which show the relation of the subject to the action. A verb is in the passive voice when the subject of the sentence is acted on by the verb 'The decision was made by the Court'. In the active voice the sentence would be 'The Court made the decision'. Passive and active voice are further discussed in our Grammar Primer.
***Persuasive writing:*** writing that seeks to persuade the reader to an argument or proposition. Appellate briefs and negotiation letters are often categorised as forms of persuasive writing.
***Plagiarism:*** using or closely imitating the language and thoughts of another author without acknowledgement of the source. (Adjective: *plagiarised*.)
***Plain language:*** communications written with the audience in mind and which present information clearly and accurately, free of excess wordiness, unnecessary complexity and legalese.
***Planning:*** the process of thinking about and organising a document or other body of writing.
***Positivism:*** in relation to law, the idea that as long as a written law has been duly enacted by a branch of government, it is valid and binding, regardless of whether the law itself is right or wrong.
***Postmodernism:*** a scholarly approach or perspective that is seen largely as a reaction against modernism. In modernism, science was the predominate source of truth and reality. Postmodernism rejects this. There are no universal truths or grand narratives. Rather, truth and reality are shaped by our personal histories and characteristics, such as race and gender. Postmodernism thus emphasises subjectivity, difference, plurality and relativity.
***Precedent:*** a legal decision that is authoritative and binding on (1) courts in the same jurisdiction that are of equal importance; and (2) those that are lower in status where they are hearing cases with similar facts. Also the word precedent is used for a document or activity that provides an example of what is considered to be the correct way to do things in the future.

***Premise:*** a proposition upon which an argument is based or from which a conclusion is drawn.

***Professionalism:*** the conduct expected of a member of a profession. 'A profession is a disciplined group of individuals who adhere to ethical standards and who hold themselves out as, and are accepted by the public as possessing special knowledge and skills in a widely recognised body of learning derived from research, education, and training at a high level, and who are prepared to apply this knowledge and exercise these skills in the interest of others'.[55]

***Purpose:*** the reason for which a document or other body of writing is created and to be used.

***Qualitative:*** relating to the characteristics or qualities of a thing or phenomenon, as opposed to being concerned with measurements based on quantity.

***Quantitative:*** considered or assessed according to measurements, concerned with the quantity of something rather than its quality.

***Random sample:*** the most basic type of probability sample in quantitative research. To draw a simple random sample, a researcher starts with a list of every single member, or element, of the population of interest. The researcher then randomly selects the elements from which she will collect data. (Noun: *randomness.*)

***Recursive:*** done repeatedly or recurrently.

***Reflection:*** serious thought or consideration. In this book, we often use reflection to mean self-reflection, that is, careful thought about your own behaviour and beliefs.

***Reflexivity:*** a circular relationship between cause and effect. In social theory, reflexivity refers to the capacity of the individual to recognise the impact of socialisation upon them, and the extent to which they can influence their future. Thus, a high degree of reflexivity would indicate an autonomous individual capable of shaping their own norms. (Adjective: *reflexive.*)

***Revising:*** the process of altering something already written, in order to make corrections, improve, or update the text.

***Rhetoric:*** the art of effective or persuasive writing (or speaking).

***Rhetorical theory of writing:*** the theory that holds that the primary purpose of writing is persuasion to a particular point of view or action.

***Rhetorical reading:*** an interpretation in which a reader makes inferences about the author's purpose and structure.

***Sample/sample size:*** samples allow quantitative researchers to make generalisations about larger groups.

***Scaffolding:*** teaching and learning techniques designed to move students progressively towards mastery and more independent learning in the subject area.

---

55 Professions Australia, 'What is a Profession?', available at http://www.professions.com.au/about-us/what-is-a-professional.

***Schema:*** a plan, diagram, or scheme. A pattern for organising different categories of information and the relationships between or among them.
***Scholarly:*** the form of academic writing suited to publication in a peer-reviewed journal in law, particularly in relation to the referencing of ideas and quotations.
***Scrivener:*** a scribe.
***Sociocultural theory of writing:*** the theory that holds that writing is a social act, embedded in a community.
***Standardised form:*** a document that is not specially set out for the matter in question but is drawn up in advance and applied to numerous transactions.
***Stare decisis:*** 'let the decision stand'. A policy that courts will follow decisions of decided cases.
***Syllogism:*** a conclusion or inference deduced from two or more assertions that are believed to be true.
***Synonym:*** a word having the same or nearly the same meaning as another (eg intelligent and smart).
***Syntax:*** the orderly arrangement of linguistic elements (words, phrases) to construct language.
***Synthesis/synthesising:*** the combination of the constituent elements of something into a single or unified entity.
***Technocratic:*** focused on a technical skill, decision making based on technical information.
***Thesis:*** a proposition that is to be proved; or a dissertation, involving original research, written by a candidate for a postgraduate degree.
***Thesis statement:*** a short statement that summarises the central claim of an essay or dissertation. The thesis statement is then developed and supported by way of evidence and authority in the text.
***Tone:*** the quality of an author's expression of their attitude toward subject, audience, and self. Tone may be for instance, formal or informal; serious or humorous. Tone is the author's response to the questions why am I writing this; who am I writing to; what do I want the reader to take from my writing?
***Transition***: The use of words or phrases to join together various parts of writing, such as sections or paragraphs. Transitions may also be used to signal relationships among ideas in writing. Good use of transitions makes for smooth and coherent reading.
***VCAT:*** Victorian Civil and Administrative Tribunal.

# INDEX